NORTH
STAR
WAY

I Don't Belong to You

QUIET THE NOISE AND FIND YOUR VOICE

KEKE PALMER

NORTH STAR WAY

New York   London   Toronto   Sydney   New Delhi

North Star Way
An Imprint of Simon & Schuster, Inc.
1230 Avenue of the Americas
New York, NY 10020

First North Star Way trade paperback edition September 2017

NORTH STAR WAY and colophon are trademarks of Simon & Schuster, Inc.

For information about special discounts for bulk purchases, please contact Simon & Schuster Special Sales at 1-866-506-1949 or business@simonandschuster.com.

The North Star Way Speakers Bureau can bring authors to your live event. For more information or to book an event contact the North Star Way Speakers Bureau at 1-212-698-8888 or visit our website at www.thenorthstarway.com.

Interior design by Jaime Putorti

Manufactured in the United States of America

10 9 8 7 6 5 4 3 2 1

Library of Congress Cataloging-in-Publication Data is available.

ISBN 978-1-5011-4539-1
ISBN 978-1-5011-4540-7 (pbk)
ISBN 978-1-5011-4541-4 (ebook)

CONTENTS

○ ○ ○ ○ ○ ○ ○ ○ ○ ○ ○ ○ ○ ○ ○ ○ ○ ○ ○

INTRODUCTION

A Letter from Keke

*O*KAY, the most important thing you're going to find out about me as you read this book is that I am who I am—and I own all of who I am (flaws included) completely! 😊

That's just always been my way, even while growing up as the boldest one in a family that's pretty damn bold already, believe me! 😁

I've always been the one ready, willing, and able to offer my opinions, thoughts, and emotions to anyone on any topic at any time! That ain't changed a bit over the years!! 😜 😝 😐 😝

Seriously, I may be young but I have experienced a lot in my life and I've played all types of roles both on- and offscreen. I moved from being the only black girl in my Catholic school classroom to being taught on the set of a feature film. Even now it feels as if I've lived two or three lives all at once. That whirlwind of opportunity given to me as a child meant growing up a lot faster than the other kids my age, which was kinda weird.

I can't even begin to tell you how often my heart and head rebelled against moving at the same warp speed as the new and shiny world surrounding me. But that is just the surface part of my life and not really what this book is about. This book is about the similar experiences we all face as we expand and grow. My life as an actor is just a different backdrop to the same story line that runs through all our lives.

I Don't Belong to You comes from deep within. It's the result of many raw experiences in my life that pushed me completely out of my comfort zone and into the open. That rawness gave me the opportunity to define and redefine, shape and reshape myself time and time again.

It may sound exhausting (which it can be) but those incredible opportunities taught me that I could make regular tweaks and adjustments to who I am at the core without ever really losing myself. Time has taught me that I can continue to evolve as a person while also staying true to the foundation of who I am. What a relief it is to know that I can stay true to myself—but I never have to be "finished." I am a work in progress and that's all right with me. 🎤

When I was younger, I was always so afraid of change and of losing certain aspects of myself, as if even the smallest change would make "ME" less "ME." For example, I was really worried that if and when I lost my virginity, I wouldn't be "Keke the good girl" anymore. Who would I be if I weren't "Keke the good girl" or "Keke the virgin"? (Answer in my head: "Keke the freeeeeak"!! 😜 😈 😆)

But for real though! Let's say Jennifer with the superlong blond hair goes and cuts her hair or dyes it black—does she stop being Jennifer? Does the star athlete who stops playing sports after college suddenly cease to exist? The answer is a big NO to both of those questions.

I'm pretty sure you are dealing with your own set of unfairly placed labels—"the poor girl," "the rich girl," "the mixed kid," "the jock," "the trans kid," "the only black kid," or any number of other simplistic titles that have nothing to do with what's really going on inside of you and also don't allow you to make room to be anything else!

Well, here's the gag—who we are and what we are belongs to us and us alone! What that means fr fr (fr = for real) is that we don't belong to other people and we don't belong to other people's expectations of us. We also don't belong to our own old ideas of who we thought we should be or what we thought we should do. You feel me?? It's pretty cool knowing I don't HAVE to be attached to anything that weighs me down as I continue on this journey we call life.

Here's the other big thing—you don't either!

We're all made up of so many different moving parts on both the inside and the outside—and those parts will often vary from moment to moment and from day to day. The most fabulous thing about that for me is knowing that I have the freedom and the flexibility to find my OWN voice in my own way and on my own time. It's on me and up to me to decide which traits of mine make me feel good about being me and which ones I need to let go. No one else has a vote! 😌

A lot of us create identities for ourselves that are based on the patterns of our parents, friends, or other people in our lives. Some of these patterns really don't work for us or stopped working for us—yet we continue to force ourselves to fit inside them. 😩

I Don't Belong to You

I've learned that sometimes we have to "kill" (not literally 🙁) our former selves before we can get to where we are meant to be. Sounds dramatic I know, but y'all know I'm extra. #LBVS (lbvs = laughing but very serious).

The outfit you choose may work for a night or for years to come, but the most important thing to remember is that we aren't chained to anything but the limitations of our own mind. 💭💭

Life transitions are never easy, but how you handle them is all a part of finding out exactly what you're made of.

I've learned through many experiences that it's best to follow my gut/instincts when it's time to make decisions. So go ahead and alter anything about you or your life that you feel isn't working—or isn't working ANYMORE! Listen to your gut, then move on—but only when YOU feel the time is right. 👌

I've also come to understand that energy really cannot be destroyed, only shifted (#POLARITY). 😎

So CHANGE your story if you want and when you want. Where are the rules that say who you were yesterday has to be who you are today? Where are the rules that say who you are today has to be who you are tomorrow? Those rules don't exist, but this one does—all of us must remain in a constant state of evolution IF our goal is to move on to the next chapter of our lives. You cannot stand still and grow, you just can't! 🙅🏽‍♀️🙅🏽‍♀️ #GROWINGNOTGROWN.

Just like you, I am the author of my story, and I can change that story anytime I please. I can flip it forward or I can flip it backward if I want. I'm in control and spiritually aware enough to know that I can trust God and the Universe (or whatever you name it, to each his own) 🙏🏽 with what is supposed to be happening in my life, and it will be okay. Remember, the caterpillar

Lauren Palmer

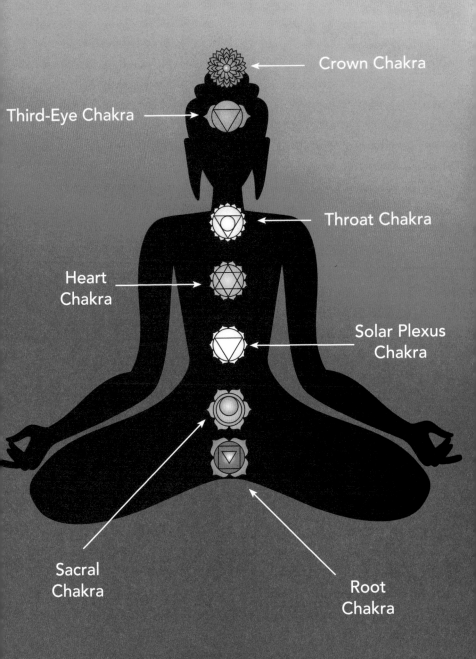

Crown Chakra

Third-Eye Chakra

Throat Chakra

Heart Chakra

Solar Plexus Chakra

Sacral Chakra

Root Chakra

doesn't ask, "When am I going to become a butterfly?" It just waits patiently until it is transformed. ⏰

I wrote this book because I have a passion for sharing and relating with those around me. I have a passion for family and God, and I have a passion for breaking down the barriers that separate us from ourselves and each other. I have real compassion for you and what you are going through right now. 💕

This is a book about you and I connecting, but it's also about us separating ourselves from what is no longer useful. Detaching ourselves from moments, places, ideas, and people that cloud our thinking, wrongly influence our perspectives, and damage the way we see ourselves. 😨

Once we realize that we belong to only ourselves and fully accept that fact, we can begin to live the authentic life we were intended to live. Real happiness can't find us if we aren't honest and truthful with ourselves and to ourselves. Can't nobody hurt you when you know who you are! 🖤

I'm not saying I'm an expert or anything, but I really do believe our life journey should be a soul-searching trip of self-discovery that never ends. 🔍

I hope I can assist you by sharing the many prayers, quotes, meditation methods, and other tools I use to guide me on my own truth-finding path. I won't lie and say it's going to be easy, because life is full of ups and downs, good and bad, and there isn't much we can do to change that fact. But once you fully accept who you are, what your true gifts are, and what you have to offer the world, I promise life will make a lot more sense!

My gift is expression (wouldn't you know 😆), and I'm happy to share with you some universal truths that can help in smoothing out many of the bumps in the road we all WILL face. I want to be an open book (literally—pun intended 😆) and I want you to

Lauren Palmer

feel my story, my pain, and my joy right along with your own. No matter how brutal our combined truths may be—we are going to get through them together I promise! 👆 Finally, by the time you finish this book I hope you can say you've learned a lot about me and, more important, even more about yourself before you enter YOUR next chapter! 👀

I Don't
Belong
to You

I Don't Belong To You

ON IDENTITY AND OWNERSHIP

When I was a kid, I loved story lines that had a beginning, a middle, and an end. That's one reason I was that kid who did not like Saturday morning cartoons. For some reason I felt they were too vapid, hahaha. No, I didn't literally think the word *vapid*, but I did hate the fact that Tom and Jerry never learned anything. I didn't get why it was supposed to be funny, when it was always the same plot with no twists and no lessons.

It wasn't until I discovered live-action shows that I really indulged in television. I loved *Mister Rogers' Neighborhood*. I think in many ways it influenced who I wanted to be in this world. I loved how inclusive his show was. I always felt like Mr. Rogers was talking directly to ME and that made me feel special. 🎬 I also loved *The Big Comfy Couch*, *Sister Sister*, and *Sabrina, the Teenage Witch*, to name a few other shows that helped shape me. *Sabrina* was actually a very important show for me as a kid. I say that because I believe it was there that I saw the good persona and the bad persona displayed on television. (You know, like the good angel on one shoulder 😇 and the devil on the other 😈.) I loved it so much because we all have voices telling us who to be and what to do. Some are thoughts in our heads (concepts, limitations, ideas that shape our opinions) and some are literal things we've heard from people around us and society (hello parents, hello friends, hello Instagram comments!) echoing from our thoughts. But we can't give them control—or we'll end up losing ourselves before we have time to find ourselves!

As a kid it was easier to trust my spirit. I believe that deep down we know who we are, and I was very aware that the voices in my head weren't me! My gut and instincts attempted regularly to show me the way to go. Did I always listen? Mostly! But being human, I've fallen into treating the mind as a master as opposed to a servant. Sound familiar? I quickly figured out how to differentiate myself from the irrational thoughts jumbling around in my brain. It was easy to tell, because one voice made me feel chill and eezy breezy 😁 and the other voice caused me to feel fear, worry, and anxiety 😟. It's a battle and a choice which voice you listen to.

On *Sabrina* they depicted the simplicity of life, which I loved. The message I took away was: *You are here living and breathing. You have gifts, some of which you know immediately or find out about later, and you have the choice to use them for good or bad.* That influenced my approach to life at a young age. I said to myself, *This is how I see life.*

⇾ WHO DO WE BELONG TO? ⇽

I was also very aware that life was a game of choices and experiences. The choices we make determine the experiences we have.

Lauren Palmer

We can decide to just drift along and let the voices in our head control us, or we can remain conscious and be a force in directing where we want our lives to go. I learned that my destiny belonged to me and that the present moment belonged to me. I belonged to me, and I had to have my back and I had to have enough awareness to make the right choices for *me*. That's the first step. In life, before we can make a good conscious decision about what we're going to eat for dinner, what activities we're going to do, what job suits us best, who we want to date, and what we're going to do—pretty much any choice we're going to make at all—we have to first determine who we belong to by accepting that we are responsible for ourselves. And we can be guided by whatever it is in our lives that stirs our passion and inspires us to dream.

Later, I learned by reading the spiritual author Eckhart Tolle's book *A New Earth* that the personalization of the ego is one of humanity's biggest dysfunctions. Simply put, taking things personally is what creates our identities as human beings. The human brain believes its reality is based off of its story. And sometimes the story can become so traumatic—which all of our stories are to some degree—that you forget your life experience is not just about what has happened to you. It's also about how you've grown and transcended. Our lifetimes are just a blip in our eternal existence, and it is our responsibility while we're here to try not to get too attached to any one facet of the story. No matter how aware I was as a child, or any of us are as children, we are not exempt from this experience. Because the gag is that is the experience that is life!

We can acknowledge and accept the thoughts we have, but we shouldn't leave it up to them to determine who we are or how we act. We should live in the moment and find peace in not

I Don't Belong to You

3

knowing what is next. I love this quote from *A New Earth*: "What a liberation to realize that the 'voice in my head' is not who I am."

➤ FOLLOW YOUR HEART ➤

Martin Luther King said, "If a man has not discovered something that he will die for, he isn't fit to live." Living your passion gives your life purpose. The good news is that the things you are meant to do are already inside you, built into who you are. Sometimes we have to simply move through all the bullshit (defense mechanisms) that have clouded us from seeing what it is we want to offer to our world in our lifetime—and what we are here to express! Not just on the surface, but in the soul of our being. There is no right or wrong per se—it's just about getting as close to your truth as possible. There is no blueprint, other than the one that is already imprinted on our soul. And it ultimately comes down to: What have you gone through that when coming out of the other side gave you a perspective that world needed to see. And I believe the best place to start is following what we are interested in. 📝

I made an unconscious vow as a child to always follow the voice of my heart wherever it led me, and my heart as a baby girl led me to my first real passion—music! 🎼 I began singing in the church. My mother was a choir director before my father even thought about becoming ordained. Every Wednesday there were choir rehearsals and I'd always beg my mother to let me sing a solo. I was so hurt every time she would tell me no, I felt like she wouldn't even give me a chance! She'd always tell me that I was too young, and I never could understand what age had to do with singing. #MOMS. 😠

Lauren Palmer

The reality was she probably just thought I was playing, but even though I was a lighthearted child I took myself and my work very seriously, haha #VIRGO. My mother was just thinking I was a kid who was not being serious, so she wanted me to sit down. She thought I was just talking. She didn't understand I really had a desire to sing and touch people until I showed her how persistent I was. You see, I idolized my mother's singing and I saw how she affected people with her voice. I wanted to do that too.

I wanted a chance at THAT! I remember the first time I got her to agree to let me sing a solo, and my song of choice was "Jesus Loves Me." 🖤 Not too long after that, I was the lead soloist singing in my kindergarten play.

My mom was so scared because we rehearsed all week for my solo, and when I walked to the front of the stage to start—they hadn't lowered the mic from the class before! My mom thought I was doomed, but I wasn't afraid, because I had watched her pull a mic out of its stand my whole life, haha. I whipped out that mic and went to town, y'all!

It was truly a special feeling to be able to touch people with my voice, and even more amazing to know that it was specific to me. I claimed my music abilities as a part of my identity.

When my parents first approached me about acting, the connection was music. There was a newspaper article about casting for *The Lion King* production at the Cadillac Palace Theatre in January 2002. The article said they were looking for little black girls of all ages, fitting this height and this weight, to play Nala. They needed a singer, and my parents thought of me. I went and didn't make it! That's how the story goes. But it didn't take long for me to realize that I liked what I saw in that audition room.

I saw that acting was another way to move people. Through playing out different scenarios and showcasing emotions as an actress, I could affect other people's perspectives and feelings just as I saw my mother do with her singing. Movies, plays, and television shows offer people a different perspective from the reality they live in, and sometimes they even offer hope. In my first acting roles I came to understand that and I thought, *Hmm, COOL!* 👯

Though I was always interested in acting, my family and I originally felt singing was my strong suit. Just a few months after my *Lion King* audition, my mother found out about auditions for a show called *American Juniors*. It was a new show on FOX that was the children's version of *American Idol*. Make a long story short, ya girl got her golden ticket! I was just nine years old. My family and I stayed in California for the duration of the competition, and it was a whole new world out there! They put me in dance classes and singing classes and my mom said watching me handle that process convinced her to really take this seriously, because I sure was!

My mom has always been unafraid to ask questions. I believe that's also a great lesson that she taught me: "Closed mouths don't get fed." She tried to raise me to listen more than I spoke—to listen and never be afraid to ask questions! To always remain humble and willing to learn, which is just what she did!

She got every phone number she could at that competition. She learned anything she could that would help with my future in the industry. And she knew that no matter what happened with this competition, she would come up with ideas and a plan of where we were going next! #MYMOMISSOEPIC.

Anyhow, we got back from the trip to California and I ultimately didn't get the call to be on the full season of the show. I was sad, but mostly itching to do more. I knew there had to be more opportunities. I just wasn't sure if my mom knew how to help me.

Lauren Palmer

Lo and behold my mom used any and every resource she had from her college and theater days, her music days, and our time in California during *American Juniors* to make my dreams happen. She even found me an agent in Chicago! The agent told us there were auditions being held for *Barbershop 2*, and they needed a little girl to play Queen Latifah's niece.

I HAD TO AUDITION! Except, they wouldn't let me!! The word was Queen Latifah (fresh from an Oscar nomination) was only going to be in town for a short while. They didn't want to waste her time with unseasoned actors, and I had been on only one audition in my short acting "career." But still, my mom and I weren't about to take no for an answer.

I wasn't much of an actor yet, but I was a singer. That was what we felt the key was—to get them to hear me sing!! I learned a huge lesson from my mother that day. She showed me how to be respectfully persistent. I mean, we didn't run up to the casting director and stalk her outside her house, haha! But we put together a tape of me doing the lines and then me singing "Be a Lion" from *The Wiz*. We felt in our hearts that if they *saw* me they would *feel* me.

Yes, they had told us no, but the point is that we knew something they didn't know: Not seeing me was a mistake! Haha! So we had to find a way around that mistake. 😊 You don't have to bulldoze, you just have to respectfully disagree when you experience, what I call, an unfair no. ☝ Because even if they don't like it or it isn't what they're looking for, people respect well-thought-out effort! And anytime you're reaching for a goal, I've found it helps to create a pattern for yourself of always giving it your all—everything you've got. That is a great habit to start with!

I Don't Belong to You

My mom and I sent in the tape and heard nothing for months. We didn't expect to hear back, because again, we'd done something kind of unorthodox. We weren't even sure when they received the tape, or if they'd actually watch it, ya know?

These were the many thoughts running through our minds, but we sent it off anyway because we felt in our hearts it was worth the shot (it's gotta always be about what you believe!). We started to lose hope until the casting director called my mom saying they'd still been unable to find the girl! 😁 They asked to see me, and they told me that the producers AND ICE CUBE were going to be in the room. 🙀

My mom said they were testing me and probably wanted to see if I would get nervous. We wanted to do more than show them I was prepared. We wanted to do something *extra* to show them that even though I'd never been on a set or met any celebrities, I was fearless!

Fearlessness goes a long way, and it doesn't mean you feel *no* fear, it just means you don't let it drive your decisions or detour you. I was fearless and CAPABLE of doing the job, and I wanted to show them that!

My mother and I quickly hatched a plan. I'd do my lines and then beg them to let me sing! Haha, I know it sounds so silly but I enjoyed this, and singing was my main talent at that time, so I felt more confident knowing I could lean on that in the audition room. Little did I know that this same plan would be my introduction for most of my early career. By the time we moved to California, every room I entered, I would beg the agent, producer, or casting director to let me sing. And when my mother was in the room with me we would really play it up.

Me: I love dancing and acting and singing. I really started out singing with my mom in church! Oh, Mommy, please can I sing for them??

Lauren Palmer

Mom: Oh no Keke, that's not what these people are here for . . .

Me: Mommy, please!

By that point they had to let me sing!

I know this might sound elaborate, and some people might think my mom and I were pulling a little *Heartbreakers* con 😄 — the 2001 movie with Jennifer Love Hewitt and Sigourney Weaver— but the truth is that this is how we got my story across in less than 10 minutes, how we bonded, and how we showed them that I was more than what they saw on the surface. We had to show where we came from and where we were going, with little to no time! We wanted them to know that it was about the feeling and we couldn't do that without a performance to find the quickest way to get there. It was about creating the atmosphere to show the feeling I was able to express through my gift. This became our "Thing."

SHINE YOUR LIGHT AND BE FEARLESS IN YOUR CREATIVE PURSUITS

My mother and I leaned so much on my singing in the beginning, because it was the quickest way to show people my heart and what I was about! Even down to the song choice of "Be a Lion," it was all about courage—having the courage to shine your light— which I had to have. It was the best song to express that Keke is about hope. She is young, but has found what she is passionate about and can't help but share it with the world.

We were asking them, in essence, to be a part of my movement! That's more or less what my mom was trying to display with her game. It's special to me in retrospect because God was

I Don't Belong to You

First simple rule in life:

If you don't go after what you want,

you'll never have it.

right beside her. He was guiding her and guiding me on my yellow brick road.

My timing was good because the opportunities were booming for child actors! There were so many child-driven projects back then. Maybe it's the same now, I'm not sure because I'm no longer a child and don't hear about those parts anymore, lol. But, in any event, when I first moved to California there were opportunities out the 🐴. I was first in line to audition for every last one!

In 2004, I appeared in two very different but equally good movies: *Barbershop 2: Back in Business* with Queen Latifah and *The Wool Cap* with William H. Macy. *I was nine and ten years old!*

Over the next ten years, I was in twenty-one films and sixteen television shows, including the television show *True Jackson, VP* and my own talk show. My mom gave me some perspective. She reminded me to be grateful for the blessing and overflow, but to also understand that life has ups and downs, and even if the work wasn't always overflowing, I should always have fun because the work was about creativity and not society's idea of success.

By the age of ten, I had received a SAG Award nomination in the leading actress category for *The Wool Cap*. I am still the youngest person to be nominated in the female leading category and it brought me a lot of attention in the acting community. The award is so special among actors because it means your peers thought you deserved the nomination. At the time, I didn't know what that meant, and I think that's good. But it was a recurring theme in my life. My mom understood, but I didn't even realize I was achieving all that, because my identity was more wrapped up in music. I was able to be more fearless in my acting because I was less self-conscious about it, but the music—not so much.

However, a very rare opportunity was given to me at the age of twelve. I had just finished *Akeelah and the Bee* and there was

I Don't Belong to You

buzz in the industry around my performance. Record producers heard that I recorded a song for the sound track and all of a sudden they wanted to sign me! WHAT? ME? An official actress, and now, A RECORD DEAL! It's ON! 😈

I was ecstatic! But something went wrong on my way to that dream and things quickly fell apart. The joy I felt singing was overshadowed by people who didn't always share the same love for my music that I did, and suddenly singing became just a job. The gag is most record labels don't have artist development. That part of the company lost its way when labels' main agenda became to sell singles, and when rappers like Master P and Birdman started creating their own independent labels. It made many of the record labels stop investing in real artist development because they depended on smaller production companies to do it and make money off the major singles from the artists. And that means, if you don't come to major labels with your *own* infrastructure in place, it is hard for them to know how to deliver you to the world. They are thinking more about selling singles because that brings in the money faster. They aren't thinking about a long-term career for the artist because that honestly does take a lot of time and effort and is not always a huge "pay off" for THEM, even though it is for the artist. "Single" records don't help build the careers of great artists the way albums do. That's why Motown was one of the best record labels in the world—if the artist didn't hit the first time, they still believed in them and they didn't stop spending money on development and creating albums where the fans were allowed to grow with them. Today, labels are more like distributors. They don't want to spend money making artists—they want to get money off artists who are already made or already made a hit. In other words, they don't want to help the artist create the brand, they just want to attach themselves to the brand once it's

Lauren Palmer

already created. That's why it is important to know who you are and follow your dreams independent of if you know whether people are going to help you or not. Because if you expect them to do it for you, you will be disappointed every time. Just like I was.

I got my first record deal as a very young artist at the age of twelve, and I didn't understand all of that. I thought once you had a deal you had it made. I didn't know how important it was to have a plan for your career going in. I didn't have my own plan. I got lost in the process, and that's what I felt like.

My problem in the early days was that I didn't know who I was as an artist yet. The record company knew I had a great voice and a growing brand as a performer, but they didn't take the time to consider where I came from, who I was, and who I wanted to be. The record labels were just thinking I could sell some records because I was well-known for being on Disney and *Akeelah and the Bee.* They knew that my fanbase was diverse and included all kinds of people. They were focused on the money, and not spreading the joy of the *feeling* that brought me to music in the first place. They didn't care that I grew up singing in the church or about the community that I was from—basically all the experiences that shaped me and made me ME! Rather than understand me, they seemed frustrated that they couldn't tap into what made me special. They couldn't figure out how to make money off that gift, and ultimately it was probably because God didn't want them to. In a lot of ways, I think God was protecting me in order to protect the message that I now know I am supposed to send. It hurt me, but they couldn't block the message!

If you look at the successful careers of performers like Alicia Keys, Jennifer Lopez, Aaliyah, Brandy, and even Taylor Swift, you will see that when they started out, you knew their histories, their backgrounds and their *stories*, which in turn helps you relate to

I Don't Belong to You

the usually unrelatable lifestyles of artists' lead. Alicia Keys was the soul singer and classically trained pianist. She was the "diamond in the rough" so well displayed in the "If I Ain't Got You" video. And even though we saw Jennifer Lopez living large with Diddy and then on her own, her videos always displayed her as a cool down b*tch from the Bronx, with song phrases such as "'cause I'm Real." And even if you couldn't relate to the "sugary sweet country girl playing the guitar," a la Taylor Swift, you could relate to her love-struck tendencies and her dragging of her exes, because honestly, everyone likes to speak their truth.

After my first record deal ended, I would watch tons of music videos from my fav artists and listen to their songs and research, wondering where I went wrong. What did they do that I have not? The record company never gave me time to establish my career and tell my story about growing up in the south suburbs of Chicago and moving to the big city of LA. I was so heartbroken by my experience with the industry that I wanted to understand how it went wrong. I would watch videos all day and night and try to see the difference between some that propelled forward and others that didn't. Their videos gave me inspiration, and it was the first time I realized the integral part that a story line plays for artists—whether it be ambiguous like Prince or straight down the middle like Taylor Swift.

I realized there was always a story. The greats always told you their stories—the ones with legacies gave you a story worth remembering. We were impressed by Michael Jackson's *Thriller* because it was a universal record. It had mainstream appeal and a kick-ass video. We were also overtaken by Michael's image—the glittery gloves and glittery socks. But would it have hit as hard if it wasn't the Michael Jackson we all knew? Would something so abstract have been understood if we didn't know Michael's story?

Lauren Palmer

That's the whole gag. Even though we couldn't always relate to Michael's lifestyle, we could always relate to his story.

He came from Indiana, big family, close to his mother and sister, problems with his father. We maybe didn't always get his quirkiness, but that's what we would expect, seeing as how he grew up so different in front of our eyes. From the very beginning, he had a different life, making hits since the age of ten for Motown Records. It made sense, he made sense. A song about going to see a horror movie made sense for HIM. And Prince, would we have been able to accept Prince's ambiguity if he hadn't so artistically expressed ridicule being a part of his life since he could remember? #PURPLE RAIN. As some people ridiculed him about his race, his sexuality, his sense of fashion, other people also shared that story line or just related to his resilience and started to root for him for those same reasons as they realized that his embracing ridicule for being different was a part of his artistic message. ("I just can't believe all the things people say. Controversy. Am I black or white? Am I straight or gay? Controversy.") #THATSTHEULTIMATEGAG.

We were invested in these great artists *because* we got to watch them grow. My previous label ALWAYS tried to take shortcuts with me because I was already a celebrity when I signed—unlike traditional new artists mentioned above. The label didn't think they had to allow my audience to grow with me as a musician, by giving them the TIME to get to know me as an artist. They thought they could ride the wave of my popularity from acting and make a quick buck, but the gag was I'm not my characters. People aren't stupid, and they didn't want a glazed-over Keke Palmer, they wanted to really get to know her if they were going to listen to her music. When my first album was released, the label threw the single out and when it didn't become widely successful (even though they didn't promote it effectively or even know me

I Don't Belong to You

well enough to know how to promote it), they blamed it on me. The single they chose, "Keep It Movin,'" didn't even represent me or my story well. A better choice would've been "Hood Anthem." They were just thinking about the money and not my fans, not the kids or the people who I wanted to positively affect with my story.

That time was scary for me because I wanted to shine my light, but if it wasn't big and it wasn't grand I felt like it wasn't good enough. They tried to get me to sing music I didn't give a f*&k about. It was bullshit.

As I said on my website, I did not spread my wings because I was told I couldn't fly a certain way, and I believed it! I stopped trying altogether because I allowed people to make me believe that being an artist meant having big-budget music videos and big record producers backing you. When in reality, all being an artist means is to be fearless in your creative pursuits. My anxiety, caused by the habit of unconsciously holding my breath, coupled with the stress of my personal life at that time, created a lot of hard years of depression for me. However, I am exalted now because God brings it to you when you are ready, not when you think you are. I am now right where I should be and I can see with my heart that I have always known who I am and who I want to be.

I was young then and I didn't understand it all. Now I'm a grown woman, and I can say to record executives that they may *want* a big single, but I *want* to tell my fans who I am first. I couldn't articulate that as a kid. No one would listen to me, and I let it steal my joy!

MOVING TO THE NEXT LEVEL

I started to shut down as a result of feeling chained by something that once set me free. What could I do other than to abandon

Lauren Palmer

music as a whole? That's what I thought at the time. Talk about a heartbreak! No guy could ever break my heart like the music industry did. 💔

This is a typical story when you are pursuing your dreams. When you start taking action, a lot of people are suddenly trying to weigh in. And it becomes easy to doubt yourself. You are also "walking through the valley of the shadow of death," which to me in many ways is a metaphor for the doubts and disappointments playing out in your mind.

When you decide to be all that you know you are meant to be, you have to face a lot of the things holding you back mentally, physically, and spiritually. (They all affect one another.) And certain situations, no matter how difficult they may seem in the moment, you MUST experience in order to get to the next chapters of your life. 🎮 It's like a video game, and the sooner you accept the tough situations as something that's going to move you forward, the more it drives you in your desire to advance to the next level.

I forgot that I belonged to me at that time, and just like that (finger snap), the negative voices that I was so quick to ignore as a child began pushing me the wrong way. These were the voices of despair that I had unconsciously vowed to never follow. They became very loud and very real.

They told me that the problems in my music career were all my fault and that I had failed. 😰 My rational, intellectual voice was quickly being drowned out by the irrational voice of my ego that had personalized the experience. The ego voice was telling me, *"The label people are smart and can't be wrong about artists. I mean, could they? I don't know? Oh no, I don't KNOW."*

That's the thing about the mind and why it should always be

I Don't Belong to You

a servant to the heart. The mind has limitations, and these limitations are because the mind is like a computer. A computer only knows what has been put inside it. Our minds cannot fundamentally understand the point of following a passion. It cannot comprehend passion, and it can only "know" the information it knows already. The intellectual mind, when nurtured, can filter out what is in your control and what is not—and when it's time to let the heart decide. When you allow your ego to take over, it often doesn't feel at ease, unless it's in control, which means it is uneasy often because you can't control the circumstances of life. So when you let your ego drive, it is a fast way to a world of anxiety. But our hearts tell us that what "we know" is relative and that there are things we can do that have never been done before. 🔑

I didn't have enough *experience* to know the difference. The even scarier part was these dark thoughts were a much more aggressive version of the not-so-positive thoughts I had as a child. This was a mixture of my own frivolous fears and the voices of real people, businesspeople, filling me with fears I never knew existed. They were putting limitations on me that I never knew were there!

The louder their voices got, the cloudier my sense of self became. I believed my fears, because to me, it *had to be true* now that others were also saying it, right? I started making associations that weren't true. I tried to equate them like A+B=C. I determined that I wasn't able to be a music artist, and that it had to be true because my first album, *So Uncool*, wasn't "successful." I was only fourteen years old, but that is when I began to belong to them instead of to *me*.

As far as I knew, the labels never made mistakes. And I told myself that if I was worth anything, then they'd know it. So I stepped away from music thinking that I wasn't a musician, and even more so, *that I wasn't worthy of being one.* I felt this way for many years, and so I focused solely on my other passions and talents. I didn't understand that those voices of doubt, whether in my head or from the mouths of real people, would always be in some ways my constant companions because that's simply how life works. The more you grow and the more you're faced with, the more your mind has to analyze and digest. *Mental constructs are a part of our humanity, and yes, haters gonna hate!* 👻 But I didn't know at the time that I could fight them. I had to fight them and I had to win!

This concept doesn't just apply to the music industry. Some people think that being a celebrity is the only extraordinary thing to "be" or that popularity is what it means to be successful. How many times a day do you judge a life event by how many "likes" it gets on social media? 😉 I've even done it myself!

But this is not fair to us. *Our worth cannot be based on what others believe, but what we CHOOSE to believe.* What I'm talking about applies to whatever you are trying to do in life—whether you are an aspiring entertainer, writer, model, trainer, doctor, nurse, hairdresser, or bookkeeper! Whatever is in your heart, whether it's pursuing a career you love or trying something new every week until you find what it is you love. It's on the right track as long as it's true of heart because "success" is what's relative to YOU.

➤ LEAVE THE DOUBTERS AND ➤ FIND ENCOURAGERS INSTEAD

As soon as you know what you want to do, and your gut is screaming out, you might have people step in with a list of "logi-

I Don't Belong to You

cal" reasons why you shouldn't do that thing you know you need to do. But you have to take a real good look at those people who are setting roadblocks in YOUR life. #YOUSAIDWHATNOW?!

When you look at where people are in their lives, their point of view becomes clear. You have to weed out the people you love from the people you admire. Does that make sense? The two things are different. For instance, if you love your brother, but your brother has never been disciplined about anything, he's probably not the best person to talk to when you need motivation to follow through with the things you are doing. If you love your mom, but your mom was always too scared to try anything new, it makes no sense to expect her to encourage you when stepping outside of your comfort zone. #CONSIDERTHESOURCE.

They may share their fears or doubts, and that's fine, but you can't wait for them to come around or allow their excuses to become your own. They may have certain wisdom, but they may be limited in their perspectives, and they are also not inside your head or your heart, so they may not know what *you* know about what *you* are capable of.

We are the heroes of our stories! And when you choose to be, that's what the work of belonging to ourselves is about. Taking responsibility for your own life requires a lot of work and you will need support. We've gotta surround ourselves with like-minded people who are on a road of self-discovery, just like us, so that we can encourage each other.

Making room for those who are all about what you're about also shows God and the Universe that you are serious about changing the world around you. By taking the steps yourself to change your path, and actually walking the walk and talking the talk, you open the door for God to assist you. You show Him that you are ready to step up each and every step of the way.

Lauren Palmer

The ego says, "I shouldn't have to suffer," and that thought makes you suffer so much more. It is a distortion of the truth, which is always paradoxical. The truth is that you need to say yes to suffering before you can transcend it.
—Eckhart Tolle

⇌ BE READY TO CHANGE YOUR PATH ⇌
WHILE KEEPING YOUR EYE
ON YOUR DESTINATION

When doing this work of belonging to yourself, there are no strict plans that you have to follow, and if your narrative isn't working for you, you need to change your story and change what you are telling yourself about it. Sometimes we sit back and say, *Well this is what my mom did and I know if I do this then that will possibly come next and I guess I can deal with that. . . .* But NO! Stop living your mom's old story line and begin creating your own story by being present in the moment—our moment.

You are unique. Your path is unlike your mother's, your teacher's, or anyone else's. Start living in the NOW and not inside your head packed with all these used story lines about other people's experiences. The moment you step outside their story and outside of your head, you allow yourself to come face-to-face with YOU. The whole point is to get as close to *you*—not your brain, not your physical body—but as close to YOU as possible.

Of course all those things are a part of you (the body and the brain), and they're important, but they're not meant to be the drivers of the ship. It's your gut, your intuition, your ESSENCE that is the magic. ✦ A great thinker once said, "The intuitive mind is a sacred gift and the rational mind is a faithful servant. We have created a society that honors the servant and has forgotten the gift." What I interpret that to mean is that the mind cannot tell you that the things in your heart are not true or real.

Lauren Palmer

These things take practice. Your practice may be prayer, meditation, yoga, or whatever it is. But it's always something that clears your mind and makes way for you to use your intuitive senses. That's how you stay in tune with your core, your essence, and when that happens you become guided to your passion.

The reason why is that you are doing the work of lifting the veils of bondage (false beliefs) that have limited you from seeing clearly. *It's like you've been living in fear, seeing this delusional world, and then when you truly reconnect to your essence you see the only truth there is—that there is love.*

It's like when you see a video of a lion mutilating a person. Okay, I know that is a terrifying image, but follow me here. If the most deluded person (a person with a perspective in life altered by fear) saw a lion mutilate someone, they might say, *"Thaaaat lion is so evil! That lion was plotting to hunt my friend. Lions hate people. That lion needs to be killed!"*

Then you may never go to the zoo again, even though you love animals! A person based in love, which to me is the reality, would likely have a very different perspective. She might say, *"What a horrible accident! The nature of that lion is to hunt and to kill. I hate that the person had to be there in that place at that time."*

You see, it isn't that danger isn't real, it's just that most things aren't personal. The emotion of fear can create ideas on top of a situation that personalize it, which makes it a lot harder to move past. *You see what I'm saying?*

Trying new things and seeking new environments is an important part of finding what you love too, because what you love may not look anything like what you grew up around. You may have to step outside your present circumstances to find your passion. I grew up in an artistic home, but that's not true of all artists. You might be an artist who grew up in a home full of mechanics, but in order to find out that you love the arts, you'd have to expose yourself to them and try them! If you allow yourself to believe that you have no future other than being a mechanic because that's all your family has ever done, or to let your mechanic family make you believe there is no future in anything other than being a mechanic (because that's how they have been living THEIR lives), you will never try something new, find your passion, and develop your gifts. You will miss out on living your dream! (Nothing to be scared about, because it's never too late!)

But if you look at the people and situations in your life more objectively and less personally, it will be easier to grow. How could I let others so easily define me in my music? I could not allow anyone else to deter me or make me question what was so insanely important to me! 🎭

I realized that I needed to understand why I let those negative voices impact me so deeply, because what happened with my music simply couldn't happen again in my LIFE.

⇥ LESSONS FROM THE HEART ⇤

The first lesson I learned was to be patient with myself because sometimes experiences, particularly the not so "good" ones, have to happen to us several times before we really get the point. 💡 #SOLISTENTHEFIRSTTIME.

I also asked myself the really tough questions that we all have to ask ourselves every time we make a decision: *Is this something I feel right about? Or do I feel right that other people feel right about this? Is this something I feel wrong about? Or do I feel wrong about it because other people told me it was wrong?*

Lauren Palmer

Now, finding a way to conquer the un-useful negative voices in my head required a few different methods, but they weren't as difficult as you might think. It all has to do with observing your thoughts and being in tune with your body so you can know how things are making you feel and ask yourself the right questions to see what is causing the negative voices. None of this comes without trust and belief. You have to start from a place where you *believe*—I mean really *BELIEVE, y'all*—that:

1) You deserve a happy life.

2) You were born with the instincts and tools to achieve it.

3) There is good that can come of bad things.

4) There are no forces that can stop you as long as you refuse to give up.

5) The world is not out to get you.

Okay, that is the mental part of this process of taking charge of your life. There is also a physical component connected to healthy habits like yoga and meditation that I will talk about much more. When I was on this path, I began sitting alone with myself for a few minutes a day. I'd take deep breaths and just quiet the surroundings around me. Doing those small things reminded me that the world was much larger than me.

Forgetting that point is a quick-ass ticket to "Woe-Is-Me-Land." Silence helped me to separate the voices, like I had done so effortlessly as a child. I feel we are all here to live and experience life using each and every one of our unique gifts. Our purpose is to spread the love that we come to know when we learn to love ourselves.

I Don't Belong to You

When we learn to let our light from within shine THROUGH us on Earth, it in turn expands our world and allows us all the space to create many amazing things that we can only imagine in the moment. I feel that it is this awareness that helps keep you fearless and courageous throughout your life so that you can pursue your passion and live your dreams. It inspires you and always reminds you that you are connected to everyone around you, and that their experiences are a part of your experience too. #YEAIMAHIPPIEOKAY. 🍵

I'm sharing this with you because it's my personal belief. I've needed to lean heavily on my spirituality more than a few times in my life, and I don't know the state I would be without it. You may not know yet how you are going to change the world, but if you are going to go out and change it, you have to be prepared to listen to what the part of yourself that is bigger than your ego is saying. It will help you follow your passion.

Here's an example.

Just a few years ago I had a great offer to be the lead actress in a very popular show that originated on the CW and then went to BET. It was called *The Game*. My offer came after Tia Mowry-Hardrict left the show. They were looking at me coming on in a big way.

This was just around the same time I was developing my talk show *Just Keke* with Telepictures, which really meant a lot to me. Telepictures is the reality extension of Warner Bros. Television and they have produced *The Ellen DeGeneres Show* since the beginning, as well as *The Real* and many other great talk shows. I was really excited that they wanted to produce mine, and it meant a lot to me! Anyhow, the role that the producers of *The Game* were offering me was a great paycheck and a move to a home in Atlanta. The only problem was that its schedule conflicted with that of *Just Keke*. 🙀

Lauren Palmer

This was a point in my career when I could have used a steady job and a good paycheck, but the conflict in the schedule with my talk show made me question whether I really wanted to be on *The Game*. I knew in my heart that *Just Keke* reflected where I wanted to go in my career and was on point with the message I wanted to put out into the world.

I kept waiting and asking *The Game* producers to adjust the schedule. All the while people were telling me I was stupid not to take the role. I waited . . . and I waited . . . and I waited. . . . Eventually I waited so long that I lost the role and, surprise, surprise, those inner voices of doubt and criticism returned with a vengeance!

The voices had a field day telling me that my career was over and that I'd always just be the girl from *Akeelah and the Bee*. The reality was I lost one job, but I didn't lose *Just Keke*. I may have gone into a temporary state of financial and career discomfort. But it was just that, temporary *(even though it sucked in the moment, lol!)*.

The rest is history. I stuck to my belief in my heart and soul. I followed my dream of writing this book, I never gave up on music, and Telepictures is still behind my talker. This is the direction my heart always knew I was headed in! 👫

I 🖤 my heart!

➤ IGNORING VOICES, MAKING CHOICES ⬅

Sometimes we have to turn down opportunities, even "good" ones, to get to those that were custom-made for us. I was scared when I made that choice. At that point I hadn't yet done *Grease: Live*. Or *Cinderella* on Broadway. Or *Scream Queens*. I feared that my career rested on this one decision. I was an actor, and this was a big gig—take it! Easy choice, right?

I Don't Belong to You

But was it the *right* choice for *me*?

My decision came down to my belief that I'm more than just an actor. I wanted to expand, and that meant thinking about things other than just "my acting career."

No one could know that particular truth but me. Few people would have made that decision for me, but I made it for myself. That is what was in my heart, and my heart guided me through the fear and insecurity of myself and others. I saw my potential past the limitations. The magic powers of my passion kicked in! #DUH. If I want to be a girl who acts, sings, writes books, and has a talk show, that's cool! Just because no one had seen a talk show host that young materialize in the world doesn't mean it couldn't be.

Sometimes we get messed up in our HEADS. It's so dramatic in retrospect, haha . . . But this is what fear was telling me:

"You will end up just being the girl who did Akeelah and the Bee."

"You are becoming just like the people you know who gave up their 'dreams' to live 'normal' lives."

"You will fall through the cracks and give up."

"You're headed for an uncreative and unfulfilled life."

"That's what life is, isn't it? Welcome to Adulthood, land of the brokenhearted and disappointed."

And then I had to say to myself, *Why am I living* this *story line?!* It was like one of those VH1 specials on forgotten child stars, hahaha. I didn't want to be a has-been at twenty. Yikes! I had to flip my story quick! The reality was, yes, my life had changed and it was a blow to my self-esteem, but I truly believed in my heart of hearts that I was meant to create my own blueprint.

I needed to tap my vision and shut out the voices. I had gotten into victim mode (#PITYPARTY). I was letting the fear of a bad

Lauren Palmer

outcome keep me from paving the path toward the outcome I really wanted. So sometimes you gotta rein all that in. You gotta rid yourself of the baggage loaded with doubts, fears, and insecurities. You gotta say, "I don't want that program. I don't want the victim program. I want the hero program!" It was time to focus on what I had to be grateful for and unleash my powers, my magic, my light, my gifts. #YASSSSBIH.

Thankfully, this time around I was ready for the negative voices, or at the very least I was better equipped to ignore them. I wasn't playing the victim. I wasn't going to worry that there were forces waiting for me to fail. I exercised understanding, observed my thoughts without judgment, and told myself that just 'cause my mind is regurgitating the same old negative bullshit, I don't have to listen if it ain't moving me toward a positive disposition.

I was ready to be the hero of my own story. #PARADIGM SHIFT.

→ GET THE REWRITE, ← I'M CHANGING THE STORY

I know our trials and tribulations will differ, but at the end of the day, I know we all have gotten familiar with the voices in our heads telling us we're not good enough or smart enough to get the things we really want out of life. We all have insecurities, doubts, and people who we feel would rather see us crash and burn than rise and shine.

It's part of being human.

My mom always told me that no one could make me feel any way without MY permission. What she meant by that was, peace is within you—it's obtainable no matter what situation you are in.

Don't let anyone tell you that you aren't worthy of living your

I Don't Belong to You

dreams. You came from God/Allah/the Great Big Spirit! Y'all know I hate labels, lol, so call the highest power anything you want. As long as you know that you were put here for a PUR-POSE.

We exist—wow, that's special in and of itself. There is a connection to magic in you—to something bigger than yourself—and no matter how low you think of you or how low others think of you, you can never break that. You came with the standard package, but the gag is God put in some extra stuff for you!

You may not feel it sometimes. You may ignore it and not make use of it. #FREEWILL. You may go low (which will make the highs all the better), but no matter what you do, it's always there for you with wisdom and patience.

Therefore, we were meant to make manifest and the world IS our oyster. Do not let life make you feel stuck. You bend; you don't break. You don't have to wait until the end of your life to look back and realize you never lived. 😖

We can start living with purpose and power now. If we're alive and breathing, then we have all the power we need to be great. Not tomorrow, not yesterday, but now. You ain't never gonna meet yesterday, and you ain't never gonna meet tomorrow. You're only gonna meet today, and today is a good day to start deciding who you're going to be and then watch your story unfold.

You have no idea how you're going to be able to change the world! 😎

Lauren Palmer

Say Hello to the Real You

ON FINDING AND EXPRESSING YOUR VOICE

I once forgot, oh I let life decide
I didn't know what was me
Because I was trying to be everything
And all I'd seen was a lie.
—"I Once Forgot," Keke Palmer

*B*ack when I had just turned ten years old, my parents had made that crucial decision, the one that would have a lasting impact on my entire family's future (dramatic score, *"dun dun DUN!"*). My mom and dad decided to move our family from Illinois to California so I could have a better shot at following my dream of being an entertainer.

After my small but significant role in the film *Barbershop 2*, the producers of the movie encouraged my mom to head west to try my luck in Hollywood. I was so excited by what the future had in store for me that I never gave much thought to the life we were all leaving behind. None of us did.

In our Illinois hometown, my mom had been working as a teacher for mentally disabled children, and my father was working in a polyurethane company where he made plastics and yellow jackets. Only a year and a half before we left Robbins, Illinois, we'd moved into a new home and my dad was so proud. To understand why this was a big deal, you have to understand how segregated Illinois is, or at least it was when I grew up. My dad went to school for communications, but when he was first hired they put him to work in the factory. He had finally worked his way up into the front office—a goal he had had the whole time. After seven years, he had gotten the big promotion he wanted at his job and that enabled him to own our first home! 🦆🦆

Up to that point, we had been in Section 8 housing, living in one of Mr. Williams's houses in Robbins. Mr. Williams was the grandpa of the neighborhood. But he and my grandma were enemies because apparently when he rebuilt his home, she said he took over half her driveway, and she could never get over it (#PETTY). But the real gag is, when my mom was a kid, he put rat poison on their property without telling my grandma, and my mom's cousin ended up eating it. So ever since then, they never got along. When he would try to say hello in the morning, she would give him the look that Ice Cube's mom gave that lady in *Friday.* 😂

Now we had a nice home, in a good neighborhood, in a house that was under my father's name. He had finally done all he had set out to do! 😁 ❗ He had just been ordained as a church deacon; he was the man.

Fast-forward a year or so and we were all packing to leave that new home that my father had worked so hard to secure. Our move meant my parents would have to walk away from their careers and the only lives they'd ever known. It meant my older sister, Loreal, would need to say good-bye to longtime friends just as she was set to enter high school (freshman YEAR? #WHOA). The twins were still babies, still too young to even understand how their lives were being turned upside down too. 🙊🙊

Lauren Palmer

For better or worse I've always been in tune with my feelings, as well as the feelings of those around me. When I came across the word *empath*, I felt I finally figured out that that was a gift. Here's a definition I found: "someone who is highly tuned to and affected by the feelings of others to the point that their lives can even be influenced unconsciously by other people's thoughts and emotions." That translates to this for me: I'm highly sensitive to the world around me. Even when I was a kid, it was an affinity for other people's feelings that inspired me to do something good in the world. Pretty much, I feel everything! Often to an extreme! Those feelings overwhelmed me a lot in my youth, but now I'm realizing that just because I feel it doesn't mean I need to succumb to it. My mom always tells the story about when I was five years old, running out of my room crying and screaming. She was so alarmed—she just knew that someone had killed a family member or worse. I yelled, "THEY KILLED MUFASA!" hahahahah. I had just been watching *The Lion King* and couldn't believe they took Simba's father away from him. I think that was the first time my parents saw the depth of my empathic nature. I was always so moved by the feelings of others, even when watching television or movies. Any time *Selena* came on, my family wouldn't even tell me. They knew I would start crying and hugging the TV. I was all dramatic because I couldn't handle that the reality was she was gone. For REAL for real, not fake like MUFASA. ☹

As a kid, and even today, I can look at someone and pick up on their energy. It's not about me knowing every little detail about their life, but I feel their *disposition* about life. What people give us on the surface, whether it be docile or bubbly, is just a little bit of who they are. Usually there's just so much more under that.

I Don't Belong to You

Even when they seem like assholes, we have to try to show them something different because clearly they've gotten this whole deal confused. #ITSNOTPERSONAL. When I meet someone mean, and they're lashing out at me—I try (verrrry hard 😡) not to lash out back. Because I know their energy toward me is them perpetuating their reality of what's underneath. Meaning it's just a defense mechanism to whatever vulnerability they aren't expressing. And the only way to combat it is to bring love into the forefront.

Love is the real reality, but pain has a way of making you forget that. Pain is a part of life, it is not a personal attack. You can hold yourself back if you don't see life as a benevolent force and pain as an opportunity to grow. We can all act from that place of loving consciousness—as a kid I would look at my mom and feel that she was sad about something. I felt it was because of the music industry. The music industry was unkind to her, like it could be unkind to a lot of people, because only a small percentage of singers have commercial success and commercial success is made to seem like it's the only success. I knew she wanted more for her life and for her children. That is how my mother discovered my talents. When my mom saw me singing, not only did it make her happy, she saw that I had a genuine love for music too. I loved how my family and I have a special connection with the arts, and watching the positivity spread between my family and me over the connection we shared.

My dad was an entertainer too. He got accepted to UCLA and didn't even go. He felt he had to stay back and take care of my grandma. It was hard for him to leave his family behind without feeling selfish. I could tell my dad was always trying to be so much for everyone, and that can weigh on a person. Both my parents were the youngest in their families and to me it seemed like everyone depended on them. My mom and dad had this bond in

Lauren Palmer

common. They held each other up. I wanted to be part of that bond and I also felt isolated because of it.

My parents, like many people, went through life with dreams unrealized. As they began having kids and building a home, that became their main focus. I wonder how their lives might have been different if they had had parents like me, for instance? Now I know how much they loved me, considering the opportunities they gave me that they didn't have for themselves. But sometimes, back then, it was hard to understand the ways they were (or weren't) communicating. They didn't know how to express their love in ways I could relate to. They were about the practical—keeping the roof over our heads, and making sure I had a platform for achieving my dreams—but I was just wanting a hug and a kiss. I can still remember days when my mom's mind seemed a million miles away while my sister and I played games in our rooms. My dad was often distant as well, and whereas I could talk with my mother some of the time, my father's guard never seemed to come down.

California was going to change all that, I just knew it! 🥚

We drove four days and three nights to California in our Dodge Caravan. The twins were barely potty-trained, so it was hell on wheels that ride! 💩 When we finally got into town it took forever for us to find a hotel we could afford that wasn't a motel. My parents took out all the money they had, including my father taking out his pension, so that we would have the money to move. This was a big deal because he had worked for that company for years, and for them to draw from his pension for us to start this new life in California was a huge sacrifice. That's how my dad showed his love—sacrificing—and sometimes I couldn't comprehend that as a kid. Each and every step of the way, whether it was leaving all his family behind, giving up his job to

I Don't Belong to You

stay at home, and sacrificing the way he appeared to the outside world because of it, he sacrificed his own feelings in order to do what he thought was best for my family. My dad's back still hasn't recovered from that drive. I remember when I was twelve him going to get cortisone shots until his body became numb to it. Even so, we were never prepared for the culture shock that is California. I will never forget the first hotel that we stayed in—the moment our skin touched the covers we all started itching! And let's not even get on what we saw when we turned on the television. 😵 Honestly though, we were happy—at least, I know us kids were. I loved having all that time to be around my dad and my mom, to have their undivided attention, and all of us in the same room.

We bounced around until we found our hotel home for most of our first year, the St. George Inn and Suites in Tarzana. After a week of being in California, I got an agent, and I also landed a Kmart commercial, which allowed us some breathing room financially. Again, it was music that broke open the door! They wanted the kids to sing the Kmart theme song: "Right here, right now, there is no other place I want to be. Right here, right now, this is the place I want to be. Right here, right now, Kmart." WOOO! I got so happy, and I thought, *Hell yeah, I've got this. I've got a real chance of doing this.* After calling us in, they gave us fifteen minutes to go out and learn the song. I told my momma, I'm going to get this! And she just started laughing. She loved when I came at her with that confidence.

When they called me back in, I did the song and added my own twists. When I left the room, little did I know that the casting director literally followed me out shouting, "WOW! I can't believe your daughter. She's FEARLESS! She rocked this audition." Everyone in the waiting room was shocked. Their mouths dropped! We

Lauren Palmer

knew then I got the role, because he had said the magic word—*Sing!*

We hit the ground running in Los Angeles and quickly found regular work in television films like *The Wool Cap* with William H. Macy. As I mentioned earlier, I received a SAG nomination for that and that success led to the film that in many ways changed my career and life—*Akeelah and the Bee.*

Later I got a role in Tyler Perry's *Madea's Family Reunion* and with Ice Cube in *The Longshots*, movies that really were great strides toward the career I imagined. I was having a blast, and the other really great thing about being in *Akeelah* was that it put me around kids, lots of kids, for the first time in a long time, and man was that fun for me!

When I was back in Illinois, I'd been living a more regular life, so of course I was surrounded by kids all the time. That all changed with our move to Los Angeles. I was being home-schooled by my mom and my world pretty much consisted of my mom and me, day in and day out, my siblings when I was in town, and a few actor kids every now and then whenever I worked on a set.

Mom would take me to auditions as often as possible and then we would spend time going over lines and studying for my next role. For *Akeelah*, since my mom loved that script so much, my entire family would do table readings of the film, with my sister and dad playing different roles. She even had the idea to help me learn the lines by running our own spelling bees with my sister and me. Whoever won got some snack money that they'd take across the street to buy candy with. 😄 We had so much fun rehearsing and I really liked that undistracted time with my mom, but that didn't happen as often as I would have liked without acting being involved.

I Don't Belong to You

10 Essential Questions To Guide You To An Extraordinary Life

From bestselling author and life coach Debbie Ford, who dedicated her personal and professional life to the importance of self-care by teaching from her own experience.

1. Will this choice propel me toward an inspiring future, or will it keep me stuck in the past?

2. Will this choice bring me long-term fulfillment or short-term gratification?

3. Am I standing in my power, or am I trying to please another?

4. Am I looking for what's right, or am I looking for what's wrong?

5. Will this choice add to my life force, or will it rob me of energy?

6. Will I use this situation as a catalyst to grow and evolve, or will I use it to beat myself up?

7. Does this choice empower or disempower me?

8. Is this an act of self-love or self-sabotage?

9. Is this an act of faith (love) or fear?

10. Am I choosing from my divinity or am I choosing from my humanity?

From Debbie Ford's The Right Questions: Ten Essential Questions To Guide You To An Extraordinary Life, *HarperOne Publishers, 2003.*

When I was fourteen, I was shooting *The Longshots* with Ice Cube, about the first female to play in the Pop Warner football tournament. It was my second film with him, and I was really excited and looking forward to all the football training I needed to do for the movie. At the same time, I was worn out physically and mentally.

I was finishing up the Jingle Jam 2007 tour with the Jonas Brothers, and my mom was planning on adding more tour dates to get the word out about my *So Uncool* album. The music industry had done a pretty good job beating me down, and I felt like I'd gone from being the most important person on my label to them not caring at all.

The whole experience was causing me to lose my belief in myself and I didn't see the point in touring. The beat-down of it all made me forget about the kids who actually liked my music and the whole point of performing, which was to create love between us through art. It's like I was saying before—I was getting lost in other people's ideas of success for me instead of being the driving force along my own path. Looking back now, I can imagine how frustrating that must have been for my mom at that time. She didn't want me to give up, but in some ways, I already had.

While I was filming *The Longshots*, I would leave on the weekends to go do a Kmart tour to promote my album, as well as do some dates for kids who lived on military bases. I enjoyed performing, but honestly I was heartbroken. My mom didn't understand that I needed her as a mother at that time. She was in manager mode and it truly made things harder for me.

A part of me loved being busy because it kept my mind off the music situation, but I hated that I had to sacrifice my relationships with people because I was on the road. It seemed the more my career grew, the less connected to others I started to feel and the less time I got to spend time with my family. Many of my films were shot across the world, and most of the time, my family couldn't come for the whole shoot. It would usually just be my mom or my dad with me. Loreal still had schooling, and as the twins grew, so did they, so one parent had to stay behind to parent them as well. I understand that now, but at the time it was painful, because there was a separation in our family that grew.

It became easy for them to feel like a family without me. I was like the father who always worked. I felt disjointed. I would try to maintain friendships through texting and Myspace, but I was really lonely. It was a catch-22. I loved being able to entertain, but it was also a sacrifice. After a month on *The Longshots*, my family was able to come on set. But even when they came I felt over-worked and just so tired. I couldn't express myself and didn't know yet how to put it into words, which made me feel more isolated.

All of that stress and anxiety made me feel very up and down personally, like I had several different personalities—and as usual, I turned that into a tool for entertainment to hide my pain and confusion. 😕 My whole theme for the *So Uncool* album was "I'm Keke," but Keke is many different characters depicting the many different ways I was pulled and what was created out of it. It was lighthearted and fun, but created in heartache and the undefin-able stress I was feeling.

The album art for *So Uncool* depicted several different Kekes: a skater, a hip-hop head, a bookworm, and a diva. That grew into a running joke with my dancers and road manager, Big Billy Clark, during my tour. We would joke about my different personalities— Keke as well as Meka, Leka, and Deka—putting names to those

Lauren Palmer

characters, different facets of my personality that I wasn't afraid to admit I had.

Meka, Leka, and Deka were my alter egos for that period of time, haha. Big Billy Clark's favorite character was Meka because she was the CRAZIEST and sassiest! Leka was the most focused, and Deka was the most docile. If I'm remembering correctly. Keke is the balance of them all. She is the representative of all sides of my personality. I played off them during the making of my album and a bit on the tour to entertain everyone.

The gag is I had broken through the mold. I had broken through so many parts of myself by just accepting who I was in the moment that I was. We all have many facets, and I think we should feel free to express them instead of feeling like we have to be exactly the same all the time. I'm actually many people at once, though I always felt the world wanted me to be less than I am.

People sometimes feel they have to be what the world wants them to be. They settle on one aspect of their personality, but I could never get with that. I always felt like I was a little of everything. On my Instagram page I sometimes call myself "Auntie Keke" because that would be me tapping into the wisdom I had collected from my grandmother and from the adults I was always surrounded by. Then there is my "Laurennnn" side, which projects more of who I am outside the entertainment business, more of the raw girl from Chicago who people don't get to see all the time—the universe-loving hippie and cosmic queen.

The real me isn't one-sided or one-dimensional. I want to express every aspect of who I am as a person, an actress, a singer, an entertainer, a daughter, a sister, an African-American woman, and a child of God. I am not the only creative person to address the capacity to access different personalities, of course. Eminem has his Marshall Mathers and Slim Shady sides. Nicki Minaj has talked

I Don't Belong to You

about the fact that she created alter egos—Nicki Minaj, Roman, Roman's mother, and Onika—to transcend her reality. Beyoncé flashed what she referred to as her "more sensual, more aggressive, more outspoken, and more glamorous side" as "Sasha Fierce."

These people show what it means to be a diamond—they are pieces of coal that allowed the pressure to shape them, and their reward is that they shine bright like a diamond. And let's not forget about Michael Jackson, who, through the power of the written word, manifested his destiny. Note by note, he created on the page who he wanted to be. He wrote to himself he wanted to be a greater dancer than before. That he wanted to be known not only as a singer but as an actor and an overall entertainer. He wrote that he was going to be the best entertainer the world had ever seen. And he added the discipline to it. He vowed to have a life of mystery because he knew he had to re-create his identity from what people knew him as when he was a little boy. And he accepted the ridicule that came with that mystery. He knew it was important to show the possibility of the depth of such expansion, and his reward is that he's a legend.

⇥ MOVING ON ⇤

The one relationship that suffered the most with the move was with my sister, Loreal. When we were kids, we were best friends. When I was little I would do anything to protect her, and I wanted to be just like her. My mom always tells the story of how my sister was being teased when we were little. She went to private school and so did I. But I knew how to relate to the private school kids *and* the kids in our neighborhood. It was harder for my sister, and the neighborhood kids always made fun of Loreal, saying that she talked white.

Lauren Palmer

One time they teased her, and I came from the back of our yard with a piece of wood and said, "Get away from my sister, you black mfs!" Hahahhaha. And that was our dynamic. She was my big sister, but I would hurt anybody if they hurt her.

While it felt pretty cool getting film work on consistent basis, I could really see the toll it was taking on my sister because the focus was shifting to me and my work. My mom had worked with her to audition for her own role in *Akeelah*, but she just wasn't as into it. I felt her begin to withdraw from me after the move. I felt like it was all my fault. I felt that she was different because of our move and I felt like I altered in some way the person she used to be. I felt like that for years, and I really wouldn't come to understand what was really going on with her until years later when we started working on our relationship and improving it.

But back then, my hope for California bringing us all closer as a family wasn't going very well. We were separated a lot and I could see us falling apart at the seams but couldn't feel the fabric unraveling. Something had to be done, so when I was fifteen, we decided that to have more time together and to still keep nurturing my career, I would need to combine the best of both worlds by doing more child-driven television work in Los Angeles (Disney, Nickelodeon). That way we could cut down on the travel and all be together again in one location.

My mom and I had avoided corporations like this since my Disney Channel pilot (a show I did titled *Keke & Jamal* when I first moved to LA; shout-out to Ralph Farqhuar), because our focus had been on making me a theatrical actress. A talent agent had told us once that black children had a better chance at getting parts in sitcoms because they were not as accepted as dramatic child actors at the time. We took that as a challenge, so it never occurred to us to explore the Disney and Nickelodeon realm again.

I Don't Belong to You

I hadn't done a lot of television at that point, and the idea was exciting to me, but I also worried about how my transition from film to television would be. I wondered if I could bring the work that I did in film to that type of show. It took me a second to realize that I had the power to make my experience with Disney and Nickelodeon what I wanted to make it. 😄

On the flip side, I did love the Disney Channel and Nickelodeon. I looked up to *Kenan & Kel*, I looked up to *That's So Raven*, I looked up to *Even Stevens* and *Sister Sister*. Those shows and the people in them inspired me, and the idea of being a part of what they had created excited me. I felt happy, even if it scared me a little.

⇥ PRAYERS ANSWERED ⇤

Not long after accepting the reality that I needed to do more television, I was offered the lead role in the Nickelodeon series *True Jackson, VP*. Wooo-hoo!! For a time, it seemed as though some of my prayers were being answered. 🙏 The funny thing about my prayers being answered is that I'd gotten out of the habit of praying shortly after we'd moved to Los Angeles.

Back in Illinois, I lived with my mom and dad, but I also grew up with my grandma Mildred Davis. 👑 Mildred Ivy West Davis 👑, who I stayed with from birth to age seven while my mother and father were at work. I loved my grandmother Davis. The things she told me and the activities we did together had a big impact on my life. She literally lived right behind our house when I was growing up. I would run through a withered forest-y pathway (think of the movies by the director Harmony Korine) to get to her house and every time I made that trip, it felt magical to me, like a fairytale, because on the other side I could see my Grammy. #LITTLERED. 👹

Lauren Palmer

Dear Self,

Promise to treasure your time.

Don't fall in love with potential.

Remember that just because you want it doesn't mean it deserves to have you.

Be patient, but don't procrastinate.

Be hopeful but not naive.

When it's right, you'll know.

You don't have to force it.

Grandma Davis taught me how to pray, and she made sure I prayed every night. She would often kneel beside me at my bed so we could pray together, and I can still hear those prayers she taught me humming in my head, especially this prayer: *Lord now lay me down to sleep, I pray the Lord my soul to keep* . . .

When we stayed with my grandma we went to bed real early. She'd lock her doors at six p.m. She'd turn on the TV but she had no cable, so after PBS, Maury, and Jerry went off, there really was nothing to watch anyway. We'd all be there talking, and my sister would play with her dolls. Then we'd go to bed.

I wanted to sleep with my grandmother, but it seemed like she never slept. She would trick me. She would stay close by to me and read her Bible and say, "I will come sleep with you in a minute."

She would come by the bed and pray with me. Then she'd sit in a chair by the bed until I trailed off. When I'd wake up she would be in the chair in the kitchen. I never once saw that she'd slept in the bed with me. In the morning, she'd give me hot chocolate, but she always said it was coffee. Then if my mom wasn't picking us up yet, we'd do fun things with my grandmother like go to the grocery store, go to the thrift shop to look for antique furniture and clothes (she loooooved thrift shoppin'), or drop off food and canned milk to her friends in the old folks' home. #OLDPEOPLESTUFF. ☺

I honestly think my grandma didn't sleep much because she had the anxiety that seems to run in our family. She suffered from that, but I think the habit of going to church, worshipping, and praying all the time helped calm her anxiety. I usually felt peace and comfort when I went to church with her, but I would get restless when the services went on and on and on, which they usually did. ✦✧

Lauren Palmer

Once we were in California, I found myself missing that sense of family and the peace and comfort that came with it. I don't know why I didn't think to pray, but it took me years before I remembered what it meant to exercise that practice again.

My show was a hit among its audience, and for a while I buried my head in the sand and tried to ignore what was happening in myself and my family. I tried to focus on my new job that I was very grateful for, and it took some doing. Channels such as Nickelodeon and Disney are machines that have many rules and regulations in terms of how their stars are presented and branded. Not only did I have to film the show, but there also were other requirements and demands I had to meet for commercials, branding and merchandise, Nickelodeon cruise trips, and other time-consuming activities. I'm not saying it was horrible, because that was part of the work, but it did leave me feeling like a zoo animal at times. Even when I would go back to Chicago, instead of just chilling with my family and getting a kick outta one another like we used to, suddenly we would have a lot of people over who wanted to take pictures and have me entertain to some extent. They wanted more out of me than anyone else, and they didn't realize how exhausting that was and how much pressure it put on me.

I signed up for it, so I didn't express my feelings because I didn't want to be the "bratty child entertainer." I ended up feeling like I couldn't feel anything at all, because I couldn't acknowledge how I felt without thinking I was hurting everyone else. People were treating me abnormally, and I denied my feelings about it.

I felt I didn't have the right to respect my own feelings and my own boundaries, and I didn't know how to draw the line. I also remember hanging out with girlfriends who would get

I Don't Belong to You

upset because of the attention I was getting and it would hurt our relationships. Guys would do it too. Whether they loved me because of the attention or hated me because of the attention, they didn't get that all the attention I received wasn't even about me at all.

I think they thought that I felt I was better than them, because of the fame, but it was the fame that made them even have that idea in the first place. Fame created the friction. Fame is an enchantment, not a reality. Fame is a motherfucker and people are affected by it even when you aren't. It became very hard to find people who weren't enchanted by the fame.

It's not like everything was always bad, but this was a crucial dynamic in how I learned to manage my feelings. Whether it hurt anyone else or not, it hurt me, and that should have been enough for me no matter what my family thought, what my friends thought, or what the people reading think. I went wrong when I didn't validate myself. It was up to me to set the boundaries to make it feel right for me.

The two most influential women in my life (my mother and grandmother) were strong, steadfast, and fearless on the outside, but full of anxiety on the inside. Some of the trauma my grandmother suffered as a child had birthed a pattern of using control as a defense mechanism. She passed a lot of her fear and need for control to my mother, who has dealt with general anxiety in one form or another her entire life.

My mother dealt with it, and she unknowingly passed it to me. Parents sometimes don't understand that their kids feel what they're feeling, even if they wear a mask to hide it or even if they're concealing the truth from themselves.

In some ways I wanted to be exactly like my mother, and in other ways, I disliked things in her that caused me discomfort. I be-

Lauren Palmer

lieve what I disliked the most was the anxiety and fear created IN her. I didn't understand back then, but when I found myself not liking my mother, I was perpetuating the same pattern that she had been subjected to: If you fear it, try to control it, and if you can't control it, resent it. 😒 And that's what I was also doing with my FAME—letting it direct my emotions instead of putting it in check.

One day when I was about twelve, without really thinking about the weight of the question, I said to my father, "Do you think you will ever go back to work again?" Though my father never answered me directly, I knew it was the wrong question to ask because the entire energy of the moment changed. I had asked it innocently because that's something I always really liked when I was a child. I liked watching my father go off to work, and then missing him, and then seeing him come home again.

The new reality of our life wasn't one that was easy for any of us to get acquainted with. When I asked that question, it was one of the first times I saw that my dad was as uncomfortable in his new role as I was in mine. My father looked for work as soon as we arrived in California, and he did find a job in his field. But eventually, with all the success I was having and the time constraints it put on my mom and me, it actually made more sense for him to stay home with the twins. I see now that was really a sacrifice for him.

➤ ADJUSTING TO THE GOOD AND THE BAD ➤

By our second year in California I'd become the primary breadwinner of my family and it took me a while to realize the shift in roles that resulted. It also took some time for me to fully understand what that role shift meant for me and my family. By age fifteen I became more aware that the success of *True Jackson, VP,*

I Don't Belong to You

Each of us is a house with 4 rooms

. . . a physical, a mental, an emotional,
and a spiritual room.

We tend to live in one room most of the time:
but, unless we go into every room every day,
even if only to keep it aired, we are not a
complete person.

—PonderAbout.com

was changing everything for all of us. And who's to say what's wrong with that? In life you have your village, and sometimes that's a problem with society's outlook—it creates shame and causes people to feel bad if their village looks different from how society says it's supposed to.

I looked around and compared my family to other people's families that weren't in the same position we were in, and that wasn't fair to my family and it wasn't fair to me. People judged us, but they didn't understand. I remember coming home one day and saying something really below the belt to my dad. I told him, "Well every bill comes back to me"—something like that. And my dad said, "Well, Keke, you may be making a lot of money, but that isn't what leads this family."

He was right. Yeah, I was making money. But so what?! My parents gave up their lives for me, and they came across the country to help me live my dreams. I let other people's ideas about our situation make me doubt my family as a whole. No, they weren't perfect, but life is never about being perfect. Life is about growing, not being grown. I let myself think I was being used, but the reality is that my parents loved me and they would love me if I didn't have a dime. There were many people who judged my parents, and at a certain point I did too. But when my dad said that to me, I got it. I maybe didn't know what to do with it, but clearly it stuck with me, because I repeated it to you right now.

It became clear that I had made it to Oz. 👠 For a little girl who grew up in Section 8 housing, that certainly felt different. My parents started giving me an allowance, and we enjoyed a larger house. 🏯 I felt the weight of adult responsibility, even though I was a kid. I couldn't internalize it, and it made me resent everything connected to it.

I thought if I stopped booking gigs, no matter what my parents said, we would be in trouble. Not just me in trouble, ALL OF US. Even though they would always say I could quit the business at any time, that didn't seem realistic. Talk about pressure. That thought really scared me. I tried to ignore it for a long time.

It's disconcerting when everyone is unsure about where they belong in a family. The role I was playing in my family was the role my dad played in his family when he was young. My dad sacrificed a lot for his family, and honestly that is what kept the villages going back in the day. The village was protected by the young who were strong and could do it, and they got wisdom from the elders. But that idea conflicts with Western thinking/capitalism that says every man for himself. That is what happened to me as I got older. My sense of community that was fostered by where I came from growing up in the 'hood started to conflict with the big capitalistic success I was seeing in LA.

Our true nature is to survive together using our strengths and sharing our assets. The world can't go round without us caring for one another. That's how it should be done. Not in codependency, but in balance. There's nothing wrong with us taking care of one another, the gag is that we must take care of ourselves first. You can't lose yourself and your dreams in the process. For instance, there would have been nothing wrong with my dad still going to UCLA when he was a kid and sending money back to his mom. But for whatever reason, that wasn't the path he wanted to go down, and it's not my place to judge it.

As I've gotten older, I don't have any shame looking out for my family, because my family always looked out for me. It's never been about the money for any of us. Everybody had roles, but it is easy as a kid to be a little self-absorbed and get wrapped up in your own story. My story is no different from someone who has no father in the household. Sometimes in those cases the oldest

Lauren Palmer

son or older daughter is given more responsibility. Or when the grandmother assumes the role of the parent instead of the grand-parent.

Family labels can have a negative effect sometimes on how comfortably you relate, depending on how you accept and handle the roles you are given or feel you need to play at the time. Role confusion over what a mother does, what a father does, what a cousin, sister, brother, and whoever else does can make us feel insecure and uncertain of what we're expected to do and be in the family. It can make it hard to figure out what is best for you to be in that moment. #THEREARETHOSELABELSAGAIN.

Whoever I thought I had been was completely changing. We were all changing and we were all resisting. Who knew my "dream job," the one that was offering us all more stability and time together, would also end up giving me some pretty serious life/family angst?

All these mini dramas circling around me presented some serious challenges to the identity I was still trying to form during my adolescence. Making matters even more complicated was the fact that the identities of my parents were also being challenged at the same damn time #GOOOOOOOTDAMN. 😵

My parents were trying their best to handle this new reality. So was I! We were all trying to figure out where we fit in the new family framework. I felt I was being cornered by life, and even though I had tried to start the habit of praying again, I found myself not knowing what to say. I found solace in this quote: "In prayer, it is better to have a heart without words, than words without heart." So many nights I didn't know what to say, but I was just hoping that God could feel it and relieve it for me. And once I became open to it, I saw that through many things and many people, He did.

I Don't Belong to You

Looking back, I think my father had the most difficult time of all, as a man who was now a stay-at-home dad, which was not typical of a "man of the house" perception at the time. It was a respectful position, but somehow I don't think he felt it was as respected by others, and even me at the time, because as a kid, I don't think I got it. Now he was the primary caretaker at home, cooking and cleaning and taking care of three-year-old twins. I felt that my father withdrew even more from our family emotionally, but my mother began to hold on tighter. Suddenly it became very important to her that I not fall into the pitfalls of some of the child stars we heard about. 😦

Both my parents for some reason became overly concerned with my being humble and felt the only possible way that could happen was by imposing the strictest rules they could. 😓 I began to feel like a prisoner in my own home and in my own life. 👨🏿 They wanted so much for me to remain a normal, humble kid, and I understood that, but I wasn't a "normal" kid. I was a kid with a television show and not many friends or time to spend with the few I did have.

Between my work hours and my curfew, I didn't have time to be anywhere but in the house, and I don't think my parents got that. As a result of them overprotecting me and confronting me with a list of things that made me either "good" or "bad," I began to feel very anxious and shameful. That morphed into me trying to hide myself from myself as protection #DEFENSE MECHANISM. I just had to deal with it and I didn't want to deal with it. 🙍🏿

I truly believed that my parents were trying to control every aspect of my life. I know it wasn't with bad intentions, but their

Lauren Palmer

concerns turned into exaggerated fears that led me to become a robot of sorts because I felt that even if I disagreed I still had to do everything my parents wanted in order to keep the peace at home. I stopped bothering to share things that would help them understand that I was experiencing an abnormal childhood and that it was confusing and frustrating to me. I know now that they weren't intending to hurt me, but I am still working through a lot of the issues that originated during this stressful time in my life. I was a young person dealing with a lot, and to not have my parents understand what I was experiencing and the hurt I was feeling, made them part of the problem. They didn't have an answer for it. Their best suggestion was "Well, we can always go back home." They didn't seem to have a complete answer for the complex situation we were going through, so I just stopped sharing things with them altogether.

One of my responses, as a defense mechanism, was to become very positive about everything in my life. It was my way of keeping the peace. This was a good approach at first, but it became a problem later when I kept trying to please everyone without considering that there should be boundaries to pair with it.

See, when I was trying to keep the peace in my home I became not only positive but a PEOPLE PLEASER. I unconsciously did it by removing my boundaries and giving in to my parents. That was my way of surviving the situation. Sometimes we create unhealthy habits to help us deal with our current circumstances that we may not be able to get out of. At that time, it made my life easier to go with the flow, but it also brought me into accepting habits that were not good for me in the long run—habits I would have to learn to break later.

I Don't Belong to You

I didn't become aware of that being a pattern until adulthood. Later, it caused me to have issues when I was always trying to please friends and boyfriends and had my boundaries crossed many times because I was not aware of what the boundary should be!

We often do that, experience the same issues with different people not realizing we are following a little pattern, and it is our lack of awareness about the pattern that is the culprit! When we get to the root of it, we can kill it and escape mental bondage. Kind of like the movie *The Conjuring*! The lead actress couldn't pass off the demon until she named it. Life isn't full of fake boogie monsters and all this "scary stuff," I mean maybe, lol. But the demon or devil in our life is truly just our bad habits and our unconsciousness. The best lie the devil ever got us to believe was that he was real. Being aware of our behavior and relationship patterns allows us to take charge of them instead of them being in charge of us.

To make sense of all the upheaval I was facing, and to combat some of my negative feelings, I started researching and reading meaningful life quotes from notable people. I began doing this when I was sixteen or so. For some reason the quotations gave me a sense of peace and lifted my spirits. I know that is what they are supposed to do, but I was surprised at how much they calmed me and helped me focus.

Up until then I would just write out my own thoughts in a journal. I started writing in my first journal when I was thirteen. (The singer Brandy gave it to me! 😄) Up until I got into quotes, I wasn't aware that so many other people questioned or wondered the things I wondered, or had feelings and thoughts so similar to mine.

As a millennial, I think that's the great thing about the

Lauren Palmer

Internet—it allows you the opportunity to see that you are not alone in your thoughts or feelings. It is a relief and validating to know that there are other people out there wondering and thinking the same things you are.

Journaling was the only place where I felt safe enough to be truthful and honest about everything that was going on in my life. Journaling is what I feel helped me to stay connected to my spirit even when I started piling up all these defense mechanisms.

⮞ MELTDOWN MOMENT ⮜

Nothing shows us what we're made of more than a major change—whether it is the one you are looking for or not. You're never prepared, even if you have a hint it may be on its way.

That's pretty much how it went down when the network decided to end *True Jackson, VP* after three seasons. *True Jackson* was a hit, but the network was paying high salaries to three child stars, Miranda Cosgrove, Victoria Justice, and myself.

True Jackson, VP had hit the standard three seasons for a series, and to do another season meant contract negotiations would have to take place, since our contracts expired after the first three seasons. Negotiations almost always meant bigger paychecks for the actors, and for multiple reasons, we didn't enter into fourth-season negotiations. That was the end of *True Jackson, VP*. It was the business part of show business and it was not personal. Still, that meant change. Even though the show had caused me stress and I was ready to move on—and had been praying for something different—change happened and it meant that the lifestyle my family and I had come to depend on was gone. Up in smoke 🚭 *cough*cough* too much AUTHORritative smoke #GETIT? 😂

I Don't Belong to You

Just like that, the role that had come to define me in some ways at that pivotal time in my life was moved from a current job to a past job on my résumé. And even though I thought that was what I wanted, I clearly wasn't aware of everything that went along with that. The impact of my career change hit my family and me in immediate ways. Without my paycheck coming in, it became impossible to live the way we'd been living, and the problems that I was facing internally suddenly became larger, because I had no show five days a week to hide behind.

My family wasn't hurt, I was. I was like the stockbroker dad who was used to making x amount of dollars and didn't know what to do without it. That was not the change I was expecting. When I lost *True Jackson, VP*, my family didn't blink an eye, and even though my parents tried to assure me that things would be fine, I didn't feel that way. When I wanted to move, they didn't hold their breath. They weren't upset about it, but I WAS, and I tortured myself over it. Nothing was more devastating to me than losing our beautiful house in a peaceful gated community. After losing the house, I couldn't bear coming face-to-face with my own family that often because of the embarrassment I had created within myself. I felt I'd let them down. 😥 #EGO.

Please keep in mind that when I say "ego" I don't mean the macho "I think I'm all that" attitude, per se. I mean "ego" in its truest definition of being the psychological construct of how we identify who we are in the world. Sad to say, our self-worth is often attached to ego, which usually is based on material attachments: people, places, and things. The whole gag with the ego is that it isn't real. The ego is attached to the human life experience, and the human life experience, unlike our eternal spirit, does have an expiration date. But no one said human life was the last stop. Instead of learning down here, we get attached to the experience.

Lauren Palmer

"SOME CHANGES
LOOK NEGATIVE
ON THE SURFACE
BUT YOU WILL
SOON REALIZE
THAT SPACE IS
BEING CREATED
IN YOUR LIFE FOR
SOMETHING NEW
TO EMERGE."
—ECKHART TOLLE

The ego tries so hard to make itself the most important thing in our life, because it's afraid of not existing. So it tries to control your life with personalizations and attachments in order to feel comfortable. A change in any of our attachments here—people, places, or things—gives the opportunity for our ego to create negative thoughts in our heads that aren't real, just like the ego isn't real.

⇒ GUILTING OUT ⇐

My parents didn't place guilt and responsibility on me, and they didn't have to. I placed guilt and responsibility on myself. The bad angel took the lead on my shoulder and in my mind, and it was telling me all sorts of things that weren't true. It was feeding me those devilish lies:

"You've let your family down, Keke." 😨

"Do you even know what you're doing?" 🫤

"Where can your career even go from here?" 😐

"Stay inside, it's too difficult for you to decide." 😔

"You're an idiot. Look at how emotional you are. All you do is let me down! How can you trust yourself?" 😤

"Talk to your mom." 😨

"No I can't." 😅

"Call her, you need her." 😨

"No, she probably doesn't love me anymore." 😟

"Why would anyone?" 😣

"Once all my money is gone no one will think about me." 😑

"'Cause no one really sees me anyway." 💀

My ego defined itself by being the breadwinner. None of this was true. My family loved me, but my ego was insecure and it blinded me from the reality and drove me away from people who loved me. This very irrational voice in my head had me believing

Lauren Palmer

every negative word and put me in a very dark place. When you allow yourself to feed into the negative voices in your head, they drown out everything and everyone else. See, that's the ego trying to be in "control" again.

⇥ GIRL ON THE MOVE ⇤

At eighteen years old I ran away to live with my boyfriend, and when I did it was like I put my life, and my dreams and my passions, in a freezer like some human embryos. 😞 😁 Reality soon set in that my man couldn't save me because that wasn't his duty. #DUHKEKE.

I shouldn't have expected him to save me, and he shouldn't have agreed to. We were both really young and we thought the emotion of being "in love" itself was enough to sustain a relationship. #LOVEISANACTIONNOTASENTIMENT.

Never mind the fact that he hadn't had time to come into his own as an adult, and neither had I. Guys kind of mature late, so even though he was twenty-two when we moved in together, he didn't know any more than I did. Neither of us had really gotten comfortable with who we were as individuals, let alone as a couple.

We didn't grasp the importance of knowing ourselves or what we wanted from each other. That level of maturity is very important when starting a relationship, especially when a couple is moving in and starting a LIFE together.

We quickly began crossing boundaries that we never knew to set for our relationship. Almost immediately we became the perfect example of a codependent relationship. My fantasy that a relationship could save me popped.

My guy couldn't help "me find me." I had to love MYSELF and

I Don't Belong to You

face everything that I had buried underneath my mask of humanity if I ever wanted to accomplish ANYTHING in life.

I'd lost my identity with the loss of my job and it took a lot of work and honest reflection and self-assessment to get back to the real me. Digging into my journals was a big help in doing that. I had to be comfortable with who I was before I could be comfortable in a relationship. I needed to step back from it. This is what I mean when I talk about how you can change your story. If an identity isn't working for you (aka Keke the child star on *True Jackson, VP*, Keke the breadwinner, Keke the perfect humble kid who I thought my parents wanted me to be), then you can create a new one.

Or even if it ditches you, take it as the opportunity to expand into something more! But I wasn't allowing myself to do that. I was trying to hold on tightly to an *old* identity and an *outdated* story line. I was spending all my time mourning my old identity, when the reality was that it was time for Keke to move on.

It was time for Keke to expand into something more. And that's when the idea of *Just Keke* started to develop in my head. I knew I had so much to say about life and that my feelings and experiences were probably not so different from other young people. The only difference was that I had gotten resources very early on that allowed me to intellectualize my feelings as a young person.

I felt I could be a conduit to relay the message to younger people that it ain't that deep, and that we were going to be all right. Before, there had always been older talk show hosts, and we didn't feel like they could relate to us. My idea was that because I was young, the time was now (I am a millennial 👽). It wasn't that I was smarter than them—I just grew up in a different world and I could create a platform to help young people tell their stories. I

Lauren Palmer

just couldn't leave them hanging. That's where my new dream was birthed. I also wanted to help them see that their stories are their testimonies! I figured out how to see myself as a hero in my life. I realized the power of perspective and I wanted to share that power with them!

➤ GROWING BEYOND EXPECTATIONS ◄

I had loved *True Jackson, VP*, and I missed the comfort of that scenario, but even before it was canceled I'd begun to feel ready for a larger role. People had started referring to me as "the girl from Nickelodeon." That annoyed the ^*%$ out of me. I'm like, *Oh really? Y'all forgot about* The Wool Cap? *Y'all forgot about* Akeelah *and* Barbershop? *Y'all forgot about my foundation?*

I was still having trouble establishing an identity outside of my career and outside the perception of others. Their labels bothered me so much simply because I knew there was more to me than that. Yet, at the same time, it reminded me that the public perceptions of "Keke" that were focused on those specific accolades or accomplishments had moved to the forefront.

I resented not being able to surprise people when they met me. I started to become pissed that everywhere I went, there was already a perception formed of who I was. I thought that public perception was too narrow. My frustration with it was also a symptom of me being aggravated by my own confusion of who I was. Maybe I wouldn't have been so pissed if I'd been more secure in my sense of self.

When you grow as a person, you're always trying to reestablish your own identity. I was growing and changing on the inside daily, but I allowed my circumstances to put me in a mental space that restricted my efforts to grow. I didn't realize that this was a

I Don't Belong to You

blessing. Now that I was no longer working on a television series, I had the freedom and the motivation to move forward. That's how it is when you lose something. It creates a space where there wasn't space before, so something new can come in.

I also realized that for others to respect my boundaries, I had to make my boundaries clear. That realization came when my boyfriend and I broke up.

Boundaries aren't just for boyfriends either. They are for anyone who is a regular part of your life. Creating boundaries up front can solve a lot of issues long term.

⇒ CREATING BOUNDARIES ⇐

You can create boundaries in any area of your life in order to develop and follow your own voice. If you don't like your sister wearing your clothes, you can tell her that if she puts on your shirt, she's crossed a boundary. It works with parents too. I eventually had to tell my mother I wasn't going to accept her not being conscious of my privacy and not respecting my freedom of choice.

My mother has been my manager all my life and she was very comfortable micromanaging everything! But there comes a point where you're ready to be the driver of your own car. And it took a lot of concentration for us both to accept that it was time for me to take the leading role instead of a supporting one.

In the transition, she'd often cross those boundaries. Thinking she was helping but really only stepping on my toes. I could understand why she did it. She was my mother *and* my manager, and sometimes it was tough to distinguish between those two roles. I wanted my manager to work for me and with me on all major decisions, but I didn't want my mom acting like my mom in front of the people we worked with. I wanted the people who we worked

Lauren Palmer

with to respect me, and for her to respect me too, outside of being her daughter.

Letting her know how I felt allowed my mom to make the needed changes for our relationship to thrive. She heard me, and our relationship began to change for the better. I started to feel like I could say what I really wanted. I finally wasn't a kid anymore, so I guess I could be seen and heard. 😏 #LUCKYME. #BLACKFAMILYPROBS. 😄

At every turn after *True Jackson, VP*, I was learning more and more about what I could handle and how resourceful I could be during difficult times. 🐶 When things begin to change, you really have no choice other than to look for the real you. Your set-backs give you the opportunity (and space!) to figure out what truly makes you happy, who adds to your happiness, and how to find the next part of your story—the one that's going to make it really interesting! 😈

Think of all the things you'd do if you knew that failure couldn't hurt you, and focus on the experiences that have been beneficial, useful, desirable, and constructive in establishing your core values. Once you begin to determine the values that truly matter to you, the *real you* and your real voice can't be far behind, and that's real! 😏

The Good Girl/Bad Girl Myth

ON SEXUALITY

*Sexuality is one of the ways that we become enlightened,
actually, because it leads us to self-knowledge.*
—Alice Walker

When I was young, my parents and grandparents and other adult relatives used to refer to me as a "wild child." I didn't know what that meant at the time, but I knew it somehow alluded to my sense of open expression and independent opinions as a female. I didn't think about it like this at the time, but I understand that their feelings about me being "wild," although said jokingly, stemmed from their own experiences about what could happen to a passionate female with a big personality.

Ultimately, reality is relative to each person, and whatever your family has experienced can be passed on to the next generation. In my family, my earliest opinions on female sexuality were based on a fear that started with my grandma Davis.

So let me take you back a bit . . .

I think you know by now that Grandma Davis and I were pretty tight. My mom thinks that is why some people call me an "old soul." I hung out with my grandmother so much as a little kid.

Mildred Davis was everything. I loved spending time with her, even on long, long, long Sunday (sometimes weekday 😑) services at her Baptist church.

Before I moved to California, every so often I'd attend church with her, and I hated it because the service lasted three hours. Yoooooooo. . . . I said THREE HOURS! It was so long, they even had an intermission, I swear!!! Lol.

That is a long time to sit as a little girl, especially for a little girl as active as me! On the flip side, there was part of me that also loved going to church with my grandmother because she was fly. I loved watching her get ready, because she put so much time and effort into it. She never left the house without looking together, and going to church was always a "moment." #DRAMATIC. Lolol.

Picture my grandmother with her hair done so neatly, dressed to the nines with the bifocals she always wore and a hat—always a hat! I was so proud to sit next to her. She was known to hook her friends up too. In her younger years she was a hairstylist, and as she got older she would still have some neighborhood clients who came by the house. This provided great entertainment for my sister and me as we watched all the many different characters who would come in and out of her care. She had this one client who she worked with for years, Ms. Wright. Ms. Wright lived right down the street. She would come over and get her hair styled from time to time. The gag was she had this one cup that she would spit in all day as my grandma styled her hair in her kitchen. It was for chewing tobacco, which doesn't sound so obscure as an adult, but as a kid, it was horrific. 🤢 My sister and I would try to avoid that cup like the plague! Hahahahahahhahahhaha.

I often wished I could have seen my grandmother back in her heyday. It always seemed like she had such a great rapport with the women who came by. Even now I wish I could go back in time

Lauren Palmer

and see what her life was like, before my mom and aunts and uncles, outside of her own perception of her life.

Still, despite her love of fashion, beauty, and friends, my grandma had to deal with a lot of disturbing experiences in her life, and there was one experience that hung over her and all of us. This dark moment in her past affected our view of sexuality and men for many years. It was always said that nothing my grandmother faced was more challenging than what happened to her as a child.

When my grandmother was a little girl living in Mississippi, her mother, my great-grandmother, was working for a white attorney in Memphis, kinda like Viola Davis's character in *The Help*. Because she was working so hard in Tennessee, she left my grandmother and her brother with their grandmother in Mississippi.

Since my great-grandmother's job was so far away she'd come down to visit maybe once a month. When my grandma turned five, she had to go to school, and that was too hard on her grandmother, who was elderly, so her mama sent her and her brother to their aunt's house, her mama's sister. My grandma would have loved living with her aunt, except for the fact that her uncle was a very sick man.

There was one story she would always tell, and this was one of the only stories she could share with her family about what happened to her as a child. As a little girl, while my grandmother was living with her aunt and uncle, she ended up spending a lot of odd time with her uncle. One time while they were alone, she told him that she was cold and as he put out a cigarette on her hand, he said, "This should keep you warm." I heard that story once, but every time my grandmother would look at her hand, she would talk about her arthritis, and then show me the cigarette scar on her hand and say, "You see this? This is a burn on Grandma's hand, now don't you let anybody touch your private parts." That was her way of trying to keep the unspeakable things that my great-great uncle did to her from happening to us.

For years, and I'm sure still now, my whole family had a code word for the children in the family when it came to speaking about the female private area—we used to call it a *tuti*. It wasn't until I was about seven or eight years old, after watching an episode of *The Facts of Life*, that I realized that *tuti* was not the common terminology for a vagina. I thought it was normal, but as I analyzed it when I got older, I realized that this was something my grandmother was doing in preparation for a sexual emergency.

This code word added a preventative factor so that in case something happened, we could say it without anyone knowing what we were talking about. There was always this secretive and overanxious sense of worry when it came to female sexuality. I remember her asking me often, "Did anybody touch your tuti?" or "You sure ain't nobody touched your tuti? You can tell Grandma." I remember that like it was yesterday. Literally anytime there was a change in my or my sister's energy, or if I had a tummy ache (it really could be anything), her first question would be, "Did anybody touch your tuti?"

I thought it was normal for people to be hypersensitive and obsessed over female body parts. But it made me highly cautious of the male species. There were even times when my grandmother would question my mother about my father. I knew there was a boundary that was being crossed, but the way my family reacted, it was as if they didn't blame her for it. It was obvious that they didn't take it personally.

My grandmother went through this type of thing for a long time without anyone knowing, because her uncle threatened her

Lauren Palmer

and told her not to tell anyone. Back then, in the thirties, therapy wasn't only considered taboo, but it didn't exist for people without money, and the most popular way of dealing with traumatic issues in poor communities was to move out and move on. Typically, they would get as far away as they could from the situation, start a new life, and never speak of it again.

Molestation, or any trauma in general, was nothing that anyone dared to bring up or really acknowledge. This was true of my family and, I believe, habitual within the black community, dating all the way back to slavery. It became second nature during the slavery period to glaze over hard times without a second thought, because to think about how traumatic your experiences were could only make you feel worse. It did no good.

I believe the cultural consciousness shifted during that time period and birthed what people stereotype as the unbelievable re-silience often seen within the black community. Sometimes such a resilient nature can drown out the necessary need, as a human, to acknowledge that you've been hurt. I believe this habit was created in the consciousness of the black people because they felt saying "you were hurt" only made their current reality of living in slavery worse.

It was natural for my grandmother to avoid talking about her feelings—therefore she never understood the importance of a tool like therapy, and she couldn't afford it consistently anyway. So she just threw that traumatic experience and any other in the back and moved on. She never really talked about it again. Or at least not in a way that led her to be vulnerable.

As we've come to realize, this method rarely works. You can't bury bad experiences that easily. Whatever we try to cover up tends to reappear because we've never really put it in its place, and because we've never put it in its place, we forget that it's there.

I Don't Belong to You

So when it reappears, it usually reappears in the worst ways at the worst times. #GOTCHA. In my grandma's case, as she grew older, she lived with the constant fear that her children and grandchildren would face the same horror she lived through.

So, in many ways, we all became prisoners of her anxious nightmares and traumatic memories. That trauma really hung over our family. That's the thing about narratives, everybody has them running through their family and their own heads. These stories shape your human life, so it's good to be aware of them. Needless to say, that entire experience did a lot to shape my views on sex, sexuality, and femininity as I grew up, and those views weren't always "clear."

➤ DESIRES AND FEARS ◄

My family didn't explain sex to me so much as they warned me about it. So instead of really understanding what was going on with my body and my hormones, I grew up being afraid of the magnitude of sexual parts and sexual acts. My ideas about something so natural were a little extreme in retrospect.

I don't fault my grandmother for that influence. She was doing what she thought was best from within her own knowledge and experience. But not all things done with great intentions affect all people "positively." It led me to desire a sense of control in all my relationships, but especially male relationships. I took on a little bit of my grandmother's need for control and became how she had become.

Naturally, as human beings, we learn by mimicking those around us. From the time you are a baby you watch your parents relate—that is your first lesson on how you believe humans relate to each other, and even on a deeper level, how humans who love each other relate to one another. By the time I met my grand-mother, she had experienced enough trauma that she had already gotten into the habit of needing a sense of control to minimize her high level of anxiety.

That habit of needing a sense of control had no way of not being passed down to me, because that is what I saw as "normal" through my grandma and my mother. My feelings about guys were always warped by my grandma's cynical perspective on men and their motives toward women, which was understandable based on her experiences with her uncle and her two ex-husbands.

The gag is I've always had an outgoing personality, and as a little girl that was often described as precocious or sassy and sometimes mischievous, lol. My grandma even got me to say an infamous phrase that followed me most of my childhood. No one ever wanted to babysit me but my grandmother because they all said I was too "bad." Well, it hurt my feelings I'd imagine because one day my grandma told me to say, "I'm not bad, I'm just misun-derstood!" and I said it, okaaay. Hahahahahaha.

As a kid, I felt that they had the wrong idea about me. Like they maybe thought I was "up to no good" or that I, in any way, in-tended to appear "sexual." Maybe it was the way that I danced, or how friendly I was to the men and women who came around me. I'm sure there was just the hypersensitivity that my family had about children and possible child misconduct, but I took it very personally. As a female I felt their oppression, based on fear, even as a child, and it did stifle me at times.

Add on top of that, my family at that time subscribed to the old adage that children should be seen and not heard. I don't really believe in that. I think children should be heard and under-stood! That idea really hurt me sometimes. I think in some cases

I Don't Belong to You

this could be true. I don't think it's absolute, but that's often how my parents used it.

"Stay out of grown folks' business" was to heed your warnings, and if you didn't listen, you knew an ass whoopin' was coming soon after. I didn't always follow rules that well as a child, which led me into more than enough trouble as I moved through my growing-up years because of my need for independent growth. Not hardheaded like in a "cut off your nose to spite your face" kind of sense, but I just wanted to walk on my own two feet.

My happy, free-spirited ways regularly had my family and friends of family suggesting I'd end up on Jerry Springer's show one day. Now I didn't see that as a bad thing completely during that time because my sister and I had a great time watching ol' Jerry every day. His show and all its wild and brawling guests were a real time for us bonding with my grandma. But I'm not sure it was meant as a positive when they talked about me as a future Jerry Springer guest. 😒

In the end, my grandmother's warnings proved true for me in a way, but the harm didn't come from the way she thought or from who she thought. The precautions weren't enough to protect me because my first sexual encounters weren't from a grown male but from another child, a girl just a little older than me. Unexpected, maybe, but it still left me feeling shameful about sex. I just wanted to suppress myself after that, just as I had felt suppressed by them.

I think a lot of people have stories that they keep to themselves about unwanted sexual encounters as children. When I tell people about mine, they often say, "Me too!" Or "That happened to me, but I never told anyone!" It's almost like they are coming out of the closet! Almost everyone has stories they are too ashamed to tell. I'm talking about my experience because these first sexual encounters really shape how you feel about yourself,

Lauren Palmer

your sexuality, and your expression of identity and sexuality in the world.

CHILDHOOD ENCOUNTERS CAN HAVE LASTING EFFECTS

Danger lurks in both obvious and not-so-obvious places, even in the home of beloved relatives. We had this set of cousins on my mom's side who had little supervision from adults. They didn't live particularly close to us, but we visited them in the city whenever we had the chance.

Sometimes it was the "wild, wild west" in that house, literally (pronounced LIT-TRA-LEE 😂 #DRAMATIC). I'd say my cousins were definitely affected by this. For example, they were learning way too much from what they saw on television.

My dad was very strict about the things that we saw because he didn't want them to infiltrate our minds with just anything, especially things we couldn't intellectualize. I still would try to watch things that were too mature to me, and I wish I'd listened more, lol, but I just didn't understand, because I was just a kid. #SOMETIMESKIDSJUSTDONTUNDERSTAND.

My cousins' home was nothing like our home, where there were rules and regulations to follow all the time, and it didn't take long before we realized why those rules and regulations were necessary. When I was five years old, just like always, my cousins would initiate a game of playing house and everyone would get their designated roles. But later on one evening after playing house, one of them, just a bit older than me, took me off to another area. I couldn't label it then but I came to realize that what was being done to me was sex play, immature sex play, but encounters that in the years to come, and especially with my grandmother's warnings always echoing in my ears, felt like acts of molestation.

What I remember is that it always started with this guise of the game house, and then it would end in something sexual sometime later. As I got older there wasn't even always mention of the house game, instead it was referred to as "playing" and I became very okay with it. You could even say I liked it or looked forward to it, which was very confusing to me for a long time.

As an adult now I realize my cousin was only regurgitating the things she'd seen. We were children who had seen too much and were trying to live out the things we saw without any concept of what they meant. My grandmother did not think to warn me against this kind of play, but I do think her warning ensured that when I thought back on what happened, I felt that I had suffered a molestation.

It was not like the adult/child "pedophile" relationship I'd been warned about. Looking back, I have been able to accept that no one was wrong in this situation. My heart, once filled with judgment, was refilled with compassion as I learned to observe the situations outside of myself. Neither she nor I understood what was happening or how it would impact us later. How could we?

⇾ CARRYING THE BURDEN OF SHAME, ⇽ GUILT, ANGER, AND FEAR

I was angry at the circumstances and didn't know how to digest the reality. Confusion mixed with the natural oversexualization that comes with such acts encouraged the hereditary habit of anxiousness. Things felt so out of control and I didn't know how to feel like a normal "girl," or "little girl" at that, knowing all that I'd

Lauren Palmer

done. I would often wonder if my tough nature was really me or a result of what had happened to me. #SELFJUDGMENT?

I felt ruined or damaged, tainted by my "situation." I was confused on the inside about what all this meant. I felt there was something wrong with me. It's common after being sexually abused to blame oneself and end up carrying all this guilt as well as anger and confusion. That certainly was the case with me. I had so many questions.

One of them was, what did this mean about my sexual identity, that my first experience was with a female cousin? It was easy to understand and forgive my cousin, but forgiving myself was another story. It would be years before I realized the depth of all that had happened to me in those moments and how that abuse, though inflicted by another child, led to certain kinds of thoughts and beliefs and behaviors on my part that were simply cause and effect. I can look at her now and know that it was not her fault or my fault, that it was simply the outcome of the situation that I wouldn't identify until later.

Sometimes it led to me giving the appearance of being "fast." One reason they called me a wild child was because I danced provocatively. But when you look back to African culture and dance style you see that is how women often moved and it was the black female's voluptuous figure that made it seem sexual, when it is only cultural.

It was no different from how Shakira moves, as hip shaking is a part of the culture in Colombia. Even little girls move like that in many cultures and, yes, it can seem sexy and arousing, but it is cultural. Twerking is a thing now, but when I was doing the same thing at the age of five, it was just some shit we did—and I was very good at it. I was a black American child doing something that is of the black American culture.

I Don't Belong to You

Still, there was a moment when I was thirteen years old that is one of the most traumatic moments of my life. 😨 I was going to a birthday party for my friend Malcolm David Kelley. We met during the filming of *Knights of the South Bronx*, and unlike me, Malcolm had many friends. He especially had friends outside of the industry, which I thought was so awesome. I was excited for his party because I very much desired that non-Hollywood existence. There was going to be dancing, or what they call "grinding" in LA and "juking" in Chicago, but most recently "twerking." Lol. 😕 My mom, however, was very worried that if I was too friendly with anyone, even other kids, I'd get warped or poisoned (like literally 😆 😷) like the child actors she'd heard about. #ANXIETYMUCH. The entertainment industry validated her extreme anxiety. While there are certainly many child actors who turned out to be normal, productive adults, there were others who drew a lot of media attention with their "wild ways" or tragic lives. Anyhow, my sister, Loreal, had gone to some teenage parties back in Chicago. In preparation for my first teenage party she taught me how to grind, and I was so excited to go and show off my moves!

Fast-forward to the party. Parents are in the house and we kids are in the garage dancing and just being kids. I hadn't found a dance partner because I was scared, really. Guys had asked me to dance, but it wasn't until Malcolm's best friend, Ronald, asked me to dance that I accepted. He seemed like a nice boy and a good first partner. As I was dancing with him, I see my mother searching through the party to find me.

Oh my Lord, calling all readers, WHY THE F*CK WOULD SHE DO THAT! 😆 😨 😆 😨 😆 😨 It's like she took lessons from *How to Ruin Your Daughter's Life 101* and *How to Traumatize Your Daughter FOREVER Volume 1*. It was literally the ONE party with my peers that I'd ever been to. I didn't go to school and

Lauren Palmer

I didn't work on a television show. I had very few people to relate to and going to that party meant new experiences and possibly FRIENDS! I wanted friends so bad.

She saw me and came and pulled me off the dance floor and said some things that REALLY hurt me. "You are acting like a fast ass like I always knew. That dance is nasty. Uh-huh, it looks like you are out there having sex! Come inside with me so I can watch you." I know all mothers worry, but I think my mother was especially sensitive to it because of what I told you about our family. She had no idea I was already carrying so much sexual shame at this point, but what she said really added on top of it.

At that point I didn't even really understand how to best interact with boys. If I wasn't feeling awkward toward them, I was wondering if I liked them at all, and I would be halfway prudent. I tried to act the way I thought my parents wanted me to be. The reality was, I was a little lost on just how to act around boys. I tried to do my best impression of being a normal kid who hadn't been sexually violated by a female when she was young, but when I was grinding with a boy my age, I got it "wrong" again. 🫣 😟

I just wish that night my mother would've taken me to the side and spoken to me one-on-one and really taken the time to understand where I was coming from instead of scolding me and making me feel bad in front of my peers. I wasn't trying to be a bad kid, and I wasn't a bad kid. I didn't even understand at the time what I was doing. I was just trying to be a normal kid and fit in. Instead of seeing it that way, I accepted her words as the entire truth of my character because they fed into the shame I was already so used to carrying.

We do that sometimes. We shame ourselves and we allow the fears of others—even the people who love us—to then add to that

I Don't Belong to You

shame story. That was a powerful lesson for me to learn. We don't have to feed the shame monster! I'm sorry to myself; I love you, self; I understand you now.

➤ A WORD OF ADVICE ⫷

As I got older, I still maintained an open spirit and outgoing personality, but I did carry a lot of anxiety, especially surrounding sexuality. I had this conflict. I wanted people to be attracted to me and I wanted people to like me, but I wasn't sure how much I liked myself. Sexual tension was something I avoided if I'd ever felt it between peers, and boundaries continued to be an unidentifiable option. This theme continued to grow, and when I was fourteen, I learned that there were levels to this shit, lololol.

When I was fourteen, I was making *The Longshots* with Ice Cube, and my tendency toward openness, having fun, and being friendly came into serious focus. It was just me being myself, acting naturally. I still considered myself a kid at the age of fourteen, and rightly so if you think about it! You are a kid until you're an adult, right? And some people are never adults! 🤓

Anyway, every day when I arrived on set I made a habit of saying hello to everyone who came across my path, and then I'd give them a big hug as we spoke. I did this with men, women, actors, directors, and the entire crew all of the time because I wanted to show how happy I was to be working with each of them and how happy I was they were working with me! I thought nothing of showing joy for the many blessings and opportunities I had been given and was still receiving.

I was living my dream, so of course I was happy beyond words and I wanted to show it. 🔺 O'Shea Jackson, aka Cube, saw things a bit differently and decided to help me out. People know

Lauren Palmer

Ice Cube from his rap music, but I didn't know him like that. I knew him as an actor and a father figure. I remember seeing his videos years later and I thought it was so funny, because I couldn't imagine him saying those things. I was so surprised that I laughed. 😂

The Cube I knew was enjoying a long marriage and this very settled family life as a husband and father. 👩🏽👨🏿👦🏿👦🏿 That's who I've met during my work with him. Settling down didn't cause him to not speak up though. Cube has never been one to mince words. When he has something to say, he will say it right then and there to whoever it is.

Not surprisingly, his words could be just as impactful as his iconic rap lyrics. One day on set, he pulled me aside and asked if he could speak to me for a moment. Of course I said yes, I was scared as a mf, hahahaha.

What he had to tell me was a bit jarring at first but I did understand in the end. He told me that it was great that I was friendly with my coworkers, but that I needed to be careful, particularly with the men. He said that while I may have seen myself as a kid, men saw me as a young woman and I needed to keep that in mind as I continued to mature and work in the industry. Especially an industry that is dominated by men.

My body was changing (translation: I got boobs), and I was becoming a woman, so being overly friendly could send the wrong message to the wrong man. Huh. 🙄 I had to really think about that! As I mentioned earlier, my mother didn't talk to me much about sex, or at least maybe when she talked about it, I wasn't as impacted as when someone outside of my fam talked to me about it.

When I heard it from Cube, it was coming from a man who was also my employer. I was intimidated. I didn't want to do the

I Don't Belong to You

wrong thing. I wasn't consciously trying to be "fast" toward the men and I didn't want to be perceived that way. I just didn't understand how it could appear like that, until Ice Cube explained it to me.

How cool was it for Ice Cube to give me my very first lesson on how much power and control women have and how important it is to be in control of that power? His message stayed with me long after we wrapped that film because it taught me that I had to keep my wits about me.

I still had to stay true to myself, but I had to be aware of the perception and message I was sending to the people around me, so I could stay conscious and be assured that no one would take advantage of my power! I find it true that as a young female, the sooner we become aware of our sensuality/sexuality the harder it is for others to exploit it.

⇒ BEING AWARE OF OUR EFFECT ⇐ ON OTHERS GIVES US GREATER CONTROL

That's true of a lot of things. We can't completely forget how our actions and behavior affects those around us and how they interact with us. Cube wasn't telling me to change who I was. He wasn't saying there was something wrong with me. He was simply advising me to be aware of my femininity and how that femininity comes across, and to consider how I was being perceived by others.

This was an aha! moment for me. 💡 I hadn't really thought about it that way. No, I didn't belong to their perceptions of me, but I did need to be in control of my body and to understand how men's minds generally work. That way I will always be the one in the driver's seat! 👑

Lauren Palmer

Fast-forward to today and I often think about the messages people project. For instance, whenever I watch television, videos, and music videos with women as the stars or listen to the conversation surrounding sexuality, ownership, and women, there is something that drives me nuts.

From Beyoncé to Rihanna to Lady Gaga to Nicki Minaj, I see women—very visible women!—who are often scolded for looking and seeming "too sexy" or criticized for not playing the game and not being "sexy enough."

What's a girl to do? This is different from what Cube was saying—because yes, as an adolescent girl, I needed to become aware of my boundaries and the danger I could face if I didn't set any.

But as an adult, that shouldn't have to be anyone's concern, as long as you are aware of whatever consequence there may be (because every action has a response). Our behavior is our choice.

People often try to put women in little boxes because that makes them feel safer and more in control over the world. This isn't new either, think of Grace Jones and Annie Lennox, two women who were bold enough to brand their own type of sexuality, femininity, and ideas decades ago. I mean, Annie Lennox performed with her male bandmate for years as they both wore suits standing side by side. #TWINSIES.

⇒ GOOD GIRL VS. BAD GIRL MYTH ⇐

This is where the good girl vs. bad girl myth comes into play. Despite (or maybe because of) my past and the anxiety surrounding it, I felt pressure to be a "good girl." It's the same pressure many of us have felt. Nobody says the bad girl is the one you want to marry, so we all want to be the good girl.

I Don't Belong to You

When I was fifteen, my boyfriend tried to get me to have sex with him in a movie theater. He was putting so much pressure on me, and I wanted to cry because I was so worried that if the cameras would catch what he was trying to do, True Jackson and her lost virginity would be all over the news the next day. #TMZ NIGHTMARES. 👻

I really thought about my private feelings and public image a lot, and I struggled with how my fans saw me versus how I saw myself. Even at seventeen I thought, *Who am I if I'm not Keke the Virgin anymore?* #MENTALBONDAGE. When I did lose my virginity, I thought the whole world would host a block party in honor of Keke the Freeeeeeak!! 🎤 😄

But after wrestling with all my experiences, I have accepted them as they were and moved forward. My being glad or not glad they happened didn't make it any less a reality nor did it make it good or bad. Only I could really decide if a situation was good to me or bad to me.

Why did I beat myself up so much? That didn't make it any better! And there aren't just two ways of being a woman, aka you're either a good girl or a bad girl, a prude or a sluuuut, gay or straight, and on and on . . . Sexuality, personality, and even identity fall on a spectrum, and you are who you are in the MOMENT and nothing more. #MENTALBONDAGEREMOVED. 🙌

As human beings we should always be growing and changing and expanding, and after really giving serious consideration to that thought, I can honestly say I don't think either the good girl or the bad girl really exists, not in the way I used to think anyway.

We can all be different versions of ourselves at different points of our lives. #YAASSS. And this "good/bad" discussion

Lauren Palmer

isn't just limited to women. Guys face a lot of pressure to behave a certain way, particularly when it comes to sex and sexual identity as well! Yes, I think the media can seem more critical of women because I feel that on a more personal level, but guys are often forced to live up to certain expectations as well. #KEEPINITAHUNNID!

➤ SEXUAL EXPECTATIONS AND EXPERIENCES ⬅

The thought of sex has been intense and confusing for me at times because of my conflicted feelings due to what I experienced with my female cousin and the anxiety that my mother and grandmother passed on to me about bad men who were controlling and abusive.

When I first started having sexual encounters, old feelings that I had buried came to the surface. The act of sex causes the female to be in a more vulnerable position, and mentally I could not adapt to that. Often I would become angry at the guy and almost feel mad at the idea of losing control of myself. It would almost make me feel defeated in a way.

I discovered that I was using sex to play off the emotional unavailability in myself and my partners in my first sexual relationships with boyfriends. Not only that but once I'd realized that I could have sex without vulnerability, I realized that I could remove my anxiety with sex by just enjoying the physical, stress-relieving aspect and dumping all the emotion behind.

I was trading sex for intimacy, and when in a relationship, I would confuse the two. I would have sex with a boyfriend when I couldn't get any emotion from him, and that isn't what sex is meant to be for.

Sex is meant to be enjoyed, and it can be in the right mutual situation, but when the individual is not clear on why they want to do it, it could be exploited as opposed to cherished. When we use sex as a substitute for feelings and intimacy we create habits that keep us right where we are. That's not a suitable environment for growth in romantic relationships. That's something I learned later. For a while, I wasn't understanding the true purpose behind sex, but now I am conscious of my actions, what is driving them, and what I am using it for each time. I am awake. I'm just enjoying it physically or connecting if I'm in love with the person. It is not a reaction, habitual or compulsive, and I think that's the important part. I don't want to be reactionary, and as long as I am conscious in my choices I can respect them.

You know how you'll hear someone say (especially guys) they don't know why they had sex and can't control it? That is compulsive behavior that you aren't controlling. If you are not acting consciously, then you are not awake, only following behavior patterns, urges, and habits. I think that guys often say that because they are made to believe that they aren't normal unless they have a ridiculous sex drive. That idea is often encouraged by society. So many dudes will act or talk about sex compulsively because that is the way they feel they are supposed to act, when in reality it is an adverse reaction to the media's social influences.

When we find ourselves being obviously affected by GROUP THINK, that is when we have to take a second look: If it is not fun or not enjoyable or you are obsessive about it or doing it just because, that's not good enough. Our choices, no matter how small, deserve to have reason.

Lauren Palmer

I've learned some pretty amazing things from the women who raised me and the women who inspire me. I embrace the fact that ultimately no one has to like my story or understand my story, because it's mine alone. They taught me that my life is full of contradictions and so is everyone else's. The human/female experience can be extremely contradictory, which is why watching women embrace their beauty and their bodies is feminism on another level.

When I was working all of this out for myself, I found women every day, like my mother, who encouraged me to keep going and to work through the pain and hurt, and to reject the labels inflicted on me by others as I continued to grow on my journey. I've also found so much strength by watching the lives of my heroes, who have embraced and showcased the many wonderful contradictions of being so fully human.

They've proven that being human and being a woman mean many things: being vulnerable, sexual, in control sometimes, and honest about admitting to being controlled at other times. It also means being playful and strong. It's A LOT of things, and that's okay. 😁

It's a journey for all for us, but here's a few thoughts that might aid you in becoming a lot more comfortable with your own sexuality, which in turn will make you more comfortable with yourself. 🖤

The first thing to know is that sexuality can refer both to what gender you're attracted to and to how happy you are in your own body. 🧑🏿 One of the most important lessons I have learned is to pay no real mind to stereotypes and/or labels. Boys can wear pink and girls can be tomboys and that means absolutely nothing. The

I Don't Belong to You

world is ever changing, so ignore what others say, and do what YOU love. 👍

I found this out myself when I released my video for "I Don't Belong to You." That video ends with me going home to a female. After I released it, the Internet exploded with people wondering if I was "coming out." They missed the whole point. I put that video out to represent the young women of today—it's not the traditional women of the fifties anymore—and it's not the specifics of "Am I gay? Am I straight? Am I bi?" #SEEYAHETERONORMATIVITY.

⇒ LIVE YOUR TRUTH ⇐

We're making the rules for ourselves, and we don't have to be stuck or defined by one label. I don't feel the need to define anything to anybody, because I'm always changing and I'm sure you are too. Who's to say that I'm this or I'm that, when I might not want to be that or this tomorrow? I'm gonna follow my own feelings and my own heart. And that's what I am praying for you. Living your truth is the only perfection there is! #STRAIGHT LIKEDAT.

I am also learning that it's okay to switch it up and to try new things whenever you can. What I mean by that is if you're a man, and you want to get manicures and go to the spa every once in a while—do it!

If you're a woman who can get under the hood of a car and fix it—get it, girl! The sooner activities done traditionally by men and women change, the sooner we can get past the whole gender difference thing overall. 💅

Finally, if we judge or ridicule others and their ideas of love and sexuality, and their opinions period, we are ultimately judging and ridiculing ourselves. We all have parts of us that we may or

Lauren Palmer

may not recognize as outside the "norm." We're all weirdos in our own way. People often work so hard to fit into society, but no matter what you do, you're never going to be what society depicts as "normal" or "perfect" because that's not real!

The only point that you have to make is that you're being you. That's being a beacon of light, that's being an inspiration—it has nothing to do with followers or popularity level. Just do you, go with the flow of your life, because that's you experiencing life #FUCKYEADUDE. 😎

If you're being yourself, then you are following your purpose. The more we get out of the mind-set of thinking there's a certain way to go about things, the more free and creative we become. Not to mention that life becomes easier when you are living authentically, because you're not forcing everything to fit your perspective but you're allowing what is new to expand your perspective. #PARADIGMSHIFT.

It's all about encouraging one another to follow our own desires in how we think, dress, like, and love by accepting one another. Giving others freedom to be themselves, in turn, sets you free. 💡 #THATSTHEGAG. If you look at everyone with more kindness in your heart and understanding, you will watch as you transform in the process.

I wish my grandma Davis was around to hear that message and take it into her heart. She wasn't defined by what that man did to her. She was defined by what she did for the world. I want to be defined that way too, and I wish that for you as well.

That's what I finally told seventeen-year-old Keke who lost her virginity: "Girl, that doesn't make you good or bad. That just makes you a young girl having an experience. And if you didn't feel great about it, that's okay, we'll pick ourselves up and try something different tomorrow."

I Don't Belong to You

I gotta tell you, as this journey continues to unfold, I've learned to be kinder and to speak nicer to myself. We treat everyone else who we love well, but too often we are down to beat on ourselves. We need to speak to ourselves nicely and treat ourselves with that same nurturing love. I want to nurture myself, because I enjoy just being Keke. You take care of yourself too! Fr fr.

Lauren Palmer

Let It Flow

ON FINDING YOUR PASSION

Be fearless in the pursuit of what sets your soul on fire.
—Jennifer Lee

I've always loved music, especially R & B. My father loved Jackie Wilson, Smokey Robinson, the Temptations, and R. Kelly to name a few, so I grew up on soul music. Every other Sunday afternoon or so we would do a big family cleanup and he would let all the old-school jams play down. My mother loved performers, especially Prince and Michael Jackson.

Music affects me the same way! It's been my true love ever since I can remember, and even now, when I'm unable to make music or work on my music, it is always on my mind some way, somehow. 🐱 I didn't know the weight of it when I was younger, but music was definitely my first taste of what passion felt like.

Both music and acting are highly creative forms of self-expression. They make me feel alive and, in fact, I've built my life around them. I have learned that to have passion like that is a gift. It provides the fuel that drives me to find something greater for myself; my purpose in this lifetime.

When we have passion, we are listening to our hearts. We have discovered the fire inside that is powerful and drives us to create the best lives possible for ourselves!! Our passions give our lives direction, meaning, and joy. They connect us to others and they motivate us to pursue our dreams.

You probably know this by now, but sometimes we forget that our passions are far more important than our possessions—especially material things like money, cars, or diamonds. I think this is because the media pushes us to believe happiness is based off products simply because they want you to BUY, lol. It's not personal, just business for them, but the gag is that you truly find your purpose by doing what makes you happy. What makes you happy is like a compass needle that directs you where to go in LIFE.

Passion helps to create who we are and defines who we are not. Our passions guide us throughout our lives. They are a constant source of inspiration. What could be greater than to live passionately, expressing our gifts each and every day, doing what we were born to do and sharing it with the world? I mean, if you're not doing that in any capacity, then what are you doing? 😕 I am not judging, just asking, because if your life doesn't involve passion, how can it be meaningful? How can it be enough for you?

Following your passion is an intuitive process. It is about listening and responding to what is in your soul, not just planning out everything in your head. 👀 Expressing our passions is how we show gratitude for being on this earth. It's how we become beacons of light to one another while we are here trying to figure it out. By sharing your gifts with the world and expressing your uniqueness, you are saying "THANK YOU FOR MY LIFE!!"

Lauren Palmer

So we ask ourselves, what are our passions and how can we build our lives around them? When we wanna find out what truly moves us, we must ask ourselves the best questions to pick our own brains. Sounds pretty simple, I know! But sometimes it is so hard to get a grasp on it. Yet that is so essential. 😶

I'm not talking about what you "should want" or "shouldn't want" based on expectations other people have for you. I'm talking about what makes you come alive! Your passion isn't a duty, it's what lights the fire in your soul!! It's all about honestly tapping into whatever excites you. Maybe that's writing poetry, painting, or acting. Whatever stirs your soul is a passion that can help you find your purpose in life.

You know the feeling I'm talking about. It's the thing, THOSE things, that bring you joy. Our passions are part of our DNA, and they often make their presence known early in life. Truuuuust me, G, I was a young drama queen long before I was a Scream Queen. 😄 The creative form of expressing it can change over a lifetime, but the passion is always there.

Think about what you were most drawn to doing as a child, an adolescent, a teenager, and now as an adult. What has been there consistently? What have you tended to nurture, consciously or unconsciously over the years? And what was it that others saw in you? What did your teachers and mentors encourage you to nurture?

What subjects were you best at in school? What talent did your friends and family members praise you for and encourage you to pursue? What comes naturally to you? Communicating? Talking to children? Writing sheet music? Photographic memory? Organizing?

I Don't Belong to You

No matter how obscure it seems, write it down, because I promise you, in life there is a perfect place for everything!

⤜ TRUE PASSIONS LAST A LIFETIME ⤛

My family has always been creative. Making music and analyzing films and television shows was very normal for us. We loved it so much that we started to guess the directors and producers of different movies and TV shows that we loved before the credits ran! My favorite game was when we would be on a long car ride and one of us would say a quote from a movie and everyone else would have to guess what movie it was from. We played the same game with songs! These games came in handy, especially when we drove all the way from Illinois to California. Four days and three nights! ☀ ☀ ☀ 😄

Many of my best memories are of my sister and me watching my mother write and record songs. She also wrote and recorded some with us when I was around seven or eight years old. Since pursuing music was my mom's dream she had all the latest recording equipment. 😄 We wrote this one song called "Summertime" that I can remember a little bit of, lol. It went like this:

🎼 *I can't control the emotion*
Something stirred so deep inside
Ya know I find it hard to sleep at night
Toss and turn until daylight.
And when I see the sun
Just like magic I am sprung. 🎼

How do I remember that after all these years? Because it sprang from the heart! It wasn't about the sales or the popularity.

Lauren Palmer

It was about the love. We created it for no reason other than the joy of it and the love of doing it together.

I was fortunate to grow up surrounded by people who nurtured that spirit. My grandmother was the one who really got the credit for letting me become SO "creative." She knew how much I loved to perform. She loved that "extra" part of me, but idk if she was laughing with me or at me or both, hahahahahahahahaha. My grandma was hella shady on the low. 😭 👯

This led to her encouraging me to sing and dance whenever her friends or clients were visiting her home. She would declare the need for a talent show at some point while company was over, and then would shout, "NEXT ON THE PROGRAM IS MISS LAUREN KEE-YAH-NAH PALMER!" Then she'd say, "YES YES YES!" and clap her hands and stomp her feet and make music for me as I did my thing, which I had perfectly planned out of course! 😎

My grandmother loved music, but she wasn't a quote-unquote *singer*. She could hold a tune, but she never claimed to have the best voice. According to all family accounts, our musical talent came from my grandpa George, who died when my mom was only ten years old, long before I was born. But regardless of her talent level, my grandma would sing. I remember her singing hymns and old church tunes all the time I was growing up. Even when we moved to California she would sing to us over the phone, "I've been missing you, I've been missing you," and that would make us so sad. 🙁

When my twin siblings were born, each had a theme song. My little brother's was "You're so fine, fine, fine." My little sister's was "Renny, is that your name? Renny, uh-huh uh-huh!" 😆 😂

We were always coming up with reasons to use our creativity, lol, and my love of performing made me the proverbial life of the

I Don't Belong to You

party and/or busybody. 😂 😇 You have no idea how much I loved those days. Grandma Davis was something else! She was my biggest fan! 😇

The shows we put on really gave me a feeling of LOVE and support along with the freedom to feel like it was all right to be myself and to express that self through my gift = passion. Everyone around us encouraged us to be creative. Their support and enthusiasm inspired my sister and me to find what excited us and to go after it.

My sister discovered her brilliant imagination very early on with her dolls. She loved dolls up until she was, like, twelve (sorry, sis, hahahahaha) and while we were confused by it, we were also intrigued, lol. She created the most elaborate and entertaining stories with those dolls. Legend has it that one of her first was named Keke, hence my family nickname. 😄 I used to love to watch her play but ultimately I'd get mad because she wasn't playing with me, #HOLLUP HAHAHA! I always wanted her attention.

I loved music and singing, but I was also into hairstyling and fashion. Not only was grandma a hairstylist, so were my aunt and a couple of cousins, but MY MOM didn't get those genes, haha. 😵 Very early on I realized I was particular about my hair and I learned how to do it myself, trying new things constantly, lol. I cared very much about expressing myself and doing it with style.

The encouragement from those around me really helped me feel I could express my creativity in any way I wanted. In fact, I grew up feeling that I SHOULD always be creative because that is how connections are made. We connect to others by expressing who we are to the world. People connect to that openness and that sharing. I loved feeling connected to others,

Lauren Palmer

and it's something that still drives me today. #OBSESSED WITHTHAKIDZ. 😍

→ FULL ENGAGEMENT AND TOTAL FOCUS ←

For me, early on, I wasn't really thinking about all of this, because I didn't even know what passion, creativity, and connection meant as a kid. I just knew it felt so right doing what I loved to do, whether it was singing, acting, or performing at backyard barbecues!

Can you remember one of the most basic of things that you have always enjoyed doing, even if you think it's silly? Don't be scurd, cuzzzzzz. 😱 My interests and desires have gone through many transitions since I was a kid. But to really understand what we want, we have to learn to listen to ourselves.

What has stayed with you? Have you always loved drawing and painting? Music? Do you have a strong fashion sense? A love of decorating? These are all passions that can inspire creativity in you. They are things you are naturally drawn to. You might also consider your responses to these questions:

- What engages you so completely that when you are doing it you lose track of time and place?

- What excites your mind, body, and soul?

- What makes you so focused that you shut out everything around you and people have to drag you away from it?

If you're STILL having trouble deciding what your passion is (omg, you killing me, dude 😫😆😛), take a deep breath and

I Don't Belong to You

relax. Don't kill yourself—learning about you should be fun—you're interesting, right? 😊 Once you woosah, ask yourself: What could I do in life that would be so fulfilling and enjoyable that I'd do it for no money? What do I enjoy so much that I'd look into finding extra time for it? What would make me happy as is, without attaching it to a future goal or outcome? It can happen, FR FR! Sometimes people have passions that they can't pursue as a career so they do them as hobbies or in their spare time. The trick is finding a way to build your passion into something you can do full-time, for a living (very, very possible!!!). That way you get to pursue your passion all the time, getting your spirit filled on the daily!!

➤ BE PATIENT WITH YOUR PASSION ➤

Don't be discouraged if that doesn't happen right away. We all must be patient for that to develop. Sometimes you have to hone your skills before you can pursue your passion as a career. It's almost like a universal test of your dedication.

You have to be patient and stay prepared for the opportunity to build your life around your passion. You may hit a few walls. You may lose (things that were really never yours anyway; else you would have them). You may get knocked down and have to review your expectations.

I've done all that. In some cases, the world hasn't even opened to certain passions of mine. But I know for sure that timing is everything and if you keep working and growing and developing your talents, you will be ready when opportunities come. #PREAAAAAACH.

My early disappointments in my singing career caused me to

Lauren Palmer

THE THINGS YOU ARE

PASSIONATE ABOUT ARE

NOT RANDOM, THEY ARE

YOUR CALLING.

—FABIENNE FREDRICKSON

step away from music for a while and I regretted doing that with all my heart. I was discouraged and felt betrayed by the music industry. My spirit was broken when my desire to express my music creatively ran up against the numbers people of the industry. I told myself that maybe a singing career wasn't meant to be for me because I was so discouraged.

I honestly couldn't even listen to the music I had made. Whenever I saw it on my computer or iTunes I would literally ignore it or disassociate because I was so brokenhearted that I'd given up on myself because of the industry. *So damn lame*, I thought.

I realize now that we can become so caught up in looking for outside validation that we perpetuate a cycle of disappointment. Like let's say you lose a basketball game and feel so bad about it that you are almost ashamed. So you don't even practice for the next game. You blame that loss on yourself. You may think you are bad, instead of accepting that you just had a bad game and maybe you haven't reached your full potential yet. You have to be patient and give yourself time to become your best.

Otherwise, we tend to repeat the same mistakes out of our fear-ridden story lines by thinking things like, *I'm the girl who never gets the job she wants.* Then we might perpetuate that negative perspective by never GOING for the job we want! The good news is that your passion will usually override your fears. True passion is a fire that burns even when water is thrown on it time and time again.

Lauren Palmer

My love of music and singing was so strong that even though I was discouraged about my music career for many years, I couldn't ever extinguish that fire inside me that drove me to keep singing. I'd sing in the shower and while cooking and driving. I loved to sing and I realized that my ability and passion for singing is God-given.

No industry could take that away. No industry could take away the fact that singing changed my mood from negative to positive. No industry could take away the fact that other people were touched when they heard me sing. NO, NOTHING can stop you from spreading love around the world. You may be discouraged or stifled for a moment but if you have a true gift, the cream always rises to the top, as my mom always says.

And even though I was afraid of going up against the music industry's numbers people again, I used that fear to drive myself to get stronger mentally and to keep working on my voice and my songwriting. Having fears gave me the opportunity to face them, which in turn gave me the opportunity to become my own hero. It helped me to understand I have the power to feel better about experiences that left me feeling defeated and insecure. The great jazz singer Ella Fitzgerald is heard to have said, "Just don't give up trying to do what you really want to do. Where there's love and inspiration, I don't think you can go wrong."

For years I let my poor situations with record companies dictate who I was as an artist and affect my identity as a musical person. Every no was *NO*, every yes was *YES*. Translation: Anything bad I saw as horrible and anything amazing I saw as not enough. The industry stole my strength when I was child, and as

I Don't Belong to You

an adult it was at first hard to tell the difference between a stagnant situation and a growing one.

I wanted to turn over a new leaf in my singing career, but I kept having the same negative attitude about every NEW music situation. I put myself in bondage by reliving this same tragic story, but then I was no longer a child. Once I hit the age of eighteen, I started to gain a little more confidence and decided to put out a mixtape.

There was also the explosion in social media that provided even more opportunities independent of corporate assistance. On YouTube, Twitter, and Soundcloud, people were revealing their talents to even greater audiences. I was inspired by all those online who were making their shit happen in their own way and just keeping it fun.

Even though I still got distracted by industry perceptions with that project, it was the start of me realizing that I didn't want my inner voice to stay dormant. I mean, it was the brains of the operation, watching over all my thoughts like Sway, having all the answers. 😂

⇌ PUTTING IN THE EFFORT ⇋

Even when I wasn't singing professionally, my love for music encouraged me to dig deep, really deep, and study the art and music of producers and musicians I'd heard about or just liked a lot. I think we can pursue all of our passions throughout our lives, but sometimes one passion might become a hobby while another becomes a career. I've always wanted to pursue my passions simultaneously, but for a long time acting took precedence because that's how others first saw me. It took quite a while for me to realize it was my consistency in acting that did that, not their boxing me in, and if I wanted to be acknowledged with something else, I was going to have to be just as consistent with that. What is a hobby and what is a career is all up to you and the effort you put into pursuing your passions.

I got the courage to do that when I was about twenty/twenty-one. Living in New York really gave me that independent push, and I started to understand that I needed to get out there in the music world if I was gonna be serious about my artistry. I needed to talk to the kids coming up, the people working in recording studios and my peers in the industry. I also wanted to show my support and go give love when given the opportunity to meet performers I admired. I needed to get out there and learn where the next waves were coming from and then I wanted to create my own waves.

Music once again became a priority to me. No matter what was happening I would make time to go hang out at house parties, vibe the scene, observe the different experiences and settings I'd put myself in, and it all gave me inspiration on what I wanted to express. It was a learning experience for me—especially in learning about myself and my anxiety. Going out on my own was a constant head conversation of, "Are you sure you want to leave the house?" But I would, and I'd hit up the dope new artist who I wanted to collaborate with on some music shit or just give props to. I took baby steps in becoming the kind of artist I wished to see. #BOUTDATLIFE.

For me this was very hard because my anxiety had increased so much by that time and it was very difficult for me to drive alone and do things by myself. I didn't wanna always take my boyfriend because I wanted this to be about me and my

I Don't Belong to You

passion, that was the love story. Still it was very hard, but I loved music so much that I was willing to face my anxieties and actually go out on my own and have an independent experience creatively if that meant inspiration and growth to feed my passion!

➤ BABY STEPS CAN LEAD ➤ TO MAJOR LEAPS

It took a lot of trial and error, but every baby step created major leaps. By putting my fears aside and refusing to give up on my passions, I placed myself in a position for new opportunities down the road. Who knew my love of music would one day lead me to Broadway and television musicals as I worked to master and gain confidence in my craft?

To tell you the truth, I hated musicals as a kid. Literally, the only one I could watch was *Cry-Baby* with Johnny Depp, hahahahaha. And this one Chicago theater musical life story of Jackie Wilson! But honestly the Universe provides you opportunity to study and to exercise for your missions and "pop quizzes." The fact that I was in New York for Broadway created the space for me to get more comfortable going out on my own. The energy in New York, the easy transpo system, the people, and the activities, it all fed my soul and made me feel like I could do anything on my own!

The city of New York gave me my independence and broke major anxiety chains for me. I know that was no mistake because it came at the perfect time. I was twenty-one and the two years before I had been making my little baby steps of connecting back with the music world and the people in it. I was ready to take that big leap, and New York was it! Of course I rose to the occasion,

Lauren Palmer

but these opportunities are often all around, it's just when we are asleep we do not see.

If you haven't been in touch with your heart for a while, you may feel some fear and anxiety about pursuing your passion. I try to just accept any fear that comes up, feel it totally and own it completely. 😨 I use the concept of fear or the *emotion* of fear against itself. By focusing that energy and not trying to fight it I can create the environment that will inspire ideas and other emotions that give me the outcome I want. Example: If I'm scared about an audition, I connect it to the fear of my character, or I connect it to the fear of the makers of the film and how they need someone to fill this part so the studio can release their money to make their movie. I embrace it and that gives me power over it! Anything other than that is unproductive. It's my way of tapping into negative feelings as a positive power source.

To live a fulfilling life, we have to quit caring what other people think and follow our passions. HELLO, you dah boss. 😼 Get in touch with your negative and uncomfortable feelings, because that is the only way to let them go! Many times when we are in that unpleasant space we often think we aren't good enough to pursue our passions. Sometimes we may feel our fears are too powerful to overcome. I've been there.

There were times when I felt I wasn't good enough because "music industry people" weren't taking me as seriously as I wanted. #VICTIMIZATION. I have learned how to cope with those passion-killing, self-defeating thoughts by taking steps like these:

I'll get physical and take the focus off my feelings of fear. I might go to the gym or for a long and not-so-slow walk. When I do this, I leave my phone inside and try to focus on what's hap-

I Don't Belong to You

"Practice any art, music, singing, dancing, acting, drawing, painting, sculpting, poetry, fiction, essays, reportage, no matter how well or badly, not to get money and fame, but to experience becoming, to find out what's inside you, to make your soul grow."

—Kurt Vonnegut

pening in front of me. Sometimes when I'm anxious and pulling my hair out, I'll text myself to get those feelings out in the universe and away from me. Then I'll wait a beat and read the text back and respond as a friend offering a less emotional perspective. And then there is yoga. Yes, I'm a fan of that whole world. I try to do yoga twice a week, I know that keeps the anxiety bugs away. 👍 Those activities always calm me, ease my mind, and remind me it isn't personal, and give me the confidence to keep pursuing my passions. Now, to keep it real, it's also true that our dreams don't always come true, but the gag is that's because our dreams are often way smaller than the ones we have the potential to manifest. We must learn that our minds do not know how to visualize our purpose. That's something that can only be perceived once it's being lived. It's understood as it grows.

My first attempts and vision for my music career didn't pan out. So I asked myself why is there only one idea of success for my expansive dream? Why does there have to be a lone thing that represents my passion being a success for me? Example: thinking that winning a Grammy makes you a great artist or that winning an Oscar makes you a greater actress than someone who hasn't won. That is so far from the reality and if you don't believe me, go to a 'hood near you and tell me all the niggas at the basketball court shouldn't be in the NBA. Or that the local homeless man's paintings aren't as interesting as Picasso's. People knowing you are great doesn't make you any greater and people not knowing you are great doesn't make you any less great.

The important thing is to never let anyone steal your passion from you. Not everyone has vision like you. Not everyone will share yours, because it's yours. Don't let them discourage you. You cannot deny what is in your heart!

I Don't Belong to You

Don't forget that you can have major passions that you build your life around while also having smaller passions that add to the quality of your life. You never know what might happen with them. I used to get called to speak at schools after I made *Akeelah and the Bee*. At first it was cool and I liked hanging with kids who were my age, but as I grew older I started to understand how much that relationship could affect us positively and the importance of connecting what you do to influence a great sense of community. I found fulfillment in relating to my peers who I used to live the same life as (school, no job and, if so, part-time, etc.), and even though my situation is a little more "unique" it doesn't mean we can't relate; it actually means we can relate better and dissect the new information I'm given through my career resources. 🙏

Now, ten years later, I jump at the chance to speak to schools, community groups, and organizations. Uplifting the community is one of my greatest passions. Bringing joy to others helps me realize the magic of my gifts, so I feel that I've come full circle when I talk to young people about making the most of their own gifts and opportunities. Speaking isn't how I make my living, but I still get great joy from it.

Working with choreographers and other dancers helps me sharpen my skills in case opportunities open up. You never know when your moment will come. When the VH1 Hip Hop Honors producers asked me to perform for the Salt-N-Pepa tribute, I wasn't afraid! Not only that but I got a chance to work with FATIMA, who was Aaliyah's main girl. Idk if I would've been prepared if I hadn't put the work in before.

I didn't know that they would call me for this particular op-

Lauren Palmer

portunity, but I knew someone would call me someday, and that's why I wanted to be ready. When you have a passion for something, you don't need a reason or an excuse to do it. You do it because you love it, and because you understand THERE IS NO LUCK. There's preparation meeting destiny, as Oprah would say (*heyyyyy girl!*).

Doing what we love can lead to exciting discoveries, opportunities, and relationships. The entire process of putting my concept videos together is so liberating for me because in my videos I share my vision and the fans can immediately see what kind of music I like, what style of dance I am into, and what kind of visual energy they can expect from MY project. Most important, they see the grind and they see I'm breaking my neck for it 'cause I love it. That's the drive, the love.

⟩ LET YOUR PASSION GUIDE YOU ⟨

I wrote my first script during my first season of *Scream Queens* and I have been directing my own sketches for the last few years. My interest in that was stirred while I worked with Tyler Perry as he directed *Madea's Family Reunion.* He opened my eyes to the creative possibilities of being fully involved in all aspects of the movie business. He wrote, directed, and starred in that film. He had the ultimate vision of the movie and he worked with all of us on the set to create that vision.

I loved it when he'd be dressed up like his lady Madea character while calling the shots on set. Tyler was a trip to watch. He created and stored all the lines, performances, and scenes in his head and then he fit it all together into a wonderful film. I loved it!! #VIRGO.

Tyler Perry and I share similar backgrounds, and although his

I Don't Belong to You

life is his life and my life is mine, I was inspired by him. He came from nothing, lived in his car and in rundown hotels as he struggled to write plays as a young guy in Atlanta, and stayed focused on being successful. He is now one of the most successful people in the entertainment industry, and he kept the faith in himself and God. His success shows that there is life after any trauma. You cannot be stopped if you refuse to quit.

Tyler is a great role model for all of us who want to build our lives around our passions. He is a multitalented creative genius devoted to sharing his gifts with the world. He has said his motivation has never been money, but instead he strives to motivate and inspire people by following his passions and expressing his creativity. He once said: "The dream will outlive the dreamer, so dream big."

God never said you couldn't enjoy the possessions the world can bring, He just doesn't want us to get lost in pursuing and acquiring material things instead of developing our gifts. While the notion of following your heart may sound cliché, don't be too quick to blow it off. The biggest gag of them all is that life is not that serious. It's all about having fun.

Facebook founder Mark Zuckerberg and Tom Anderson, co-creator of Myspace, are huge examples of that. They weren't trying to figure out how to access marketing and advertising dollars. They were pursuing a passion, and the material rewards were a blessing they received from connecting the world through social media. Lol, they created a space where people could connect and their blessings were the bonus.

I'm always interested when people like Tyler Perry and Oprah Winfrey say they are driven by passion and not money, because they are great examples of individuals who've reaped incredible rewards by being true to their hearts. They inspire me.

Lauren Palmer

In making decisions about my career, I've learned to listen to and weigh the advice of other sources like my parents, agents, and financial advisors and other people who are where I wish to be. I think that's so important when sharing ideas or asking advice to know who it is you're speaking with and if they hold the qualities your wish to acquire.

You can't expect everyone to buy into your goals. Even people who love you may not get them, because they don't share your passion or the vision you have for your life. They usually have their own visions based on their perceptions and experiences. I listen to them, but mostly I follow my heart, my inner GPS that is plugged into my creative core. Sometimes all of my advisors give me good advice that is well intentioned. All too often, though, their guidance is more about what they want for me than what I want for me. I'll listen to other voices, but I don't blindly follow anyone's advice.

My decisions made from the heart and based on my passion may not always turn out for the best, but I've found that when I make my own mistakes, I tend to learn from them. That's not true when I make mistakes because I've taken the advice of others. In those cases, I just get pissed off at them and at myself for listening to them!

Life is trial and error. You have to trust your instincts most of the time. If you don't, you'll become dependent on others too much. Following your passion won't guarantee success or solve all of your problems but it will help your mind become a servant to your heart and not the opposite.

I Don't Belong to You

⇒ BUILD STRENGTH AND ⇐
LOOK FOR OPPORTUNITIES

I believe our greatest passions can serve as our greatest guides and driving forces throughout our lives, if we always continue to grow and build upon them. Nelson Mandela was one of the most passionate, powerful, and wise men to ever bless this earth and I love his philosophy on taking our passions as far as they will go. He said, "There is no passion to be found in playing small—in settling for a life that is less than the one you are capable of living."

Mandela was telling us that you don't get what you are looking for by following the rules and the blueprint created by other people. His life is an incredible example of patiently following your passion, waiting for the right time to step up and make your move. The South African leader stood against apartheid in a nation that was ruled by a racist government. He paid a steep price, but in the end, he changed his nation and the world.

Mandela went to jail for twenty-seven years because he opposed the government's discrimination and demanded racial equality. I can't imagine how hard that was, but he was passionate about elevating the lives of his people. This great man could have played along with the government, but he preferred to be in jail rather than accept the atrocities of the apartheid regime. He wasn't looking for fame as an inspirational figure, but he became just that because of his determination and principles that came from the heart.

When you are doing things from your heart you're constantly inspired by the things around you and creating new ways to share

Lauren Palmer

"IT'S A TERRIBLE THING, I THINK, IN LIFE

TO WAIT UNTIL YOU'RE READY. I HAVE

THIS FEELING THAT ACTUALLY NO ONE IS

EVER READY TO DO ANYTHING. THERE'S

ALMOST NO SUCH THING AS READY.

THERE'S ONLY NOW."

—HUGH LAURIE—

your passion with the world. I was thrilled when I officially got a part on the show *True Jackson, VP*. I'd already done so much more "serious" acting in films, and one kid movie with Disney, *Jump In*. I was ready for the change a television series might bring and the different sort of professional challenges it posed. Being cast in that series also kept my family financially stable for a long time and we did enjoy how comfortable we were because of that during that period.

But money has never been my driving force, and after the second season of the show I was ready to move on to something more stimulating that allowed me to grow as an actor and performer. It was a children's show and I was a teenager who didn't want to be seen as a kid forever. I also felt my love for music was being pushed to the back burner and my identity was becoming too tied to that character. That didn't make me very happy at all and added to my overall angst.

I had accomplished a lot, but I thought I was capable of doing more. I didn't want to settle. The fires of passion were burning, driving me to take risks and keep developing as an artist on many fronts. But sometimes you have to fall off the bike to get back on. It takes time for a flower to bloom, it takes time for a caterpillar to turn into a butterfly. Once you become enlightened by your purpose, the metamorphosis begins. You are ready to grow and reach new levels of achievement, so you build strength and patiently wait for your opportunity to take flight. I have done that and will continue to do that, and so can you!

If you try to take off before you are prepared and ready, you may experience problems. You may become overwhelmed. For example, you should never quit a job without having a plan in place, whether that is a better job or one that brings you a step closer to

Lauren Palmer

your dream job. You have to invest in your dreams to achieve them fully, otherwise you will be #SETUPFORFAILURE!

When I don't rush things and instead go with the flow and prepare myself to succeed, the ideas, opportunities, and direction come to me more naturally. My preparations might include reading the industry blogs and checking the Web for the latest projects in the entertainment business. If I get impatient, I tell myself to take a step back and look at all the options while staying grounded in the present moment.

You can do the same in your field of choice, following your own passions and dreams. Don't settle for a smaller life than you are capable of living, but give yourself time to grow and prepare for that bigger stage wherever, whenever, and whatever it might be. Say you have a job you'd like to quit because you hate it. You don't like the people, or the pay sucks. Odds are you can't just walk off, because you need the cash to pay your bills. Don't allow yourself to feel frustrated. Instead, think of your situation as the perfect chance to take the time to get ready to move to that next space.

Work on your skill sets, plug into your network to find new opportunities, and put away a little extra cash. Don't lose your passion. Instead, use it to drive you to the next level. Be ready. Those who pay their dues and really put in the hard work for their dreams can spot a blessing, but those who live entitled are usually disappointed by life.

My interests and desires have gone through many stages and transitions since my *True Jackson* days. I'm sure your passions will take you on your own journey too. My goal is to always push myself to make the most of my gifts and to share them with as many people as possible. I hope that will be your goal too. Pursuing a passion-driven life means never settling, constantly growing, and doing your best to break through any barriers or limitations that others may have placed in your path. It doesn't mean you're perfect and everything will be great. Your feelings will be hurt, things will upset you, and you will be frustrated, but you will also get back up and keep trying because you owe it to yourself. You owe it to yourself, duuuuuuuuude!

⇒ PASSION IS NOT RATIONAL ⇐

Following your passion is not a rational act. You don't have to know where you are going. 🙄 You don't have to know where to start. You just start. It doesn't matter how you do it or what age you are when you start. Never stop moving forward toward your dreams.

Be warned: This will drive some people who love and care about you absolutely out of their minds. By some people, I mean your parents, your grandparents, and maybe all of your friends and relatives. 😂 🙊 Some of them will get it and support you. But too often people don't follow their dreams and when they see someone else doing it, they tend to shake their heads and tell us we're crazy, foolhardy, or even the ever-popular *insane*. 😂 So be it.

My mom used to ask me all the time, "Do you love acting? Would you want to act even if you had to do it for free, with no benefits?" To be honest I never quite knew what she meant because at the time I didn't realize that there WERE benefits for actors! 😂 😂 😂 😂 #IWASSTRESSED. #SHIT. #KIDDING. #KINDA. Hahahaha.

The point is, a lot of times we stop ourselves from doing

what we feel we should do in the moment because we play a game of if/then. If I do what I feel I should do right now, then what if xyz happens?! We start trying to predict the future and possible negative outcomes and then we miss the moment and all of the wonder in it. We also talk ourselves out of what we are meant to do!

Again, you cannot depend on your mind to rationalize acts done out of passion. That's like in the third film of *The Matrix* trilogy when Neo is fighting the AI. The AI tells Neo that since he's human he's obviously going to die because his opponent is an AI.

The AI asks Neo why he keeps fighting when he knows he's going to lose. Neo says because it's his choice.

That's free will, and it's also allowing God to stand right beside you. Neo had faith in himself that no matter where it led him, it was the right thing. He was guided by his interest, starting with the Internet surfing and then the swallowing of the pill. It guided him to the unthinkable, but he kept going because he believed and found passion in this growing and in this knowledge pool. Where he ended up is not the point, it's that he went for it with goodwill and that goodwill was enough to make his life worth something in the time he was living it. That's what life is about! To me at least. 😄

Passion produces the greatest magic in life. The mind is a processor, the AI couldn't understand passion because it had no spirit. The AI was only a brain and the brain only knows what can be known in the material form, not what can be felt or manifested. That takes passion. Your passion is a creative force unique to you. It is a manifesto of your life experiences. No one is the same, and that means no one's passion can be expressed without them expressing it. You have to let the spirit of passion guide you if you want to become all that you are meant to be. You have to stop the if/then game. You can't question your instincts.

There is no way you can compare yourself to someone else. You cannot rely on your mind to make your dreams logical. They are dreams. They are meant to seem illogical and completely out of this world. They are "mind-blowing," get it! 😶

You can live a strictly logical life if you want, but first you must understand that not everything in life can be solved with logic, or "solved" at all. Though logic is needed, the use of intuition cannot be avoided. How logical does it seem for a little girl who grew up in a family in Section 8 subsidized housing in one of the country's poorest towns to think she would one day star on Broadway, host a talk show, and work in Hollywood, appearing in eighteen films between the ages of eleven and twenty-one?

It's not logical at all. That is the great beauty of daring to dream. It's not about logic. It's about passion and following your heart's desire. And that is the magic of passion! It defies logic. Passionate people do things and accomplish things that logic would find impossible. #THATSTHEGAG.

There is nothing rational or logical about Tyler Perry's rise from a life of abuse and neglect, homelessness, and despair to one of incredible achievement and financial success. There is nothing rational about Oprah's incredible life story either. Unless you figure in passion.

As you've already learned, I am a big advocate of that. As to the highly rational people who may question you, criticize you, mock you, and refuse to support you, my suggestion is that you smile and offer them two words: "God bless."

God put that passion in you for a purpose. Your responsibility is to take it and run with it and see how far you can get. How can that not lead to good things? Following my passions and my heart's desires has brought me more joy, more happiness, and an incredible connection to the mystery and magic of life. I wish the same for you.

I do I do I doooo oooooh (read in my Kel voice from Nickelodeon's *Kenan & Kel* sitcom). Lmfaoooooo!

5

With My Mind on My Money and My Money on My Mind

ON CAREER AND HUSTLE

See, I have refined you, though not as silver;
I have tested you in the furnace of affliction.

—Isaiah 48:10

I have a confession to make: While writing this chapter, I was also working on a movie and playing a role that was quite a departure for me. It was a long, long way from the characters I played in *Akeelah and the Bee* and *Cinderella*. Well, a long, long way doesn't really cut it. This role is actually *light-years* away. In a distant galaxy, far, far away, hahahahahahaha! The movie is called *Pimp* and, as you might guess, it's not a fairy tale.

It's about a badass named Wednesday, someone we have never before seen as the main character in a film, at least I think. My girl is a pimp who struggles hustling the rough streets of the Bronx "for a chance at love and a better life out of poverty and the streets." I wish I could have all that press release material read to you in the standard movie-trailer-guy voice. It always sounds better when he says it. 🙄

My *Pimp* character is a *lesbian* pimp; not that she's defined only by her sexual preferences. Still, it is another major departure from my past roles of the innocent girl, the shy girl, and the girl next door. Wednesday is in a relationship with a woman named Nikki, whom she grew up with. My character grew up in the pimp business because her father was a pimp and her mother was a prostitute.

Wednesday quickly gets caught up in the pimp life and things turn seriously nasty when she starts pimping her own girlfriend too. There is no sassy Keke or flirty Keke in this movie. You see a completely different side of me in *Pimp*, and that's the POINT. I fought to get this role and to get the movie financed and made.

I saw this role as incredibly important to my career because I did not want to be forever cast as cute, adorable child star Keke. My mom and I could see that Hollywood was locking me into the nice-girl niche; nice girl next door, nice best friend, nice girlfriend, and nice sassy girl.

I knew I could play other roles because I love to stretch myself as an actress. I also grew up in a community where there were many women like Wednesday and the girls working for her. We knew a role like Wednesday in *Pimp* could change the game for me when it came to people wondering what roles I could play. This movie showcases my versatility as an actress.

⇉ DOIN' THE HUSTLE ⇇

My mom and I discussed the need to be versatile a lot. We both refused to let me get typecast. We've always kept our eyes peeled for new and interesting projects that allowed me to grow and demonstrate my depth as an actress. I have definitely gone through many transitions in the industry and I have been blessed to learn so much at a young age.

There comes a time in everyone's career when you feel you've done your internship. You've served your apprenticeship. You've

Lauren Palmer

shown that you can handle anything they throw at you. Now you are ready to raise the stakes.

How do you do it?

You *hustle*!

In any business, you have to keep stretching and growing. I had to explore a wide range of roles in all sorts of films, plays, and television series to continue to expand my opportunities as an actress. My character in *Pimp* may be unlike any roles I've played before, but she has one major characteristic that we share: We are both hustlers.

The word *hustle* is both a noun and a verb. As a noun, it can mean a swindle or a con. As a verb, *to hustle* is to go after what you want forcefully and persuasively. I'm all about the verb when I say that to make the most of our gifts and to build lives that are fulfilling and accomplished, we *all* have to hustle. We have to go after what we want forcefully yet persuasively.

Even though I've done very well so far in my career, the nature of show business is that there are ebbs and flows. There are times when my work schedule is just crazy and the offers are rolling in. There are also times when I'm hearing nothing but crickets and the buzzing of bees. 😂😂😂😂

That's the way of the entertainment industry. You can't wait for the phone to ring. You have to hustle. I've learned that any great opportunities brought to me or handed to me are the icing on the cake. I don't count on "lucky breaks." I am always looking for opportunities and I'm always creating my own. My mantra is *"Don't wait for it to come, get on it, girl!"*

There is no standing around just *hoping* something good happens in your career. If I want to succeed, if *you* want to succeed, we have to motivate ourselves, invest in ourselves, and prepare ourselves.

I Don't Belong to You

Staying positive is good. Praying doesn't hurt. But even God expects you to do your part and hustle. The *Universe* rewards hustle.

⇥ TAKING RESPONSIBILITY FOR ⇤ OUR OWN SUCCESS

I was eighteen years old when I heard they were casting roles for an independent movie about a female pimp. I decided almost immediately that I wanted to audition for the role of Wednesday. Even so, it took me nearly four years to nail down the *Pimp* part. I was so determined to win the lead role that I made an audition video at my own expense!

My mom and I flew to Chicago with my brother-in-law. We drove to my hometown, Robbins, which is just south of Chicago, and set up the cameras in my aunt Nene's beauty salon, which is named Ladies with an Attitude, get it, Lololol #NWA. I grew up in an area of poverty, but my life wasn't *poor*. My childhood was filled with wonderful and unique people who weren't afraid to express themselves and their personalities. I may have played some real characters in my acting roles, but my hometown crowd has many *true* characters.

You couldn't make up people with stories like theirs. They live in their own world. It's a little behind the rest of the world, like it's still in the nineties. You still see people walking around Robbins, Illinois, talking on flip phones, it's old school but that is what makes it special. For our audition film session, we invited a lot of women from the community, and they included hustlers of all kinds.

We had some real-life Wednesday women in there, and that raises another point. *Pimp* is a true woman's project. It captures a

Lauren Palmer

very harsh woman's world. Its writer and director is a woman. All the lead characters are women, and the screenplay is basically a love story between two women fighting to survive in a world dominated by men.

My mom and I really related to the characters in *Pimp* because they were so much like the real women back home and so much like us. My *Pimp* character is a strong woman forced into a series of life-changing decisions based on choices inspired by her environment. She has to make them quickly because her survival depends on it.

That's how life is for people who can't escape poverty, who have to fight every day to get by. It's just so hard because systematically poor people aren't even given the same access to the knowledge that would help them get out the 'hood. I know from my family's experience that many poor people feel like they are always chasing their own tails, and that can be frustrating.

We thought of this movie as a female version of *Hustle & Flow*, with a little female *Rocky* thrown in. Wednesday is a tough woman, so I had to prepare myself physically too. I worked out for two months with a trainer who toned my body so you could see more muscle and fewer curves. I even studied how guys in the 'hood walk, talk, stand, and hold their money. I got into some detailed method-acting shit! 😂😂 And it happened without me even realizing I was doing it. I was into all the details of that lifestyle. I love this character and wanted to do her justice.

Once we had all those badass ladies together at my aunt's salon to make the audition film, we let the liquor flow and the cameras roll. There were no lulls in the conversation, *at all*! We talked about the world of pimps and hoes and lady lovers, the good, the bad, and the fugly. It was very real.

I Don't Belong to You

Kevin Spacey taught me about method acting when I worked with him on *Shrink*. He told me to lose myself in my roles and never to judge the characters I was playing because that's the job of the audience. The actor should just play the role and let the audience decide what they think.

When we were filming the demo video in my aunt's beauty salon, I let myself become Wednesday. I said things Wednesday would say, I told stories she would tell, and I tried to get in her skin as much as possible. I must have done a pretty good job because even some of my cousins were believing me as Keke even though I was being Wednesday! Hahahaha! I'm like "Natalie, no that ain't me" in my head, but in reality I just said whatevs and stayed in character hahaha.

⇒ PUTTING IN THE EXTRA TIME AND EFFORT ⇐

I found it hard to shake Wednesday after I left the salon that day. That's the gag on such extreme characters, you lose yourself in them. But immersing myself in that world gave me the opportunity to show the producers of *Pimp* how dedicated I was to approaching such an intense role. That is the same dedication and hustle I always apply to my career.

People in the entertainment industry respect hustle, and they expect it too. One day after we returned to California from Illinois, we ran into Snoop Dogg in the recording studio. We had the finished *Pimp* audition video with us and we showed it to him. We wanted his professional opinion because I consider him an icon.

Snoop loved it, which made us feel very good about all the time, money, and effort we'd put into the audition video. He also said it was wise for me to step outside of my acting box in such a

Lauren Palmer

major way. He said the video would show people in the industry how serious I was about my career.

Snoop said, "You have to go left when people think you are going right. Always keep them guessing."

I believe in investing in myself, surrounding myself with the right people, and always going the extra mile. I did it in my first major film, *Barbershop 2*, and it ain't never gonna change. I do whatever it takes because I accept responsibility for my own career success, my own happiness, and my own life.

When I talk to schoolkids or young actors, I tell them the same thing I'm telling you. If you want it, go after it with all the hustle you've got in you.

➤ LIVE IT LIKE YOU ALREADY OWN IT ➤

Success is no accident. It comes with hard work, perseverance, learning, studying, sacrifice, and, most of all, loving what you do. This isn't just about mo' money, mo' money, MO' MONEY! 🤑 😂 If you expect others to buy into you and your talents, you first have to value yourself enough to invest your time in whatever way you feel is necessary for your growth. Real talk: If you're an actor, where's your reel showcasing some of your best shows or monologues? If you're a musician, where is the hook up in your car with your music on it? Or have you taken new photos for your portfolio?

We're always hearing about investing money to pave a path to financial success. Sadly, we don't hear nearly as much about investing your efforts, discipline, sacrifice, consistency, and work. All of those are necessary to pave a path to personal success!

Again, I'm not just talking so much about investing money in your career dreams—although it takes some of that. Success over

I Don't Belong to You

a lifetime requires constantly building and rebuilding the brand, learning new skills, improving old ones, and having the RESPECT for yourself to create scenarios that allow you to stay #ON POINT. #ACCOUNTABILITY.

Seriously, if you don't show that you believe in yourself by giving yourself the resources TO succeed, why would someone else?

⇝ THE KEKE BRAND ⇜

My parents instilled this in me, bless 'em. And they kept on me about it because they knew that staying connected to the community is important. They wanted me to succeed, but to never forget where I came from too. From day one I knew that my mother/manager and I were an unsinkable, unbeatable, and solid team. 👯 We are like Batman and Robin. We've been tag-teaming since I was a kid, and we're still tag-teaming. She is my soul mate and she, above all else, has my best interests at heart. Together we built my career, and I have to say I don't know if I could've accomplished any of the things I have up to this point without her and my family by my side.

After my first few films were released, my mom started talking to me about the significance of my peers and my generation being aware of my career and knowing my name. She understood that people knowing my name would be the first step in their knowing my story/brand, and she was the first person to ever talk to me about building my brand.

By *brand* I don't mean some fake identity just to create popularity. Your brand should authentically communicate to the world who you are and what you stand for. I think that's a concept that can be applied to anyone in any career or even personally. Think-

Lauren Palmer

ing of yourself as a brand helps you get a handle on how you want the world to see you and where you see yourself in the world.

My mom felt that most people knew I was a little black girl from Robbins who'd made it to Hollywood, but she wanted them to truly know my story. She wanted to build upon that by spreading the word so that other people growing up in all areas across America could relate my journey to their own. It wasn't just about me; it was about every little girl like me. We felt that telling my story could help stop the negative thoughts that keep so many others from thinking that their dreams couldn't come true. My mom really believed in me, my talents, and my dreams, and that made it possible for others to believe, and for me to believe in myself.

My mom wanted me to own and take responsibility for my story so that nobody else could do it for me. That is so important because if you don't believe in, build, and protect your own brand, other people will stick labels on you that might not be accurate and then you are stuck with the story that they are telling about you. They may misuse and abuse your brand for their own agendas.

My mom talked about protecting my story, my image, and making sure it was authentic to who I really was. In my earliest days as an actress, I did not know that I represented so much to the community. People would stop us in the streets to say how *Akeelah and the Bee* had inspired their kids, and my mom and I really felt a responsibility to that. In fact, right after I'd had success in a couple of films, we invested a few thousand dollars a month in hiring a publicist. We felt early on that we had to get our message out on our own terms. Not all child actors back then were paying a publicist because that was an extra fee that many people didn't want to pay, but we thought it was necessary to help get my

I Don't Belong to You

name out there. It was important so that people would know who I really was, and an added benefit was that producers and casting directors could hear about me too. We also paid to create my first website at a time when few child actors were doing that. We took flak from some of the parents of other child actors who thought it was a waste of money, but before long, they realized they needed to do it too, #AREYOUSURE. Hahahahaha. 🙄

➤ MY QUEST TO BUILD A BRAND ➤

I wasn't making huge amounts of money at the time, but my parents wanted to keep my name out in the industry. I had already made a few films, and every now and then I'd get an interview request, but you can't depend on other people to tell your story. And depending on the publicists for films wouldn't be enough because their concentration is about promoting the film, not the talent.

My mom thought what I was doing was important, and she wanted the community to know about it because she thought I could succeed and be an inspiration. She'd always say that it wouldn't do to be a dim light. I had to put all my energy into it so I could shine brightly for everyone to see. My parents nurtured me and I knew they wanted the best for all of us.

I loved the new world built around my passion for performing. The more I worked, the more doors opened up. I jumped at the opportunity to learn as much as I could so that I could be all that I could be. It was my quest to be in the industry, and I was COOL with putting extra work into it! I've come to really appreciate that my parents were so caring and encouraging. They invested in me too. They made sure I had access to all that I needed

Lauren Palmer

to know as we built my career. They put me in position to succeed as a performer and as a person.

Even taking me back to Robbins to make the audition video for *Pimp* was part of their plan to always keep me in touch with my roots so I would appreciate my gifts and the opportunities I had to build a better life. They made sure I didn't take anything for granted. Every step of the way, they explained the value of what they were doing, whether it was hiring a publicist, building a website, or setting up speaking engagements in underserved communities.

Not to sound like an old-timer at the age of twenty-two, but the entertainment environment was completely different when my career started ten years ago. Social media wasn't out there like it is now, and you didn't become a star or a household name with just one film, one record, or one guest-starring role on television. Today someone can make a YouTube video and, overnight, become larger than life with millions of fans and followers. That's how it is now, but not back then.

Today there is a new flow to business, thanks to social media. It has given talented performers more access to TV and record executives, as well as new fans, via the Internet. That's nothing but a good thing. That means you can think of an idea and put it out into the world without anyone stopping you. So what *is* stopping you then?

I try to use every tool that is available. My motto is you have to GET READY and STAY READY. That means finding ways to stay on your game BEFORE you get that opportunity you really want. If you do that, you will be ready at the time that opportunity does arrive. By taking that attitude and approach, I'm motivated to keep working to better myself physically, mentally, and spiritually.

I Don't Belong to You

⤞ ELEVATING YOUR GAME THROUGH ⤝ SELF-MOTIVATION

I do this in every aspect of my career. As I mentioned earlier, before I dropped my first single with my new label, Island Records, I decided I wanted to work on being a more polished dancer. I realized that it was harder to motivate myself to work on my dancing if I was just practicing, so I began making online dance videos for my social media sites instead. Knowing that thousands, and maybe millions, of people would view the videos, including professional dancers and recording label executives, gave me motivation to work that much harder.

This was a great way to set an intention (#MUSICCAREER) and work on perfecting and polishing my dancing, while still keeping it REAL. I wanted there to be some level of "stakes" for myself. Knowing I was going to put it out made it real for me, so I couldn't slack off. I had to take it seriously. In the process, I gave my fans a video to enjoy, and potential directors and producers had another opportunity to check me out.

So even though these were *practice* rounds for me, I had to give the same level of effort I would for the real thing. I don't want to be a mediocre dancer. I want to be the SHIT and that takes serious effort, trial and error. I filmed it, produced it, and then studied how my fans responded to it. I learned what excites them so that I can give them what they want.

Even if you don't have major cash to invest in doing *sophisticated* videos for your social media sites, I bet you have people in your circle you can collaborate with. There are also trades you can make. Maybe you wanna take photos for your portfolio and a hairstylist you know needs a new look book. Barter a deal!

Lauren Palmer

Offer your photos for her book in trade for helping with your look. 👏🏿👏🏿

There are solutions and ways around most things, we just gotta look for them. When you look at situations with the attitude of "I'll find a way," then a way is usually found. An optimistic mind creates an environment that offers solutions. 😊 #HUSTLE-ANDFLOW.

⤙ SACRIFICING FOR SUCCESS ⤚

Ten years ago the money wasn't exactly flowing from the heavens for me either. Hiring a publicist took a chunk from our extra change. But it was a key element to expanding my brand. You can't do everything yourself, and finding partners to help you build your brand very early in the game is major key. My mother had a vision for me and she saw that a publicist was an investment that could reap rewards far greater than the expense of paying one.

There are few of us, in our careers or in our side hustle, who can really prosper without putting in some real thought, some real work, and real money. That's the real truth in reality. #CANTCHEATTHEGRIND. Even though I was pretty young when I started out, I was quick when it came to sizing up my surroundings. I got the gist of the Hollywood game from the moment we arrived.

Before the move to Los Angeles, I had tons of friends. I was living a normal life but I knew there was more, and I believe my family shared those feelings. Though I didn't know it at the time, to get to my dreams I would have to sacrifice some things about my childhood and life in general so I could focus on becoming the best entertainer I could be.

I Don't Belong to You

My cell phone was just about my only connection to my friends once I hit Hollywood. It's kind of funny now remembering how chained I was to my phone once I got one. #STILLGUILTY. 😒 My parents barely let me hang out anywhere, lol, and I was often filming on location outside of California and away from my siblings.

Many of the movies I was in didn't have other people my age on the set. Even if they did, it wasn't like we would always have chemistry, or much time for socializing. Whenever filming was suspended or I was done for the day, I'd be texting and calling friends to stay connected to the outside world.

I had FOMO big-time, Fear of Missing Out! What was going on in LA? What had I missed? I tried to still be a part of the teen social scene even though I was working so much on the road and far from my friends and family. My focus had to be on pursuing my dreams. I was grateful for my opportunities, but we all want to be connected socially.

⟩ TRYING TO CONNECT ⟨

Brandon was one friend I made then (boyfriend alert). We met on Myspace when I was about fifteen. 😄 I quickly developed deep feelings for him. We would talk and text all day long and then I would fall asleep thinking about making out with him the first time I had the chance. 😄 Oh brother.

I loved having my little boyfriend, but the truth was it was too stressful when I had so many career demands too. I couldn't be a normal girlfriend because of my work schedule. We were both too young to understand such odd dynamics. We were kids, but I was working like an adult and experiencing things he couldn't understand. It created a maturity gap because we were just living in two different worlds.

Lauren Palmer

I still have to work on bridging that gap with friends today. No matter how "relatable" I am, there are some typical teen experiences I missed out on—and many experiences I had that most people my age can't relate to at all. I had to mature fast because I worked with so many adults. Movie sets have tight schedules and the stakes are high. This left me feeling disconnected from my peers in some way.

I guess what I'm saying is I just didn't realize at that time that I would be sacrificing peer-to-peer engagement. I felt like I experienced a lot of the social dynamics you experience in high school late. My mom's favorite phrase with me is, "You're only surprised because you didn't go to high school." That is so true!

They say high school can be the best time of your life, and the worst, but it certainly does prepare you for life in the real world. In fact, I've heard it said many times that Hollywood is just like high school for grown-ups. Whenever someone in the entertainment business does something that shocks me, I think of my mother's words: "You're only surprised because you didn't go to high school."

My point is that when you are working on your dreams, whatever they may be, you too will have to make sacrifices. The tendency can be to think you are missing out, but when you begin to achieve your dreams, you will realize you put your energy toward the things most important to you.

ALL-OR-NOTHING GOALS

Every now and then I think back and regret missing some of life's touchstone events and experiences. But I don't dwell on them because regret serves little purpose for any of us. Then there's the fact that I wouldn't want to trade in the memories with all the people I met and art created from my film sets and Hollywood events.

There are trade-offs in anything you do. You have to decide what you want now for what is to come later. Prom now or an empire at thirty? The past is past and since we can't change it, we love what we have and embrace the future. I still found ways to connect to other people my age, both personally and through social media.

Recently, I went to speak at a college in Texas, and they gave me an honorary admission letter to their school. That really touched me because it gave me a small taste of an experience I missed. This showed me that we can still experience the things that we want to experience, in different and unique ways. Not to mention, high school is overrated so I am told. 😝

It's a hard fact that in the pursuit of what we want, we may sacrifice some other things along the way. We have to find a way of making peace with that before committing to whatever amazing future we are seeking. Otherwise, we'll never achieve our goals. For those of us with big dreams, our motto has to be, "I did this while you were sleeping."

⇥ REINVENTION ISN'T AN OPTION ⇤

With my mother's urging, I've learned to stay focused on the future and the importance of always moving forward. It's *always* been about the future for me and the importance of moving forward. Most of the characters I played early on in my career were the "sassy girl" and that persona worked well for me for a good while. It helped that I was the new kid in town from Chicago and no one had seen me cast in much. It also helped that I was seriously sassy in real life, so I had a good base to build on for playing sassy characters.

Those things didn't work for me as I got older, because then I became "that girl who got all the roles" in the minds of some casting directors and producers. They were still stuck on wanting the "new girl," lol. They'd think that Keke Palmer had already played that role and beat it to death, lmao, so I had to reinvent myself.

The important thing to remember about Hollywood (that I know all too well) is that it's all about the next big thing, including the next "It" girl or the next "hot girl" on the scene. I don't play into that because that's a trend game; life is a marathon not a sprint. Building a career isn't about everyone loving you all the time, it's about you being proud of the work you choose and develop. Your best strategy is to keep building on your skill sets and your knowledge and be prepared.

I was very aware that I needed to constantly step up my game at every level. I kept creating new looks, adding skills, and offering to take on roles different from what I'd played before. During my "sassy girl" time it was such a blessing to have notable actors like Samuel L. Jackson, Tyler Perry, William H. Macy, Ice Cube, and Laurence Fishburne to work alongside. That's another rule of hustle: If you look around, there is always someone to learn from. I didn't grasp at first that these were major stars, but I was always curious to learn about them and from them.

I had so much fun "playing" with them. I mean, it was play for me in a sense because I was a kid working with adults. More often than not, I realized that they were adults acting like kids! I learned to improv first from Tyler Perry. I didn't know what I was doing at the time, but he let me improv a lot in *Madea's Family Reunion*.

I Don't Belong to You

Tyler inspired me because he showed me that it's possible to have it all—to direct, produce, write, and act. I took mental notes. #SOAKINGUPLIFELIKEMYNAMEISSPONGEBOB.

I believe that once you recognize your gifts, you are obligated to go #HAMMERTIME and develop them, express them, and let them take you as far as you can go.

Going overtime is standard in my craft because it's a way of expressing gratitude for my gifts. At every opportunity, I shine my light, share my truth, and hopefully create a ripple effect by inspiring people the way so many others have inspired me. That is the cycle of inspiration and creation. It's the right thing to do.

⇒ DOING THE LIFE HUSTLE ⇐

So now that we've determined life is a hustle, you have to decide what's worth hustling for so you can get to where you want to go. Ask yourself what is missing in the universe, or at least your chosen field, that you can provide. And how hard are you willing to work to provide it? I go over this in my mind all the time as a performer and I think it's a must-do for anyone trying to achieve a dream.

Maybe your dream is to create new software that'll make life easier for teachers in the school systems. How cool would that be to actually create computer software, apps, and groundbreaking websites for emerging industries? If that is your dream, do you have the skills to help you get in the front door? Do you know basic Web development or do you know binary code? Do you have a plan with step-by-step goals that will take you where you want to go?

It's never too late, y'all! What is in your heart should not be denied. You never know what skills from your last gig can be helpful for your new one. It's never too late.

Nothing is by accident; God is always on time. You can be assured in that concept, that everything is on time. You have to be patient in pursuit of your dreams, but you should never stop moving toward them. Life can take us on very circuitous rides en route to our dreams. Whatever your goal, mapping out the skills you have and obtaining those that you need to develop is essential. Remember God's got your back, and you are never too late to make a shift in your life!

I'll tell you something. I audition for roles that I know I don't have much of a chance for because I'm too young or not the exact fit or whatever. I do it for the experience and sometimes as an opportunity to meet producers and/or casting directors. Just showing up for a big audition puts me in the company of other actors, directors, and producers who may not know me or my ambitions. Maybe these actors, directors, and producers will keep me in mind the next time they have a project. If that's the least that can result from an audition, I'll take it. I go into every audition with a victorious attitude, looking to take whatever I can get from the experience. And more often than you might think, the takeaway is a golden opportunity *somewhere* down the road.

STEPPING IT UP ON A BIGGER STAGE

I can be brutal in my ambition, but baby, Hollywood is not for the faint of heart. That attitude has served me well throughout my career, and my *Cinderella* story is a perfect example. I didn't see any Broadway shows as a child in Robbins. But I'd seen a play before. I'd always felt that at some point, when I

I Don't Belong to You

was older that I'd love to try Broadway, but it always seemed like an unachievable dream, being so prestigious. Honestly, I hadn't done any theater before I took a shot at Broadway, which is unusual.

Playing *Cinderella* was no fairy tale! It was hard as a mf!! Lol! That role was the most difficult thing I've ever done. Of course I loved every minute of it. Broadway transformed my career, my self-image, and, literally, my life. Talk about discipline and stress rolled up into a giant ticking bomb with a short fuse!! Broadway is all of that and more. You do whatever you have to do to bring your A game onstage for every performance, or you're out. That wasn't an option for me. 👑

Broadway was a giant leap for me, and I reaped incredible benefits from it because it really established me as a dedicated entertainer in the eyes of my peers and in the industry. You know what they say, if you can make it there, you can make it anywhere!

There were times during rehearsals and performances too when I wasn't sure I could even make it out of bed. But in the end, that's what makes it all so sweet for you when the curtain falls and the audience is still standing and cheering. That's the way it is for us when we are willing to put it all on the line. I had to turn my entire life upside down to get ready for this "iconic role," but that's the hustle.

I put myself on a strict regimen that wasn't limited to dieting and working out. It also included turning off my phone and not staying up to all times of night texting friends. Lol! No smoking either 😫, and I'm not talking cigarettes, kids, lol. (Okay, okay, on Mondays I'd light one.) 😂

I ate the same meal every night more or less. Chicken and peas OR BRUSSELS SPROUTS! I didn't eat for pleasure. I ate for protein and clear vocals. I needed tons of energy to endure eight

Lauren Palmer

shows a week, two and a half hours each night. I also had to lay off anything with yeast so I didn't coat my vocal cords and cause swelling or overflow of mucus. #TMI. Most days, I'd wake up and eat, do vocal warm-ups or take vocal lessons. Then I would head to the stage to rehearse whatever I needed to touch up from the show the day before. We did one show every night, but two days out of the week we'd do a matinee as well.

There's another thing to consider: Just because you get the job doesn't mean they think you are perfect every day and every night, my friends! That's showbiz, and most other bizzes too. You gotta keep the hustle going, work at it, work it, and work some more. There were a lot of tricks in *Cinderella*, meaning I had a lot of costume changes. There was this big gag with one of Cinderella's dresses similar to the one I did in *Grease: Live.* That trick was inspired by my work in *Cinderella* and was designed by the same costumer. (Hey, William Ivey Long!)

I literally had to change from rags to riches right in front of the audience. We'd rehearse these costume changes as often as we could and we'd also rehearse the big waltz scene because it had a lot of lifts. 😫 Then I would take my much-needed nap, get up and stretch again, and then begin the process of getting ready for the show.

While I did my makeup, my wig and microphone pack was being put on by Shari—she was my wig girl and she was pretty awesome at it. Whenever I had a free hand and open view, I'd read fan mail and sign autographs with the help of my dresser, Marissa 😍, who was so sweet. She would read all my fan mail for me out loud before every show, setting aside photos for me to sign and send back to them! And made sure I had my tea and cough drops, and really anything else I needed. #LOVEYOUGIRL.

Being on Broadway meant negotiating with my body, and I

I Don't Belong to You

learned a lot about balance and discipline. I had to be very careful with both my time and my energy because I owed it to my audience. I'd had some disappointments in the music business before *Cinderella*, but Broadway brought back my confidence.

⇒ DON'T BE AFRAID TO MAKE A LEAP ⇐

Making a major leap in your career will do that for you because it reminds you of how powerful you can be when in control of your will. When I did Broadway, I gained so much more confidence in performing, especially in my ability to deliver deep emotion while singing again. I had to stretch to the point of breaking when I took the *Cinderella* role, but I grew as a result.

If I had failed at *Cinderella* by not giving it my ALL, I would have been disappointed beyond belief. And by failing I don't mean not being perfect, I mean giving up. I learned that you really can't go wrong when you take a leap. Don't be afraid to test yourself.

My time in New York gave me even more of a reason to dig deep and go after the singing career I'd always wanted. So many of the homies would come through New York while I was there, and hanging out after shows and listening to them plan their tours, videos, and merchandising; chilling at the clubs to hear music, watching the dancers; and just talking music encouraged me to really begin to invest even more in myself by acting on my musical visions. Ty$, one of my best friends—it was this period in which we became close. He would be working a lot in NY during my Broadway run and it would be a movie every time we linked up. I saw firsthand how he imprinted himself in the game because a lot of dudes wouldn't unless there was a trade. I got to see firsthand that my peers weren't waiting for someone to call; they were going for it themselves just as I did with acting. They weren't waiting for

Lauren Palmer

labels like I had in the past; they were politely refusing to hear those nos and firing off audition tapes at every opportunity. #GETIT, hahaha.

My Broadway experience really did teach me that if I was willing to put in the time, to hustle, to work my ass off, to sacrifice, and to never give up, I could make it anywhere. #WAKEUP CALL. The same is true for you. Go after your dreams with relentless ambition.

When you get to the mountaintop, tell 'em Keke sent you. 👌

ON BODY IMAGE AND BEAUTY

Beauty starts in your head, not in the mirror.
—Joubert Botha

I have a job in an industry that places value on beauty far beyond the norm, at least it seems that way at times. It also means being pressured to believe in one concept of beauty that often does not reflect who you are or what makes you beautiful on a nonartificial level.

Like it or not, beauty is a major concept that we all constantly have to deal with in life, so it's pretty essential to decide what beauty is and what it means to us on every level so that we don't get confused by someone else's meaning.

Of course there are different categories of beauty because it appears in nearly all aspects of life. In a personal sense, you can have a beautiful mind, a beautiful heart, a beautiful soul, and a beautiful face. These things are subjective. Ideally, in a perfect world, we would feel beautiful through and through all the time.

That ain't easy, but why not try it?

I try to look for beauty everywhere in life (my grandma Davis did too). I love beautiful music, beautiful artwork in any form, and just the simple beauty of a rainbow outside. ❀ I look for beauty in the mirror too, simply because it's me and I love me! I know now that beauty is in every person and comes in all forms, but when I was younger I sometimes struggled to see the beauty in myself. I started my acting career at a very young age, and that brought a lot of stress. As a growing adolescent, I also dealt with a lot of acne, which added to the stress because looks are so important in the entertainment industry.

I was around eleven or twelve when my acne first started showing up, which was the same time I became hyperaware of my self-image and the importance of looking "polished" because of my career. In some ways, being "onstage" was perfect for me because I always liked getting dressed up and made up as a little girl. I watched my grandma Davis get dressed up many times for no reason and I too made every situation a "moment," haha.

People forget, though, that entertainers are regular people. There is a stigma of perfection that comes with the profession. We are under incredible pressure to look our absolute best on camera, while being photographed or even when we are off work. It's unrealistic, almost fake, and it can make people who watch our television shows and movies feel horrible for being natural.

I learned early on that my looks from head to toe are on full display in every television show, movie, and red carpet I step foot onto, so by Hollywood standards—and let's not talk about social media, lol—I am expected to be *flawless* at every turn. Of course, my acne made looking *flawless* a challenge. For a long time, I suffered from severe acne problems, which wreaked havoc on my self-esteem.

Lauren Palmer

Fear of being judged is one of the worst parts of growing up. You can multiply that fear by millions when you are an entertainer. My skin problems often left me feeling ashamed because I felt like I had to do so much concealing of my acne as part of the job. Ugh, it made me feel like I was constantly saying to myself, *You aren't cute enough on your own.* My acne made me less confident. I didn't feel beautiful at times.

Not long after I filmed *Madea's Family Reunion*, my mom and I ran into Tyler Perry at the Black Movie Awards show. I felt self-conscious because I was having one of my biggest acne breakouts. We started talking to Tyler about whatever (can't remember because it was forever ago, lol). As we finished the convo and I started to walk away, Tyler quietly pulled my mother aside and told her that he knew of a good dermatologist. He said she was a great doctor and he offered to pick up the tab for my treatments. 😱 He only asked that we not tell anyone he was footing the bill. What a blessing you are, Tyler! I kept quiet as long as I could #SORRYITOLD. 😭 💚 And thank you, Dr. Pearl Grimes, you da bomb!

⇾ SHOWING YOURSELF SOME LOVE ⇽

My skin cleared up and my self-esteem improved some. Of course self-confidence isn't connected to just one or two things, and those things don't all relate to looks, but we can't underestimate the importance of doing something for yourself that makes you feel better about *you.* There are many basic ways you can learn to look your best to the outside world, but we all know the real hard work begins when we decide to become beautiful on the inside!

Aside from the fact that my skin was clearing, just going to the dermatologist and following her instructions made me feel that I was taking positive action to relieve a source of discomfort for me. The fact that I was going out of my way for myself made me feel more confident too. Tyler helped me understand that there were remedies. He put me on the path. And it felt good to then step up and take positive action that boosted my self-confidence and benefited my career.

That's showing yourself love—taking responsibility for your happiness by creating a way to be the best YOU that you can be! If you and I had a friend with acne problems, we'd want to help them, just like Tyler helped me. Sometimes, though, we aren't as good a friend to ourselves as we are to other people. I'm not sure why that is true. Maybe we're afraid to love ourselves. We might be afraid of being egotistical or narcissistic.

There is a difference between indulging in what may make you *feel* beautiful and tackling the real issues so that you become the best all-around person you can be. I love doing my hair and makeup. Getting ready in the morning, plucking my brows, etc. If hair products and makeup aren't your thing, that's cool too! There are tons of things you can do to improve and feel good about yourself, whether it's for health, fashion, or both! The most important thing is that it works for *you*.

We have to love ourselves enough to take care of ourselves, in order to see life from a positive viewpoint. That takes being healthy in mind, body, and spirit! Choosing to do what's best for yourself isn't selfish when doing things for your overall state of being. You have to love yourself before you can be loved by others. When you build your self-esteem, you tell the world "I am worthy of love. So love me!"

Young women and men can feel pressured about their physi-

Lauren Palmer

cal appearance even if they aren't in a business like mine that is so intensely focused on it. I wish that wasn't true, but it is a reality. The truth is you shouldn't worry about what other people think, their ideals and labels are their hang-ups, not yours. Don't listen to critics and bullies who judge your appearance and make cruel comments.

Don't take care of yourself to win their approval. Do it for YOURSELF! Take care of yourself because *you* care about you, not because you care about what others think. Yes, beauty care is part of my *job* as an entertainer. But even if I wasn't constantly exposed to the public eye, I would want to look good, feel good, and be good because that honors my Creator and it enhances my quality of life.

It goes far beyond paying attention to my makeup and my outfit for a day. Those are just some fun things that interest me that I like to treat myself with. The way I feel about myself doesn't come from the cosmetics or beauty products. It really has nothing to do with any of the products. It's really about loving who you are enough to make the effort necessary to take care of yourself. Exercising, washing your hair, brushing your teeth—these are signs to the self that it is beloved. It is true that the first thing most people notice about you is your physical appearance. That's a fact, but whatever look you are going after should be the look that makes you feel your best.

⇒ FAKE IT UNTIL FABULOUS ⇐

Fabulous is a great goal. But your body doesn't always cooperate. Even with the help of a great dermatologist, my skin still has its ups and down. Like everyone, I still have good and bad days on

I Don't Belong to You

the *beauty* scale! 😂 Like most who want to look their best even when their body is at its worst, you learn to accentuate the things you do like about yourself and spice up the things that may bug you.

Makeup is the gift that keeps on giving to all of us, but it really is to those of us, male and female, with serious skin issues. After all, makeup is just another form of self-expression. It allows us to look extra cute and feel fierce! #FUCKHETERONORMATIVITY.

The best part about beauty products is experimenting to figure out what you like, don't like, or what looks the best on you. I experiment a lot and am always willing to learn more. I had a best friend who wanted to learn how to do her own makeup but the big problem was, she'd never wear it. I told her she had to experiment to find the best products for her skin type and the look she wanted. If you don't try all kinds of makeup, how can you learn?

Wearing makeup and getting your best look exactly right takes practice, lots of practice! Wouldn't you know practicing is my favorite part because—true life—*My name is Keke and I am a makeup fanatic.* 😂 💅

I love, love, LOVE makeup. I adore the idea of foundation, eyeliner, and lipstick and how it can help me showcase my favorite features a million different ways. 💄 Thankfully, working on shows, movies, and videos, I have had the good fortune of meeting some of the most amazing makeup artists and hairstylists in the industry. They've shown me many tricks that taught me how to beat my face. 😁

As with anything else in life, if you're around people with knowledge about what you value, I recommend getting out your notebook and taking notes like crazy! Some of the best lessons don't come from books or classes. You can gain so much knowledge by listening to and observing the gifted people around you #SOAKITUPLIKEYOURNAMEISSPONGEBOB.

➤ EXPRESS YOURSELF ➤

My auntie Nene, who owns the beauty salon we visited to make my audition video for *Pimp*, was a real rebel during her heyday when it came to her looks. She didn't mind going short and black one day and long and blond another, lol. She had her eyebrows and tongue pierced, which was so cool to me as a kid, haha. 😎 Auntie Nene is still the bomb!

Today, I am a little like her in that regard. I love flipping the script each morning in an attempt to reveal different layers of myself to the world. If you've followed my career long enough, you know I've had short hair, long hair, and every other kind of hair in between. I've shaved one side and then the other when the mood has hit me. I've sported braids, weaves, wigs, and any other hair accessory that can be used to enhance my look, and I've loved every minute of it. 😍

Of course with each change of my eye shadow, hairdo, or lipstick came comments from those unhappy with the frequency of my changes. Being an entertainer requires understanding that people feel free to comment on everything you do. In my case, my fans watched me grow up from being little "Akeelah," so they often feel very close to me because they saw me as a child.

Growing up on television can create that feeling simply because people don't always comprehend that child actors are truly acting. Fans often don't grasp that even child actors can genuinely analyze their characters and play their roles, lol. But the re-

I Don't Belong to You

ality is I was conscious of every acting choice in that movie. I was playing a character and the gag was people bought into it to the point that they thought that was me. However they felt about that movie they felt about me and boom, I became a part of their families.

As a result, they feel that any major changes I make in my fashion style, makeup, hairstyle, or personal life should be discussed with them, right? Yes, but not really. I don't buy into the celebrity craze of my generation and I don't encourage others to buy into it either. We are in a huge time of worshipping and praising celebrities. I don't agree that they should be the pinnacle of the world.

If a celebrity does something that's interesting, inspiring, or thought provoking, it's not bad to have a conversation about it. That is totally necessary. But the idea that celebrities are perfect beings who exist for only our pleasure and affection is a bit—no, a lot—out of reality, lol. It's a concept we bought into that can be a huge distraction. Of course, I love my fans and I am committed to sharing my art, but at the end of the day, we all need to do what makes us the happiest, and we should base our decisions on what it is we truly want!

⤚ BEAUTY ON THE INSIDE ⤙

In many ways, feeling beautiful on the outside is the easy part. The real hard work and the most important part is feeling beautiful on the inside to the point where you can truly admire what is your existence in its totality: your uniqueness! I've always been up front about my struggles with anxiety. These issues ran through my family's history due to many horrific experiences over the generations.

Lauren Palmer

I've written a lot in this book about how much I appreciate my parents and all they've sacrificed and done for me. 🙏 There have been times in my life also when I felt my parents were overcontrolling. It's not unusual for a person to have "baggage" with the authority figure they grew up with. But hindsight is a mf and it never occurs to me that they could have been afraid of losing me—acting out of fear often leads to extremes. It took me years to understand how those patterns of theirs affected me so tremendously as I was developing into an adult. I began to suffer from anxiety and panic attacks early in my career and that anxiety continued to grow in leaps and bounds as I continued.

When my career became a major focus of the family, the stress quadrupled. Being the breadwinner was a heavy burden to carry while riding the roller coaster of emotions of a teenage mind. 😵 Something had to give and it did.

I sat my parents down when I was around sixteen or seventeen and told them I wanted and needed to enter therapy as soon as I could. I was clear with them that if I didn't get help, they should be afraid for my sanity. I knew I couldn't survive long-term if I didn't go to a professional who could help me sort out my feelings of anger, frustration, and confusion toward myself, my family, and the world around me.

We all feel stressed out and overburdened from time to time, but I think that's why finding a way to release your feelings through creative self-expression, like singing, writing, painting, or acting, is so important. Our minds are churning all day, every day, and to assume they do not get jumbled or tired is just not reasonable. The teenage years are especially challenging for our brains. It's during those years that they are actually rewiring themselves to prepare us for adulthood. 😨 😨

I Don't Belong to You

For example, studies have found that because the brain is working overtime to rewire even as teens go about their daily lives, certain parts of the brain actually aren't functioning at full capacity. This is why teens often have trouble assessing risks, or making judgments about what to say and do. So go easy on yourself and the teens you know. Understand that between all the raging hormones and brain adjustments going on, they are bound to get overwrought, confused, and conflicted from time to time.

Even when I was a teenager, I was aware that success, particularly success in the entertainment industry, is a double-edged sword. It's wonderful on one side, but it often is accompanied by tremendous pressure. If a studio casts you as the star in a movie that costs $80 million to make, that's some serious responsibility to be capable and accountable every day.

There is also tremendous pressure to stay on *top* and to never have a *bad day* in public, which is absurd because who's to judge what that is, even. I remember the overwhelming feeling of wishing people would give me a break. I would wonder why they expected my young ass to have the maturity of a thirty-year-old, I was already handling so much that every time I was scolded for anything it was like "DON'T YOU KNOW WHAT I'M DEALING WITH IN MY HEAD!?!"

I was a teenager with typical teenager issues, and I worked in fickle-ass Hollywood, and I was well aware that my family's quality of life was largely dependent on how I performed in my career. That was a lot to handle even if my parents did tell me I could quit. I did not see that as a realistic option. 🧑

In truth, most of us have a lot of day-to-day pressures and anxieties. Yours may be far worse than what I was dealing with. If so, I encourage you to first of all know that this is a very human problem. You aren't alone, and there are professionals who can help you, whether it's a therapist, a school counselor, or a local pastor with counseling training.

Our brains are beautiful instruments and they are finely tuned. They are also physical organs that can break down or have blips and bloops just like any other body part #THISIS NORMAL. Going to a therapist is similar to going to your doctor. You need physicals and checkups throughout the year, and that's the same thing as seeing a therapist regularly if you feel stressed out or just need to talk through issues. Your brain is like a computer that never shuts off, so weekly therapy is the usual suggestion for dealing with challenges that you feel you can't handle on your own.

Therapy is just you speaking with a person who is trained to help you find ways to help yourself. They specialize in finding healthy ways to mirror your thoughts and feelings back to you so you can understand yourself better. They are there to help you observe yourself without judgment. They can help you rewire mentally to overcome blockage by a fractured thought process.

There is no shame in seeing a therapist. If there was, 90 percent of the people in show business would be living in shame! Instead, most of them talk openly about the benefits of therapy. A good therapist will help you monitor and control negative thoughts while switching over to a more positive outlook. Those dark voices in your head can be controlled, and a therapist will teach you how to find ways to do that.

I Don't Belong to You

The defense mechanism and mental constructs we create often make it hard for us to see outside ourselves. Eventually, we can reach a point where our minds aren't allowing us to move forward anymore, and we all react differently. I started to realize that I was disassociating from most things around me. I was forgetting how to feel.

I'd put up walls because I had felt SO MUCH and never learned how to process it. My mother cried and my dad had shown frustration, but our family mostly just moved on over shit. We never discussed the process of feeling hurt and accepting that as okay. Crying was okay, but only in a limited capacity—not when it was coupled with your own mistake.

I had issues, and they were piling up like a twelve-car collision. I felt bombarded by pressures and responsibilities with my career, my family, and all the things that come with being an adolescent. 😆 😅 My mind was exhausted from trying to rationalize so much on my own. I didn't want to shut down emotionally or become comfortable resisting the feelings of life. "Good" or "bad," I wanted to be able to be there, to be present.

I knew I needed help and I had to get it, for me. I had to have my back. Make me a promise, please. If you ever feel the same way, don't talk yourself out of it. Don't curl up in a corner or hide your despair. Get help. Feel good about having the courage to ask for it. Know that you can take actions to ease your mind and even save your life. Please don't suffer in silence.

Many times during my bout with depression, I'd wonder how much better my grandma's life could have been if she'd had the opportunity to speak with a professional about all the problems in her life. What obstacles in her and my mom's world

Lauren Palmer

could have been avoided if my grandmother would have had the opportunity to speak with someone trained and skillful in therapeutic methods?

I knew both my mom and grandmother wanted me to have better opportunities that would lead to a better life, one free of fears, self-doubts, and insecurities. With that knowledge, I began therapy and it was one of the best decisions I've ever made for myself. It was such a relief to talk freely to someone who had no dog in the fight, so to speak. Someone trained to look from the outside into the heart of a situation and pinpoint what was causing me to shut down emotionally. Therapy is an awesome experience.

TREAT YOURSELF LIKE YOU'D TREAT A FRIEND

There were so many times before when I felt I was losing my mind, and the escape I had was journaling. There was no other outlet for me to unleash all the chaotic feelings rolling around in my head. Now journaling has its definite values, and I recommend it to everyone.

With therapy I found someone who validated my painful past, who helped me understand how to define my experiences and how not to let them define me. My conversations with my therapist challenged me to see myself and my anxieties more objectively, as a pattern, nothing more.

If your insurance doesn't cover therapy or if your finances are really in a jam, look for community centers that offer counseling, or reach out to your church to find out what services they offer for those struggling emotionally. One of the best and recent addi-

I Don't Belong to You

tions to the world of apps are those that offer email exchanges between you and a certified therapist for a weekly or biweekly fee of twenty-five dollars. How cool is that?

Imagine if that app had been around twenty years ago, thirty years ago. I wonder how many people and how many minds would have been helped? #THANKFULFORTHESEOPTIONS NOW. 🙏

Maybe our parents or people we loved didn't have those opportunities, but we do. If you need someone to talk to, please go out and find that help. There are so many things that I took away from therapy. I see things so clearly now thanks to tools that are now must-haves in my life. I learned that I needed more self-compassion, and I began to resist the urge of being my own worst critic.

We have to forgive ourselves when we make mistakes, because others are all too happy to remind us of our shortcomings. We don't have to help them be hurtful. Self-compassion builds up resilience because it shows you how to have your own back. I also learned how to be brutally honest with myself by asking myself questions. Simply getting to the root of my issues by asking myself *Why?* or *What makes you think that?* and forcing myself to open up to me has been very helpful. These are all tools that a trained counselor or therapist can help you master.

ALTERNATIVE PATHS TO HEALING THE MIND, BODY, AND SOUL

Therapy is a widely accepted resource in the entertainment industry. It's almost as common as going to the dentist or working out. Show business is so stressful that most performers are extremely

Lauren Palmer

conscious of staying healthy in every way. They are also open to trying alternative approaches that go beyond traditional methods of healing and building strength.

One of the coolest things about my job is meeting so many smart people who have a wide range of interests and beliefs. Friends and contacts I've met on the set or at parties and dinners have opened my eyes and my mind. Since coming to California, I've been introduced to yoga, meditation, and chakra cleansing, all of which have been very helpful.

I've also discovered intuitive counselors and emotional healers who've given me methods for self-healing and tools to empower my mind. You know me, I love to explore and experiment, so I found myself reaching out for more knowledge on these "healers" and their methods for exploring deep-seated emotional issues and painful memories. There were things I'd buried inside so deep I forgot where to find them. 😖 According to many of these healers, once a deeper level of awareness exists, change occurs and real healing can begin.

I don't want to come off so millennialish, but the gag is I AM! 😄😄😄👽 I believe in trying new things and using my own spiritual compass (gut) to figure out what might help me. Don't we all want to find our soul's deepest purpose? I, for one, believe there are many paths to that knowledge.

If you read more about these alterative healing methods, they aren't as "otherworldly" as they may sound. You might find some stuff that speaks to you, but if you deem it not cool, leave it where it's at. At the end of the day, you gave it a look and that's what is important. Trying things, being open to new healing methods, is the first step toward good health. You are free to choose only those methods that appeal to you. The key

I Don't Belong to You

is to learn about many things, so you have many options and a wide perspective that allows you to do what feels genuine to you.

Through my own guides and teachers of alternative paths, I became intrigued by the world of chakras and crystals, and the impact they have on our bodies and minds. The idea is that we, though human, are spirits made up of energy, and because we are made up of energy we must be sensitive to the ways in which we choose to vibrate (based on our actions) in the world around us.

Our energy vibrations are impacted by what we choose to invite into our energy space and what we decide to keep out. When our chakras are balanced and we are eating well, exercising, and meditating, we are operating on a high vibration level because our energy is supported. When our chakras are imbalanced—maybe because we aren't eating healthy or aren't exercising enough—we end up at a low vibration level. This usually means we have low energy levels and a lack of motivation, so we aren't inspired to do much of anything.

Chakras are said to be the seven central energy points in a human energy field that can easily become imbalanced with the daily frustrations of life. When we are unaware of this concept, we might be tempted to blame ourselves or others for our mood swings, but it's really more related to your lifestyle habits. #IT AINTYOUITSTHEWAYYOULIVINBOO. 😂 To counteract that imbalance, crystals can be used to produce corrective vibrations that promote well-being in whatever area you may feel most lacking. Chakra balancing is done through a combination of meditative practices, such as yoga or prayer, as well as adjusting your diet and exercise levels.

Lauren Palmer

FURTHEST THING

This pose is often times referred to as the Mountain. Keep your feet hip-width apart, spread your weight evenly with your arms by your side. Then breathe slowly and deeply at an even pace, keeping your neck aligned with the rest of your spine and extending the pose through the crown of your head.

CHANGE LOCATION

This pose is often times referred to as the Downward-Facing Dog. Get on all fours with your hands and knees shoulder-and-hips-width apart. Move your hands forward and spread your fingers for better stability. Curl your toes and lift your knees off the floor. Now carefully push your hips away from the floor.

OWN IT

Stand with your legs four to five feet apart. Turn out your right foot 90 degrees and your left foot in slightly. Keeping your shoulders down, raise your arms to the sides with your palms down. Kneel on to your right foot at a 90 degree angle, making sure the knee doesn't pass your toes. This pose is also known as the Warrior.

I'M THE PLUG

Begin with the mountain pose. Then shift your weight onto your left leg. Keeping your body and hips facing forward, place the bottom of your right foot on the inside of your left thigh and find your balance. When you're there, create a prayer pose with your hands. This pose is also known as the Tree.

CONTROLLA

This pose is oftentimes referred to as the Bridge. Lie on the floor with your arms by your sides. With your knees bent, keep your feet flat and push them into the floor as you lift your hips. Then clasp your hands under your lower back, and press your arms down for support. Raise your hips until they are parallel to the floor as you bring your chest to your chin.

THE FAKE LOVE

This pose is oftentimes referred to as the Triangle. Take warrior pose on your right side without lunging into your knee. Exhale slowly as you touch the inside of your right foot with your right hand. Reach up to the ceiling with your left hand. Turn your gaze toward your left hand to stretch your back.

UPTOWN

Lie facedown on the floor with your palms either side of your chest, legs extended with the tops of your feet on the floor. Squeeze your shoulder blades together and slowly straighten your arms as if you were doing a half push-up. This pose is also known as the Upward-Facing Dog.

BEST I EVER HAD

Sit on the floor and extend your legs. Cross your right foot over the outside of your left thigh. Bend your left knee, keeping your right knee pointing up. Keep your right hand on the floor behind you for stability and place your left elbow to the outside of your right knee. Keeping your spine straight, twist to the right as far as you can. This pose is also known as the Seated Twist.

CHILD'S PLAY

This pose is oftentimes referred to as the Child. Begin by kneeling on a yoga mat or the floor. Bring your knees together and your buttocks to your feet. Extending your arms forward, lower your chest to your knees as close as you comfortably can. Hold the pose and breathe into your torso.

FIRE AND DESIRE

The pose is oftentimes referred to as the Pigeon. Start in a push-up position, your palms under your shoulders, raise your left knee on the floor near your shoulders, with your left heel by your right hip. Press your hands to the floor and raise your body slowly upward so you're now in an upright position.

There are many components that go into keeping a spiritual balance, and crystals are a fun part of that too! 😎

Another big help to my mental fitness and wellness was learning to meditate. I'm sure you've heard of this method of clearing the mind and relaxing the body. It was once considered something that was practiced mostly by monks, hippies, and Buddhists, but meditation is now widely practiced in corporate America. Many big companies have meditation rooms for their employees because they see the benefits of this practice.

It took me a while to understand how meditation could be helpful for me. Meditating is a practice that creates an accessible way to center yourself, come into the present moment, and consider the bigger picture.

Even if just for a few minutes, meditating has many health benefits. Think of it as a deep sleep that works like a Swiffer. Once you enter the meditative zone, you can Swiffer away all the emotional baggage you'd forgotten you were carrying around! #HELLYESS! It can lower your heart rate and decrease your overall stress level too.

Meditation can be tough to master in the beginning. You will be trying to quiet your mind instead of letting it blabber on as you watch, lol. That is the practice, learning to not try to control it but to respect it as it is, a chaotic brain. Learning to focus on absolutely nothing even when your thoughts are going nuts can be a challenge at first, but the end result is worth it. #PATIENCE.

Lauren Palmer

My Rules for Quick and Easy Meditation

1. Try finding a comfortable place to settle down, either at home or at work, and sit with your eyes closed. Make it relaxing and peaceful, maybe with scented candles, crystals, and other items that soothe you. This is your sacred place. 🙏

2. Set an intention for your practice. Maybe you're feeling confined and your word is *Freedom*, or you're feeling guarded and your word is *Love*. Whatever you feel you need clarity on, set that word as your intention.

3. Breathe deeply, in and out. When you inhale softly count one and when you exhale softly count two. "One, two, one, two."

And yes, your thoughts will be running wild at first, but the trick is to LET THEM. Don't try to stop them, but instead welcome them as you focus on your breathing and your counting. You will eventually get lost and forget that you are not counting. However, if a thought slips in and takes your attention again, don't you fret!

Just repeat step three and you will be back in meditating land in no time. You can do this for as long and as often as you like, but again, if you're new to it, don't be hard on yourself. It's okay if you can only do five minutes or something.

Be patient and kind to yourself. It's cool when you try something new #PERIOD. Don't give up. It's practice, and just like I said with makeup, you can't get good if you don't do it! 🖤

I Don't Belong to You

⮞ THE GREATEST HEALING POWER ⮜
IS LOVE FOR EACH OTHER

We are all beautiful, especially when we rise above prejudice, jealousy, hatred, and distrust. I want to leave you with my thoughts on what constitutes true beauty in individuals. I hope this inspires you to love and celebrate the person you were created to be.

#1: FEARLESS INDIVIDUALITY. I think so often in our world we allow the societal "standard" to turn us into robots. We should encourage individuality in one another because that's how we get closer to who we are meant to be. It's trial and error in life, and there's nothing wrong with someone who is still "figuring it out."

#2: GLOWING SELF-CONFIDENCE. There is no reason we should feel ashamed or less confident when we don't look like we are walking in a runway show twenty-four/seven. It's very beautiful to be secure and confident in ourselves, even if we don't fit, or even if we defy the typical standards of beauty.

#3: A READY SMILE. Everyone has a beautiful smile. I know everyone wants perfect teeth, but I promise you, snaggle-toothed, gap-toothed, toothless, braces, or WHATEVER, I have never seen an ugly smile if it was offered up without any fear or insecurities.

#4: KINDNESS TO ALL. To be kind is to be open, and to be open is to connect. Making connections is what life is all about! That's what makes the world a beautiful place!

Lauren Palmer

#5: JOYOUSLY YOU. Just you, a beautiful creation brought to this earth to serve a purpose. You are interesting and different and I feel that that's the most beautiful thing of all. There is only one you, and only ONE me. THAT is magical!

Love Unlimited

ON LOVE AND RELATIONSHIPS

Perhaps we should Love ourselves so fiercely,
that when others see us they know exactly
how it should be done.

—Rudy Francisco

When I was thirteen years old, I was a year into using Myspace and I thought my page was fly (don't hate! Hahaha). I remember my bff Taylor told me she went to school with a boy named Josh who had a brother who was two years older and super fine, hahahah. His name was Brandon, and after searching for him through the Myspace system, I agreed with Taylor that he was indeed FINE.

Brandon and I became good friends, we would talk all the time on Myspace, then we were texting and calling and eventually we met. He was the first guy I liked in that boyfriend way. I'd say we were in a cyber relationship for about a year before I could get my parents to let him come around every now and then.

I wasn't allowed to have a boyfriend, really, until I was sixteen, but they gave Brandon a pass. Puppy love! It wasn't until I was seventeen that I embarked on what I thought it meant to be in a real relationship. I met Joey (aka first "real boyfriend") when I was fifteen, and it was a "movie moment" for me, haha . . .

We were on the set of *True Jackson, VP*. Joey was really good friends with Patrick, a guy who I did a Disney original movie with when I was twelve called *Jump In*. #CLASSIC.

Patrick would visit the *TJVP* set often and one show night he brought someone with him. I literally remember the moment I opened my eyes and saw him. I had just finished jumping on Patrick, hugging him, and when I released the hug I saw Joey behind him. I couldn't take my eyes off him!

Joey was about 5'10" and clean-cut, a lighter-complexioned pretty boy with a low-cut fade and prominent bone structure. He was an unusual mix—half African-American and half Guatemalan—very strong features and a bombbbbb-ass smile. 😍

At first, it seemed like he had his act together. He said he was modeling, working on a fashion line, and also had a job at a bank. The only problem was he was nineteen (soon to be twenty), wayyyy too old for fifteen-year-old me. Right? 😑

We did a little harmless flirting on set that day because he, like most peeps at that time, assumed I was older. After he and Patrick left it took me no time to hop right on Myspace and find his page! 🖱️ Immediately we started talking back and forth and he was totally surprised and disappointed at the age gap. However, we had chemistry and we couldn't stop talking. We quickly went from Myspace to texting and then calling each other.

I loved talking to Joey. Even though we couldn't hang out a lot, I really enjoyed having him to call because he was so easygoing, very shy, and even introverted, which made him easy to talk to for someone like me who can hold up both ends of a conversation no problem. 😄

During the *True Jackson* days, I was going through some de-

pression and it truly made a difference to have him around. It really made me sad at times that people might judge him over the age difference and his having feelings for me.

⇒ MY LITTLE REBELLION ⇐

It upset me not being able to hang with Joey or do whatever we wanted. Thinking back, I feel like the distance in my relationships with Brandon through my not being truly able to have a relationship at that age—and the age difference with Joey—made it all safe for me because I wouldn't have any anxiety with that physical *space* between us. It made me, and can still sometimes today make me, anxious to be face-to-face with people who I like on a romantic/emotional level as our relationship builds. When I was younger I think I was more aware of that, at least on a subconscious level, because I sought relationships out that were *impossible* to a certain extent. As I got older I just found ways to sabotage the power that physical connections can add to an emotional connection. I either wanted one or the other—having both was too close.

Not to mention—this is gonna sound a little crazy, but it's really just the way I was thinking back in my early teens—I thought guys who were four or five years older than me were safer in general! I thought they wouldn't try to push me into doing anything sexually because they'd be afraid of going to jail. 😂😂😂😂

That was such a young-ass idea! I thought I could control them because I was legally a minor. I played the "Go to Jail" card: "You can't touch me REALLY because I'm underage!" I also had it in my head that dating older guys made it easier to evaluate their character. If a guy over eighteen tried to have sex with me, I'd know right away he was a butthole.

I Don't Belong to You

Yes, I played Rapunzel games, hiding in the "minor" tower to protect my virginity until I was ready to give it up. That game got old and also enslaved me. Attaching that to my identity and using that as a game ultimately oppressed me when it came to my sexuality. When I turned seventeen, things became official with Joey. For a year and a half before that, on and off, we started trying to hang out without my parents knowing. 😨 My best friend at the time, Karen, who was around the same age as Joey, would drive me to see him under the guise of going to CityWalk! 😄

I felt terrible about lying to my parents, but at the same time I was thrilled that in my mostly "sheltered" childhood I was having a moment of rebellion, haha. It was like I told myself: My story is gonna be a little exciting. I mean, come on! 😈

That lasted only a year because I couldn't bear living a lie. (My conscience SCREAMS at me.) Around my seventeenth birthday, I started asking my mom how she felt about me dating someone like Joey and specifically, someone his age. He was twenty-one at that time and my mom surprised me with her response. She said that while I'd need to get my father's approval on something like that, she wasn't all that opposed to me dating someone that age if she knew them well.

I'd been working on television with adults for a couple of years by then. Mom said because of my high level of maturity (and men's natural immaturity level) it wasn't a totally ridiculous concept for me to date a guy four years older, considering that was also my parents' age difference.

Even so, it took much time and a personal conversation between my dad and Joey 😦 to clear the way for him to become a real part of my life. Finally, I thought, nothing was holding us back anymore from having complete and total love and HAPPINESS! 😄

Lauren Palmer

I loved Joey before, but I infused my depression into the relationship at some point. I think in an attempt to ignore what was actually bothering me inside, I told myself I was just unhappy because I couldn't be public with my relationship. NOW that was GONE. So I would be happy . . . right?? I beat the level for this love game, or so I thought. Joey and I continued to date. At first we were only allowed to hang in groups, lol, and then six months into my eighteenth year I was allowed to date him privately. My dad was EXTRA with those rules, lolololol!

But, as soon as we were fully allowed to be together, I was over at his house twenty-four/seven. I got my driver's license a little late, but once I had it I was rushing to the freeway to hit the 101 and see that Woodland exit right before Van Nuys. That still brings back fond memories for me when I drive past it to this day. I always had to leave before one p.m. or after six thirty p.m., otherwise I'd be f*#&ed in traffic, haha. #LALIFE.

I moved out of my parents' house at the end of my eighteenth year. I tried to wait, because I didn't want my parents to feel bad, but I wasn't happy being with them for several reasons that I didn't want to address, so I had to get away.

I wasn't all the way happy with Joey because, again, I wasn't all the way happy with MYSELF. I thought living together would bring us closer. Note to self: That doesn't work! Your relationship isn't supposed to MAKE you happy, but my conclusion was "He can make you happy if you just get closer. You told yourself you would get away once you had the chance. Get out of this house with your parents and just be with Joey like you always wanted. Then you will be happy! That's the trick!"

I Don't Belong to You

I was too young to understand that I was deflecting, focusing on tiny problems rather than the real internal problems that were keeping me stunted emotionally. I couldn't realize that I needed to create my own happiness through addressing my feelings and nurturing my gifts! My parents surprisingly didn't make any type of fuss about it. My mom tells me now that my dad always told her that I was smart and she didn't have to tell me the same thing a hundred times (even though she did.). 😠

My parents let me make my own mistakes as an adult woman. "Once you're eighteen we can't tell you nothing" and they actually didn't for the most part. 😄 They gave me room to figure things out. It was also true that they knew Joey was friends with Patrick and his family. Patrick was like my big brother and he'd taken me under his wing since *Jump In!* They trusted Patrick and his family, so they assumed Joey was the same type of guy.

So off I went. 🏃🏾‍♀️💨🏃🏾‍♀️💨💨

On top of everything else, it had been a year since I stopped working on *True Jackson*. The money flow was slowing, and we thought it was best to move the family into a smaller house. As I said before, that was a shot to my ego/identity. Around this time, I also asked for a release from the record label I was with. They told me it would take too much money to break an "R & B artist" and it would be less expensive for them to pay and release me from my contract. I put $70,000 of that release money into making a mix tape. I was wrapped up in society's idea of a success. When the mix tape didn't gain immediate "popularity," I took that as a failure (which is unfortunate because an artist's relationship is with their FANS, not the labels). #IHADITBACK WARD.

Lauren Palmer

Suddenly I felt even worse about myself and a little lost. I listened to "myself" and moved in with Joey for a year at his place and then into a separate apartment of our own.

⇒ WHAT IS INSIDE WILL COME OUT ⇐

When you are in a relationship with someone and there are things inside you that have not been dealt with, it will show up. Not only will it show up, it will kick and scream until you acknowledge it. You have to name the things that you haven't dealt with to be able to expel them! #MESSAGE.

I couldn't put my finger on the "problem" though. Everything seemed right. I wasn't living with my parents anymore. I had a cute boyfriend, a contented way of living, work wasn't "outrageous," and I was acting, which was always enough for me. Joey and I were more than public—we didn't have to hide our relationship anymore—yet I still wasn't "happy."

I thought all of that should have made me happy, but still I wasn't. It didn't help that I couldn't speak to Joey. It didn't make sense to me that I was unhappy in our relationship and he wasn't. I didn't understand how he could act like, in the very least, MY unhappiness didn't affect him. It seemed so fake, almost like he was doing it on purpose, pretending there was nothing *wrong* when there obviously was.

This was my first experience with emotional unavailability outside of my family. Emotional unavailability was my family dynamic, I thought it was attached to THEM. To experience it outside their home was so disappointing. I didn't know what to call it then, but Joey was emotionally unattached. He couldn't properly address his feelings and definitely not his feelings for me. He

I Don't Belong to You

would even tell me that he loved me but that he didn't have the ability to be affectionate and/or show in general his disposition. #POKERFACE. I couldn't break through his emotional walls and that made the relationship hard, especially when it came to dealing with our problems.

The fact that he was "self-employed" but lacked self-discipline was wearing on me. He wasn't consistent in his work. The real problem was he lacked certainty in himself (how funny the people in your life mirror your issues). One day when we were living at his mom's I came across three or four college applications, which he had started but didn't finish, and I soon realized he never finished anything. Our relationship became a push and pull of him and me depending on each other to make the other happy. It was depleting us both without us even realizing the cause.

When things went wrong, I would try to fix him or help him—and he became dependent on me for a lot of things. He and I thought that that was love, the fact that I encouraged his co-dependency by setting no boundaries and doing everything for him. My tendency was to let that happen, but in truth I hated that burden because it was all too familiar.

I started to realize that I was staying in a relationship that was dragging me down. I was holding on to something that wasn't good anymore because I was afraid of letting go and being alone, really alone.

As my resentment grew, my darkness started showing up: old bad habits/defense mechanisms. #HURTPEOPLEHURTPEOPLE. Sometimes I went off on him just to get a rise out of him. I couldn't express MY pain and the fact that he couldn't see I was hurting caused me, I think, to subconsciously show him through

Lauren Palmer

making him feel that same hurt. And just like that, our relationship became physically and emotionally abusive, and mostly on my part. Sometimes we think only guys can be abusive, and it's not true. Things can get out of hand for anyone when you have feelings you ain't dealt with. There was one time in the middle of the night when we got into a crazy fight. I should say morning because it was like three a.m. and I wanted him to leave! He wouldn't, and he wouldn't let me leave. I was texting my best friend, Jamie, the whole time and like in a movie she hopped out of her bed without question and came to pick me up. He left when he realized I'd called her to come, but when she dropped me off the next morning he somehow was right on the couch. 👀 He never *hit* me, but we fought for the first two years of living together. I started to feel so ashamed, as if I was turning into the monster that I promised myself I would never become. This wasn't me!! *Who was this?? How did I end up on this end of it, how?* I thought to myself. 😠

By the third year I told myself I couldn't be that person anymore. If that's what this relationship brought out of me, I didn't want it. I was tired of feeling like he was my responsibility, and of the fact that our relationship had become codependent in every area.

We tried therapy once but he wasn't available there either. I felt like he couldn't hear me and that my words were falling on deaf ears. I hung on a little longer, secretly hoping he would leave. There were many months when all we would do was hang out on the couch, smoke, and eat good food.

It was a very uninspired life and in the midst of it I would be filled with anger, depression, and anxiety over the fact that I couldn't muster the courage to leave the relationship and take the

I Don't Belong to You

5 MANTRAS FOR DAILY SELF LOVE

I AM WORTHY OF LOVE AND I AM FULL OF LOVE FOR OTHERS.

I MAKE TIME TO NOURISH MY MIND, BODY, AND SPIRIT.

I AM ABUNDANT IN ALL THINGS THAT BRING ME JOY.

I AM A POWERFUL FORCE FOR GOOD IN THE WORLD.

I AM BEAUTIFUL AND RADIATE WITH LIGHT FROM WITHIN.

Repeat these kind & positive messages to yourself every day & you'll greatly increase your level of health & happiness.

life I really wanted. This is when forgiveness of self comes into play. It's very *human* to let yourself down and to *keep* letting yourself down just because you're so disappointed in yourself, thus creating a habit of believing you are not responsible for how you feel about your life. Turning away from God or spiritual practices is another thing that tends to happen when you start self-shame—you almost don't think you deserve it, thus creating the habitual idea that you are "forsaken." #USHUMANSARESO DRAMATIC.

I was afraid he wouldn't survive without me #CODEPEN DENCYATITSBEST—I was stuck in a rut. Looking back, I think I was afraid to face all the shit I knew I would have to face once I made that major CHANGE. Even though the relationship was making me sick, literally, I couldn't bring myself to stand up and make him leave.

Then one day I looked around and saw that continuing to live this way gave me one future—the one lived by many people I knew back home after they'd given up on themselves, not coming through for what they wanted and allowing themselves to be let down by THEMSELVES. I saw that future and I knew it would kill my spirit.

I'm very protective of my spirit and when I could see where I was headed, I knew I had to do something to take me off course. Even if I couldn't see where that course was, it was better than an overindulgent, compulsive future! I couldn't let myself down, I couldn't! I swear to you, guys, my conscious was SHOUTING and I felt a fire in my chest! It was either settling for his happiness or leaving for my own, and just like that I said to myself, "Take him away!"

I didn't want him to feel like I was forcing him to be responsible for my happiness. Even though he thought that was fine, I

I Don't Belong to You

knew it wasn't. I didn't want him to bear an impossible burden and I didn't want to either. We just weren't good for each other anymore. It was unhealthy and suffocating for me. I couldn't grow and expand in that environment. You also can't have a real relationship when both you and your partner aren't trying to acknowledge your issues. Darkness can't cast out darkness, and it's only the individual who can turn on the lights. #CHOICE. I wanted my lights to turn on and in order to gain electricity back in my house, I had to cut him off from the energy source.

I knew it was time to work on "me" and I knew that with that, there would have to be some changes. It took me a year of wanting to leave Joey before actually getting the courage to break up. Shout-out to one of my best friends, Matty, who helped me so much during that time. He and I were going through the same issues, and just speaking with him, and us both giving each other the strength to do what was best for us, was invaluable. Love you, Matty!

It had gotten to the point where I had to leave town physically to film a movie in another state in order to truly break ties. I breathed a sigh of relief thinking finally I wouldn't be distracted and could try to spend some time on the real issues. I was going to figure out how to be "happy" like I always wanted to be. Joey was no longer around, so I could be alone with the space to focus on myself and just be!

⇀ DISTRACTIONS AND OTHER ATTRACTIONS ↽

I feel it's important to have some alone time when you leave one relationship before you even think about getting into another. Giving yourself time to process your thoughts on what you've just walked away from in order to determine what worked and

Lauren Palmer

what didn't for you is so important. Without that I feel like we give ourselves a greater chance to repeat the mistakes again and again. Guess I needed a few more rounds before I took it seriously. 😄 😫

In the beginning of my breakup with Joey, I was filming a movie and falling for someone else at the same time. 😄 😔 🥶 😫 We were playing love interests, and the circumstances created a scenario where I was not only NOT alone, but all up in somebody else's face, and he was in mine. 👀

I was again distracted from my self-work and this time his name was Camry: a tall, boyish-faced pretty boy I'd known since I was a teen. He had always had a crush on me, but I hadn't liked him at first because he seemed really pretentious and I was afraid he was fake in the Hollywood sense of the word (opportunistic). Unlike Joey, he was very self-confident and expressive, except when it came to what was underneath the surface.

There's that "wall" I kept running into. #MOTHTOFLAME. But on the outside he was fun, playful, and exciting and more open than most guys at the start. He had a real childlike quality. He actually took me on one of my first real dates back in the day, and would often invite me to family parties, but there was never any consistency in the history of our relationship.

The Camry I got to know while working together was a totally different Camry from the one I knew as a kid. He was seemingly more open from the start of filming. It felt like he was making a genuine effort to be more invested in my life. He cared about the breakup I was going through. Even though we had known each other since childhood, he'd never been consistent enough to get that much out of me.

While being stuck out of town working, we had nothing else to do but connect. We would have these hilariously long talks about life and everything in between and I loved our meaningful exchanges. You can't have meaningful exchanges with everyone. I think that's what makes finding people you can connect with so special!

We had a great connection. We would talk all day and all night, just best buds. It was my time with him that made me realize that there was passion and excitement in relationships, friendship! It just means that TWO people are showing up to the relationship, as friends or otherwise. He always said he just wanted to be best friends, but then he'd do such romantic things, publicly. He would give me foot massages with my girlfriends around and tell me how beautiful he thought I was. He would hold my hand in front of other cast members and act like he really liked me, but in private he'd run hot and cold.

I had to stop in the middle of our movie to promote another film I'd done some time before. I was so shocked that even though back home while his grandma was very ill, he didn't stay in LA for the time off that he and the rest of the cast had during my promo time. He joined me when I was promoting the movie and we slept in the same bed, but didn't kiss or do anything other than cuddle. I later thought I should have paid attention to how someone who was important to him was being prioritized in his life, as opposed to how he was treating me in that moment.

This was all new to me, I hadn't been that close to anyone other than Joey, and Camry and I were sharing deeper intimacy than that. We weren't sexual at all when we were making the movie together. We didn't even kiss until the movie was like a week from being over.

Having said that, I got tired of being teased. #THATPART. 😒 I honestly started taking it personal that he hadn't made a pass at me and I started to get nervous he was just using me. For what, I

Lauren Palmer

didn't know, but the lukewarm feeling I was having was starting to aggravate me and activate all my insecurities.

I finally asked him what the deal was, that most other guys would be trying to have sex with me by that point. I asked was it that he just wasn't attracted to me? I wasn't afraid of rejection, to be rejected for me would've set me free at this point because I didn't like the uncertain place he was capable of putting me in. I pointed out that one minute he'd say he just wanted to be friends, but then the next minute he acted like he loved me, literally telling me I'm *fabulous* and saying things like, "Why aren't we married yet?" He seemed so nervous, like he was a rat I'd pushed into a corner with my broom. Then he kissed me!

It was such a movielike moment, honestly, in the most HI-LARIOUS way. From that moment on we were even closer, like two peas in a pod—as close as close could be with this added element. But he said he still wanted to be *best friends*.

For a long time that bothered me. It confused me so much, a fresh twenty-year-old, that he didn't want to be my boyfriend but wanted to spend time with me and kiss me and all this. It honestly bugged me because I couldn't understand it; it didn't fit in my head. I felt like I wanted to sleep with him but couldn't, because he wasn't my boyfriend. I felt like I couldn't open up, because he wasn't my boyfriend. I felt like I had to be mad at every female who was with him, because he wasn't my boyfriend.

I honestly was chained by those words and found myself in bondage that I created. I feel like so much of my early relationship with Camry was defined by other people's ideas. I felt like certain things had to happen or I would get dissatisfied. If we didn't hang out, if he tweeted before texting me, if he didn't text me back till a few hours later. My anxiety was tripling because I didn't stop to take some time before my breakup with Joey to evaluate my

I Don't Belong to You

needs. I hadn't worked on ME, and it was showing. What was really happening was that I was having separation anxiety, on top of the anxiety habits I'd already inherited. This was the most excruciating process for me because it was me at my weakest.

Camry didn't want to be in a relationship and because I was wrapped up in my insecurities I created another rejection that wasn't really a rejection because I honestly didn't want or need to be in a relationship any more than he did. I just felt like I should be in a relationship and now that the guy was a LITTLE cooler than Joey, he was the one! It was such an identity thing. . . . I was Keke, guys want me to be wifey—he doesn't? Omg, why!? It never occurred to me that I attract people like myself. The fact that I was dating someone unavailable and finding him attractive or worthy to be in a relationship with means that subconsciously I didn't want one either. Those are just the facts, kids!

Still, my bond with him was strong and I even became close to his entire family. I adore them and I believe they adore me.

Although we had a spring romance, the inconsistency habit soon came right back. My anxiety took it into overdrive but there really were strange things happening between us that motivated my alarms. He was very up and down in his emotions, hot one day and strangely distant the next. I remember we went out to his fam's house and his grandmother was always in her room because she was severely ill with cancer. He loved his grandmother and I wanted to meet her, but he wouldn't let me near her room.

It was like she was the queen of Egypt and I wasn't allowed to meet her. Then on Valentine's Day, he invited me to his house. I took a rose for each of his family members. When I got there, he was sitting on the couch with his grandmother in his arms, I guessed he was finally ready to let me meet her! 📸 🙆🏾‍♀️ 💐

He introduced me to her and she said Camry had told her so much about me. She and I laughed and spoke about how proud we were of him and his thriving career. It was a really special moment and I felt that he had to be genuine! Not to mention he wrote me the most amazing Valentine's Day note. 😁 Even though he had gotten inconsistent once we got back to LA, I felt that he meant well and did care for me to some degree. He had to, right?

We spent the rest of V-day together and it was a chill time, but I still felt like Camry wasn't being completely real and that old pretentious energy started to come back into the forefront. The whole time he was saying nice stuff but honestly seemed like he'd rather be somewhere else. It was often that feeling of me getting the idea that I was some sort of chore. I wanted us to have fun like we did before but it seemed like the added romantic element made it somehow draining for Camry. He was doing all the right things, kinda, but the intention seemed based off a perception and not like he really liked me like that. It felt like he was acting out a movie role and in some ways I felt like he resented me for *making* him play that role.

Our feelings about love are based on our experiences, our personal histories. We bring our pasts into the relationship with us—our hurts from previous relationships as well as our insecurities and fears.

There was something that kept Camry from going all in with me. After Valentine's Day, the hot and cold Camry was at its WORST. He was passive-aggressive, saying he liked me one minute and telling me to back off the next. When his grandmother passed away, he didn't want me around to be there for him.

Yes, again I was confused. I thought he was a great guy. I just felt like he wasn't really being himself, like he was hiding something and wanted me close sometimes but at arm's length. He was warm and romantic, but still emotionally distant.

The difference between him and Joey is that Joey was soooo laid-back that his emotional unavailability didn't seem like so much of a stretch. But because Camry was much more talkative and a *charmer*, his emotional availability was much harder to identify. Camry would talk about his life, but then when you approached real inquiries on certain topics he didn't want to address he would either laugh it away or become passive-aggressive in a way that would make you feel stupid for asking, lol. He would always use the "you're being 'intrusive'" card, making it seem like you were always in breach of his privacy. That card was like my Achilles' heel because I was embarrassed to care.

I wanted to know the real guy, the hurt Camry, the disappointed Camry, but he only had the "happy" Camry. He had that dude on autopilot twenty-four seven *huuuuuuge eye roll*. His grandma's passing happened around the same time I was in preproduction for *Just Keke*. We had a really intense convo about my best friend, Jamie (who you'll hear more about . . .) because I felt like she was being similar to him. Saying one thing but acting like another, and in so many ways he used her story as a way to express his feelings. He tried to act as if that wasn't what he was doing, but it was plain and clear that he was using my situation with her as a scapegoat and pushing me away. I even asked him if he loved me the way I loved him, and he was so upset I'd asked because he felt it wasn't a yes or no question. #BULLSHIT. He told me that he didn't love me the way I loved him but that he did care for me deeply. After all the push and pull to hear those words were a relief kind of, but also I was crushed . . . CRUSHED! My ego for sure was! 💀

This was the toughest heartbreak of my life because it was the first time I'd ever felt a way about someone who didn't feel the same. I felt like my feet were numb and my heart was in my stomach, I didn't want to do anything, talk to anyone. I remember my mom coming to my house during the "Camry Storm" and at first I was so tough when breaking the situation down to her. She couldn't seem to understand why it upset me so much. She couldn't understand why I was letting him affect me so much esp because she'd known him and spent time with him during our movie too. She knew that he pursued me and she knew our past history. My emotions, she felt, didn't match the situation. To my mother I am the coolest and most confident and she couldn't understand why I was taking it/ him so seriously when I had so much other good stuff going on.

I remember bursting into tears and admitting probably for the first time that it JUST HURT. That I was HURTING, for a multitude of reasons, and I wanted Camry and me to pan out. It was like, if that went good it'd make up for all the shit that went wrong, but even it went wrong. It didn't work out as I'd wanted, my plans didn't turn out and you know what, it hurt. This had nothing to do with my career. In fact that was just like it'd always been, my career trudging along and my personal life six feet under. I didn't want to be resilient Keke, I wanted to let myself hurt instead of sucking it down deep. My mom just stood and started crying with me and started hugging me. That was a nice moment for us, an intense one, but special.

Anyone going through a breakup, know you ain't alone. We all go through it and it's OKAY that it hurts. You don't have to be strong all the time, give your other emotions a chance, that's why they're there. 😊

In the end, it not only left me brokenhearted but it also forced me to deal with the heartbreak from Joey that I'd never dealt with.

I Don't Belong to You

Jamie and I ended up getting back to cool, she was there for me during my getting over Camry. There she was again, saving the day. Everywhere I went out of town she came with and we were inseparable; she was the only person I wanted around. Really, I honestly don't know what I would've done without her. Her positive energy had a huge impact on me because she didn't judge my emotions. She didn't make me feel ashamed for feeling poorly, but she reminded me that it would get better and it was nowhere near the end of the world. That it was his loss, not mine! That's what friends are for, eh?

Even though Camry and I were never boyfriend and girlfriend, he was still someone I loved, and someone who loved me. We loved each other in different ways, but the way anyone loves is based off of what one has seen or come to know on the subject. It really isn't about our feelings toward the other person as much as it's about the way we learned to express/intellectualize them. It really wasn't my job to figure out Camry's problems, to judge him or label him. It was my job to understand my OWN problems and what made me comfortable with an uncomfortable situation.

⇒ GETTING TO THE HEART ⇐ OF RELATIONSHIPS

It took me a long time to realize that, with Camry, it wasn't personal about me. It was about him and the journey he was going through. He was trying to find himself just like me. And I couldn't make my separation anxiety and inability to stand on my own two feet his problem. No, he wasn't a perfect person, but where did it say he had to be?

By the end of my overly emotional phase with Camry, which, unlike with Joey lasted under a year 😄, the only question I had

HEALTHY
RELATIONSHIPS

BE DOWN

It's always important to know the people around you care about your dreams. A relationship isn't a one-way street. You can't just give. You can't just take. You gotta do both.

ACCEPT YOUR SHIT

In a relationship, everyone makes mistakes, but it takes admitting you're wrong when you're wrong. Accountability is important for a relationship. When you know you can do better, #DoBetter. Move your pride aside.

YAGLC

YOU AIN'T GOTTA LIE, CRAIG.

No matter what ups and downs your relationship goes through, it's always better to be truthful and lay it all out on the table—FROM THE BEGINNING.

RESPECT

NO GAMES

Nobody wants to overthink a relationship. It is easy to connect when your ego is down. You can't have a relationship with someone when you're always trying to be a step ahead of them.

LET'S GET ALONG

Why can't we try our best to be on good terms? #Compromise. Let's get along. It makes more sense to try to get along, instead of trying to always be right. Try to be reasonable. Why not?

BE REAL

If you want to have something real, you have to be real. You can't have trust if you're not trustworthy.

was: "Why did I keep pursing an obvious dead end??? What about a dead-end relationship interested me so?"

It alarmed me that I became so anxious because I couldn't control the situation, I couldn't completely READ Camry because the script he sold me was filled with half-truths already. There was literally no way to "get" through to him. I had NO bread crumbs to follow. But my need for control, where did that defense come from? I'd grown up on movie sets where everything was definitely controlled, minute to minute. I knew how to gauge what was going to happen next. I enjoyed that security. So, this was one of the first times I'd been in a situation where I felt threatened by the lack of control and forced to be . . . VULNERABLE. 😱 😱 😱 😱 😱 😱 😱

Though Camry had his own issues, he wasn't like Joey, who fed into my ways in a codependent sense. Camry did not feed into my ways because he simply didn't need me. The unhealthy hierarchy in my relationship with Joey made things easy. I never fully had to BE vulnerable because I ultimately was always in control. Camry was selfish but also totally clear on how much of himself he was willing to give, which made my anxiety and need for control more paramount. It was literally moment to moment with Camry, which I liked but also hated because it brought my weaknesses to the forefront. With Joey I learned I had a hero complex. I was compelled to make everything all right in his world. With Camry, I learned I'd been controlling all my past relationships. Even though Camry was telling me we were closer than his actions displayed, it was ultimately me who was sticking around for it. It was me who was allowing myself to only exist in this space. . . . Why did I need to know Camry's every move? Why did I stay even though it was causing me such grief? Why was I choosing to take everything so personal with Camry when even I didn't want a relationship? Was I taking this rejection because for once I was finding someone I couldn't control with my bank account? Oh no. I wasn't liking seeing that truth about myself. It really disappointed me. 😠

Those realizations caused me to switch gears and focus on why I had such a need to control, learning how to let go of the need to always know what was next. I hated that I allowed Camry's inconsistency to disrupt my sense of peace, so I promised to look deeper inside for the answer to why my peace was so easily disrupted. I also vowed to work on accepting every outcome while still being fearless in going after whatever it was my heart desired.

During my time on Broadway, I knew that there was something with me that needed to be addressed. My anxiety, why I had it, where the mechanism originated. . . . So many questions that at first I had no idea how to ask. While in New York I did a lot of personal work. I spent more time looking around me than in my phone, and I spent a lot of time reading about spiritual practices and other people's peace-finding journeys. I spent more time with my mom, and I think those new memories healed a lot of past pain. My friendship with Jamie showed me how important and valuable a relationship with your mother can be. Jamie and her mom were very close. I admired that and invested time to develop that with my mother while in New York. Of course I didn't change overnight, I think it's good to be constantly under construction, but I will say I felt different by the end of my living there.

Once I came back from vacation after Broadway, I slowly started talking to Camry again. First it was platonic and then it was more romantic. This time it felt different. I found myself still feeling like I loved him, but I was not as fazed by his inconsistency. I hated that we developed this walking-on-eggshells type of vibe. I wanted him to know that I wasn't trying to make him my boyfriend. I wasn't caught up in trying to control my feelings with a label anymore. I finally saw beyond that.

I wanted Camry to know that who I was before in the relationship wasn't me (the true me). It was the manifestation of the behaviors I was using to cope with other personal things. It was part of uncovering the layers of myself on the journey to finding myself, #IMNOTCRAZYIPROMISE, 😵 lol. I stopped judging myself because I knew that I wasn't the "crazy girl" or "the girl who didn't realize when a guy wasn't into her." But the fear of becoming those "things" and my need to control caused me to react in ways I didn't like.

I didn't make up his back-and-forth behavior or his inconsistencies, but I now understood that was his problem for not knowing what he wanted, just as much as it was my problem for not realizing that caring about people is always a risk. #ESPECIALLY IFTHEYARENTREADY.

I wasn't a little girl anymore and the boyfriend and girlfriend stuff was a different ball game as an adult. I was a girl who was going through a lot: a girl who was afraid to look at herself, so she threw herself into anybody and everybody else's problems so that she wouldn't have to focus on her own.

It wasn't my job to be aware of Camry's flaws, but it was my job to be aware of mine. #BOTTOMLINE.

It was all about my growth, and in a lot of ways, I wanted to see if all of the self-work I'd done on myself during my time away on Broadway had helped. So I kinda tested it a bit.

Around this time, I'd just filmed the pilot for *Scream Queens*, and I decided to go to Camry's house for the Super Bowl. When I got there, I noticed his ex-girlfriend was there. Now the old me

Lauren Palmer

probably would have left or acted out, but this time, I just chilled. I chose to watch the situation and see how it played out instead of reacting hastily.

All I did was enjoy the party and monitor my feelings, and what I noticed was that I didn't really feel any *sadness* at all. I was content in accepting the situation as it was. Camry was my friend, not my boyfriend, and the ex was his ex not mine, which equals not my concern. 🔫 I didn't try to label my feelings or the situation, I just observed. I now knew I had the option to choose the way I wished to react, and I chose to not be affected by things that don't concern me. My days of finding out just how cool I could keep it were just around the corner . . .

⇒ WE BRING OUR PAST INTO ⇐ OUR RELATIONSHIPS

Though Camry and I continued to hang out, we still weren't "together." I needed more, I suppose, and more came along. While working in the studio I met Sammy. He is an amazing musician and writer and so dramatic, hahaha. I thought he was really weird-looking at first. He had that look of "I'm gonna kill everyone at my school" mixed with a Spanish pimp/rapper style. 😳 😄 It sounds crazy but I felt it was bold and really unique.

He's of mixed race, black and Thai. He had shaved sides with a man bun, about six-two, with a beginner's beer belly and a bunch of tattoos and piercings. He had at least three piercings on his face, and I remember looking at him and thinking, *Wow, you're interesting!* He had the look of someone trying to look scary to throw off onlookers, lol. Though they didn't look anything alike, his wearing the mask of toughness reminded me of my dad, who once told me that he initially started drinking to see if it would

I Don't Belong to You

toughen him up and not be such a pushover when it came to the ladies, lol.

I watched Sammy as he drank his third beer and thought: *You intrigue me, but I don't think I find you attractive.* Hahaha!

You know how you do that sometimes when you see someone who is really different and ask yourself, *Am I attracted to you?* LOL. The first day we worked together, I thought Sammy was cool, but we didn't get anything done. At the time, he had written one of the most popular pop records on the radio, and it was a song I really liked. The next day when I got to the studio, he waited outside while the producer played me what they'd recorded after I'd left the night before.

OMG!! I LOOOOOVED it! It was spunky and chill at the same time. I literally thought he was the coolest person ever. After that we started working together a lot. I could tell that he really liked me, but I felt that his defensive nature made him become very aggressive toward me in conversation at times. One night we got into a hot texting match and it was such a sign that we weren't that compatible because we hadn't even kissed yet, lmfao! 😑

But there he was trying to force me to think the way he did, and I found it to be just really annoying and sexist and I let him know it. The next thing I knew, he was opening up to me about how hard he had had it, and how he'd been homeless because no one supported his dreams and how his success was ultimately scary to him. In so many words, he was trying to express WHY he was so difficult. As another human, I related to that so deeply and respected his vulnerability. He told me how hard it was for him to find happiness and to relate to others truly but that he felt something exciting with me. He felt a chemistry that was hard to find and that if I didn't feel it too, then he'd leave me alone.

That triggered so many good and bad things in me—it was

the hero complex. I felt a need to save him now (as if that's something anyone is capable of, people change their lives when THEY want to). I had not yet created any boundaries on what I was responsible for and who I am responsible to.

⇒ CODEPENDENCY ⇐

Sammy had kept me up all night playing me like a violin, lol, and I felt so sympathetic toward him—but also like a drug fiend, except a codependent fiend, looking for an opportunity to over-help someone to the point of being a disservice to them. The next day I didn't really want to see him, but I had to because we had a session. 😑 The whole day he was annoying me, he flirted kind of like a child and that often meant picking on me and trying to contradict me. 😠 Then during the session, he started texting me— telling me how special I made him feel. Again, he was pushing those buttons, the ones that speak to my old, draining relational habits. The ones that are uncomfortably comfortable only because they are FAMILIAR. I don't think he was faking it. I honestly think he felt we had a connection, but that doesn't mean he or I was capable of being in a relationship, or a romantic one at that.

Relationships take vulnerability, accountability, trust, honesty, etc. Neither of us were capable of that. I was just starting to hold myself accountable for my life and I was looking for the same in the people in it. That's one reason my relationships didn't last. None of us wanted to take that responsibility for the part we played in it.

Sammy, for example, had drinking problems. His father told me he had over five DUIs. He didn't want to be held accountable for his drinking, which hurt our relationship. He didn't want to take responsibility for anything, it seemed, and only he knows

I Don't Belong to You

when, where, and why that started. Still, Sammy and I connected through music. It was a song he wrote the night after our big fight, when I had to go to the studio the next day, that sealed the deal for me.

"Oh, I'd . . . Break . . . Rules . . . For . . . You . . . 'Cause ooh, You'd. Em. Brace. This. Fool."

It brought tears to my eyes because we shared the language of love through music. That was his way of speaking to me through our shared passion. It was a way we related that was different from others I'd dated. That night we drove all the way from the studio, which was in Malibu, to where I was living with my parents in Pasadena (long drive) and when we got there, we stood outside for a few seconds before we kissed for what seemed like an eternity. In that moment I felt I had the greatest spark with Sammy.

He was so gifted, which was truly something I admired! He was relentless in trying to get me to like him. When he pressured me into sex, it should've been a red flag, but he kept introducing my favorite distractions, so all the signs were going unnoticed, which I'm sure were his own favorite distractions. Having sex can be a surefire way to undercut the road to intimacy-ville.

Though still focused on my creative work, I allowed Sammy to distract me on my personal work. He wasn't assisting me on my road to recovery. He didn't even ask enough questions to know how to do that; all he did was enable me with more of the same vices.

I found him to be quite insensitive, and the moment I'd bring it up he'd be begging me to just forgive him or let it go.

I really didn't want to give him a chance; he was obsessive, but at the same time my ego was saying, "Wow, I have never had a guy that into me before!" I thought: *OMG this was the difference, the*

Lauren Palmer

ATTENTION! This guy REALLY likes me because, unlike Joey and Camry, he actually is obsessed with me and that's why he's trying so hard. #DUH. #THISISGREATRIGHT. *THIS is exactly what I need, this is how I'm supposed to be treated, as an object of ego gratification.* 😎

⮞ SHEDDING THE BLINDERS ⮜

My relationship with Sammy, though my emotions were true, was again about my desire to live out the habits/trauma I experienced at home that I never came to terms with. Sammy was one of the final pieces to the puzzle of me realizing my relationship problems were my personal problems. They were the problems I kept running from, and any time I tried to get close to anyone they would rear their ugly heads. Or they would blind me to being able to correctly choose the kind of characters that I wanted in my life.

I had been doing some soul searching after Camry and Joey and knew I wasn't really looking for a boyfriend, but I also knew I needed to experience life to keep growing. I didn't want to shut myself off. But I also knew I was blind to certain aspects of Sammy because I was still looking through rose-colored glasses.

Like Camry and Joey, Sammy was emotionally unavailable, but for different reasons and with one shining reason—his drinking. This problem made me revisit similar feelings I hadn't dealt with. Sometimes we form relationships that force us to confront the past.

Sammy's drinking didn't bother me, at first, because my ideas on drinking were always skewed. It didn't occur to me that the healthy relationship I desired could not include problems with alcohol. My dad came from a drinking family and he and his broth-

I Don't Belong to You

MAYBE LIFE

ISN'T ABOUT

AVOIDING THE BRUISES,

MAYBE IT'S ABOUT

COLLECTING THE SCARS

TO PROVE WE

SHOWED UP FOR IT.

ers had a habit of over drinking at times. Same for his dad and same for my mom's dad.

I felt guilty many times when I would want to speak up on his change of attitude when my dad drank. I never wanted to judge him, but I felt he was not always the same when he drank. I learned to ignore it and I just accepted it as normal.

My relationship with my dad suffered because of that. As a kid I often personalized his behavior. Because I didn't understand drinking and its effects I never thought that it was the possible culprit for his mood swings. I just felt like he didn't like me very much. I felt that there was something between us, keeping him from being real with me.

On the surface you could say that the drinking comparison alone created my attraction to Sammy. And though, to me, God WAS saying "YOU WILL SEE THIS," that wasn't the MAIN similarity between someone I dated and my family. With Sammy, it just became especially clear. Sammy's alcohol induced mood swings triggered old habits in me that brought up faded memories. I needed to examine my relationship with my parents if I wanted to heal and move forward.

⇒ RELATIONSHIP MELTDOWN ⇐

By the time I started filming *Scream Queens*, Sammy and I were boyfriend and girlfriend. We only lasted about five months because over the course of his visits to New Orleans he became increasingly more peculiar. He came down while I was filming and doing a *Scream Queens* promo for the ESSENCE Music Festival and I could tell that he was disappointed. I think in many ways he felt that way because of his inability to really focus on his music career.

I Don't Belong to You

I think Sammy knew he was talented, but I feel that just like me, because he got successful at something else first, songwriting, that is what most people wanted from him. He would try to hide this, but I could tell my new ability to go for it really affected him because of his inability to go for it. Not only that but he was also dealing with a lot with his family and just questioning his foundation of trust.

How crazy is it how the people you choose to let into your life can mirror you without you realizing it? Lol. I spent many nights trying to make Sammy "happy." I put myself in the unhealthy position of being responsible for other people's happiness. That's an old habit that actually birthed my purpose of being an entertainer in the first place, still having no sense of boundaries. Sammy was draining me, but also intriguing me because through him I was learning soooo much about *me*. I would often discuss this with Jamie, as she was out there with me working as my assistant. Especially on the days when Sammy would be moody and cruel toward me. She was there to hold me as I cried. 👭

By the last trip Sammy made to see me in New Orleans, he'd become very verbally abusive. And much to my surprise had crossed boundaries when I saw his text thread with JAMIE. 😱 I know, what a bitch, the both of them. 😡

I know they say it isn't good to hire your friends, but I actually love hiring friends and working with them toward our goals. I think it's just important to know where your friend is coming from when deciding to work together. I hired her initially so we could spend time together while I was gone and so she could save up money. She was living at home and hated working in retail, so it made sense. Not to mention, I too was really trying to stand on my own two feet without my mother.

Lauren Palmer

At the start things were great! She was pretty okay with order, and neither of us knew much about "assisting" jobs. I didn't know how to really be a *boss*, and she didn't know how to really be an assistant. I feel we can both take responsibility when it comes to the business aspect. I think Jamie cared for me, but I feel like she started to resent me at a certain point. Instead of just telling me she wasn't passionate for the job, or that she felt I was acting like a tyrant (obvi not that one 😌), or that she wanted to go home or whatever, she instead spoke about me behind my back to coworkers. I later heard that she talked bad about me to my boyfriend and some cast mates, and just a few months ago, y'all, I was told that she had bad-mouthed me to music peers and past and potential baes. #DAAAAAAAAAAMN #AINTTHATABITCH smh.

All these things tell me that there were things going unsaid between us. I think Jamie became competitive with me and maybe I did too with her. I think we were both going through a lot with our significant others as well as ourselves. I don't think we were mature enough yet to express and communicate our feelings directly, and they came to the surface in the most petty and passive-aggressive ways. I don't know how she felt exactly, because she's never told me, but I could've been hard on her. I was frustrated in my relationship and can sometimes be really critical and passive-aggressive. #KNOWYASELF. Jamie was known for her beauty, she was always the pretty girl, and I often felt Jamie's mom promoted an idea that because she was pretty, her focus should be getting a man locked down who can take care of her.

Jamie would never really share her feelings on the subject, but I know it must have stressed her out to continuously be told who she should put up with because of who they are or what money they made. To have it implied that your identity is attached to how good you are at getting others to do things for you seemed like hell to me. At the end of the day, I don't know what all she was struggling with, because she didn't tell me. But I'm sure she had reasons for her actions, just like we all do when shit goes left and we are there looking like the "bad guy." I just know that she hurt me by violating my trust on more levels than one and it's still hard to believe today. 💔

I loved her so much and honestly would've done anything for her—we were best friends I thought, and I couldn't understand why she would f&^% me over, something I learned that I may never get the answer to. THAT was what I had to learn to accept. Sometimes people will hurt you and you will *never* know the reason and even if you do, you will probably not understand it because you weren't the one who did it. Of course I don't think I deserved what Jamie did, but who's to say she doesn't feel like I did things that prompted passive-aggressive action back? Friends can be mean to each other at times, and that doesn't mean they don't love you, it just means they are human. She was my main bitch 4 life, but sometimes things change.

The final straw was when Sammy and I were out to a bar one night with her and other friends and she was talking to everyone about me. I didn't know this at the time but I knew the energy wasn't good. It was like *Mean Girls*, the movie. Which in reality means this was high school 101 stuff because if you remember in the movie all the girls were mean at some point, even Lindsay. But I completely missed the high school phase, I'm socially inept in that sense, so it all felt really intense for me. I could feel they were all judging me. I couldn't figure out why Sammy was being cold until I learned later Jamie had been saying bad things about me.

Lauren Palmer

They'd been drinking for a while and I'd come to the bar only because Jamie begged me to. The night before, I had called it off with Sammy and made him stay at a hotel. He hit me up that morning and I realized I loved him and really wanted us to work out. Jamie was gonna go out with some of our gang, and Sammy was alone and wanted to go with them. I was going to stay home because I was all in my head, and Jamie kept texting me to come out. By the time I came to the bar I sensed the energy, I swear to you Sammy had again flipped.

As we left the bar to head to where one of the cast members was staying, I thought long and hard about approaching the subject of us and when I did he shut me down. It went from zero to a hundred REALLLLL MF QUICK. ●● Sammy started cursing at me, saying everyone talks shit about me, and it was happening so fast I couldn't figure out what was going on. I was so hurt when he screamed at me in front of everybody. I felt abandoned, embarrassed, shattered, and I would've loved to be as cruel as he was but I refused to show my ass. If there was one thing I had control over it was myself. I would maintain my dignity. I simply said, "Sammy, you are out of town for *me* talking shit about *me* to *MY* friends. Who does that?" I started to walk to the car and as Jamie started walking behind me Sammy told her she didn't have to go with me. When I asked her if she was coming, she said, "Well do you want me to go?"

I was shocked that she'd even asked that question.

"Stay," I told her.

She stayed, and I was torn apart because Sammy had disrespected me and she hadn't defended me. She didn't even tell him to leave, she just went right back to hanging out as if nothing had happened, leaving me to stand alone. I went into my "be strong" habit and blocked out the pain, but just like them I pretended it

I Don't Belong to You

was okay even though I was hurt. I didn't express that they hurt me and I didn't tell Jamie that I really needed her in that moment. Was I wrong for expecting her to know what to do? I thought, *Guess what, I'm stronger than this moment and y'all will have to reap what you've sown!* It's the karmic rule. When you treat people badly, it eventually comes back on you.

That was where I drew the line, with them and myself. Something had to give, I was tired of waiting for other people to hurt me because I didn't know how to love myself. I was getting more and more creative with the pain I was bringing into my world and I had to put an end to it.

⇀ NURTURING FEMALE FRIENDSHIPS ↽

I've always tried to nurture my friendships with other women. In today's world, the media, mutual friends, and even guys we like will pit women against one another and that really upsets me because it works all too often. Sometimes it is hard for me to find and keep good female friends, because I am regularly compared to or placed in competition with my female peers in the industry for jobs, opportunities, and visibility. Not only that but I made a choice a long time ago that I'd forgotten, which was, *trust no one.* That can cause all kinds of negative energy into your perspective of life if you don't realize that that's a habit that can't be active when building relationships.

As a result, I make it a point not to let that type of controlling mind-set seep into my spirit and I learned that that means keeping people around to make me accountable. It's normal to sometimes wish you had a certain look or body shape. Admiring the qualities of other women isn't a no-no, I'm just not interested in tearing another woman down because of it. We all have done it

Lauren Palmer

but we don't HAVE to and as quiet as it's kept it's stupid. If she's successful, I would like to follow in her footsteps and LEARN from her. We are so much better when we come TOGETHER.

Self-love means having enough intelligence to see the beauty in someone else, and the importance of having people around you who have their own goals and dreams and keep you accountable to yourself.

Now that doesn't mean you won't get hurt by those who love you, but it isn't about labeling the people who've done you wrong, it's not about harboring pain and victimizing yourself. It's about understanding that everyone is in different places in their lives and your ability to weed out who's who depends on you knowing yourself and what you desire in friendships. I never wanted to be that girl who didn't trust her girlfriends. But I was wrong too in this situation because I ignored important signs and I didn't speak my mind. People aren't mind readers and if you want people not to hurt you and you don't spell it out to them what's hurting you, are you giving them a fair chance to know how deeply it's affecting you? #DONTPLAYITCOOL.

I think it is smart to pay attention to those around you, no matter how close you are. "You can be friends with a thief, just don't let 'em into your house," my mom says. Before shit hit the fan I did notice texting between Jamie and Sammy and some of the texts were about me. It was clear that they'd crossed a boundary line right before my eyes. I had dealt with many people in my life treating me like a subject, like it was okay to talk about me like a thing because I seemed like I had the charmed life/position. Them having conversations behind my back was like reliving a moment of my childhood.

However, who's to say that wasn't something I could've expressed and experienced contrition from one of them or both?

I Don't Belong to You

The gag is I actually did, and my agreement to never trust anyone put my possible mending with them in a choke hold. So they both got the axe, and I kept it moving. That experience didn't turn me off from forming friendships with other women, or men for that matter. But it did teach me a lesson that there is no love, no relationship, without FORGIVENESS and making the choice to TRUST. People won't always get it right, y'all, but it's about who is trying to get it right to be a good friend to YOU! You gotta pay attention to the people who deserve your time and your love and you have to make sure YOU are in the right mind to determine that! Don't be a pushover but don't expect people to climb your Great Wall of China either. #THATSEXHAUSTING.

⇀ PAYING ATTENTION ↽

After the Sammy and Jamie situation, I decided to take a serious look in the mirror because I had not been in a situation that lethal since those beginning years with Joey. I was just getting better with dealing with my emotions, I thought, and yet here I was— right where I had begun. I wasn't paying *enough* attention!! I was repeating the same mistakes!!

I got back to Cali and promised myself there would be no serious dating. I was interested in someone, but my vow to myself ultimately made me unavailable to anyone. Sammy was constantly reaching out to me, but I hated him at that point. He had finally told me how my "best friend" had told him all these lies about me and about Camry. It was just so hard to accept that not only did she lie, but he believed her.

That whole time was eye-opening for me because I was back on my practices with yoga and therapy, so I was able to view my decisions objectively as opposed to judgmentally.

Lauren Palmer

Camry and I were on cool terms and he was actually there for me when the whole Sammy and Jamie situation went down. I knew who Camry was at that point—instead of who I wanted him to be—and I knew how to not get ahead of myself, but to instead pay attention to his consistent actions. That turned out to be a good strategy when my moment of truth arrived. We were back on great terms, and I was over at the house a lot. He lived at home, and he started wanting me to hang with his family, even if he wasn't there. I felt really welcomed.

One night, after attending the Grammy Awards after-party, I went to hang out with his mom and aunts. At the night's end, I ventured to his room to say hello. He had given me the code to his door lock, and I with entitlement punched it in.

Just as I started to open the door, I caught a glimpse of Camry's face freaking out.

"Stop, somebody's in here!" he said.

I hadn't walked all the way in, and I couldn't see who else was there. I didn't try to see.

I immediately said "Sorry!" And ran out . . .

I shut the door and stood there for a second, feeling embarrassed. Then, I literally started laughing. 😂 I honestly wish I could've snapped a photo of his face, hahahahaha. I was still outside his door typing up a text to send him to say "my bad," but before I could finish he came out of the room. He was acting very cool and nonchalant, and asking me about the party, lol. I had just come from a party, so it wasn't COMPLETELY weird, but it was odd because he first of all knows I'm not crazy interested in industry stuff and I had just walked in on him with someone in his bedroom.

He literally didn't address it and I tried to, a couple of times. It literally was the weirdest thing because all this time I had waited

I Don't Belong to You

for the perfect opportunity to show him I wasn't "crazy" over him and there he was ignoring it when it came. I don't know what I expected, but I guess I felt proud that I didn't let it affect me and I thought he should have too, lmfao. 🙄

After that I tried again to address the awkwardness of the situation, but Camry pushed me away. #TYPICAL. Then things were never the same. Camry had worked so hard to make me feel a part of his family, but I kind of distanced myself from him after the way he dealt with the incident, yet I had already gotten close to his family and they would reach out to me! It wasn't like I only liked them because of Camry: I liked them period, and it was nice having older women to talk to besides my mom, but it was getting weird.

They wouldn't ask about me and Camry, but when they mentioned certain things it gave me the idea that Camry was telling them something totally different from what was really going on. Camry would literally NEVER text me to hang out or anything, but when he would hear that I had come over to hang with his fam he would be peeved with me. All of a sudden it wasn't okay that I wasn't working to make things comfortable for HIM. It's hard to play in a game you don't believe in anymore.

➤ REPEATING THE SAME PATTERNS ➤ BRINGS THE SAME RESULTS

My therapist once told me if nothing changes then . . . nothing changes. In other words, if you don't change your actions or yourself, you'll never see different results. I saw what my therapist meant. My relationship with Camry changed. For forever, I'd wanted Camry to care or to say certain things to me, and he never did. Then, quite honestly, it seemed like once I changed, he

Lauren Palmer

The capacity to be alone
is the capacity to love.

It may look paradoxical to you, but it

is not. It is an existential truth: only those people

who are capable of being alone are capable of love,

of sharing, of going into the deepest core of the

other person—without possessing the other,

without becoming dependent on the other, without

reducing the other to a thing, and without

becoming addicted to the other. They allow the

other absolute freedom, because they know that if

the other leaves, they will be as happy as they are

now. Their happiness cannot be taken by the other,

because it is not given by the other.

—Osho, *Being in Love*

changed. Camry's inconsistencies couldn't bother me anymore because I knew who I was and what I wanted. And for the first time, I was okay with both of us just being who we were, even if that meant we wouldn't be as close as I once wanted us to be.

Our bedroom incident provided an opportunity to balance the dynamics in our relationship. It gave me and him the opportunity to see I was above the drama and it gave me the opportunity to see that a part of him did like that. #GAMEOVER. The paradigm was shifting because I was choosing to shift it. My personal work was paying off bit by bit because I was starting to see a bit clearer. I was happy. Right? I was starting to get happy-er. I was learning that happiness was a choice with each action I made toward the betterment of me. I knew I was choosing to be happy by my actions and the people I was accepting in my life. That was a very good feeling.

However, I still felt like I was close to something really important, but not there yet. I thought I was doing great until I started having feelings for a new distraction, well actually, an old one. Sammy had returned to my life.

Why? I thought maybe I could do with him what I did with Camry and be in control. You may still wonder why I let it happen after all Sammy had done to me. But yes, I got back with Sammy in all the wrong ways. It took seven months of him begging and pleading and taking a lot of bullshit from me. What started as me accepting his apology turned into me insulting him all the time, into our "joking" conversations, and then into me hanging out with him again.

Having sex with him wasn't the problem. It was the way I was using sex. I wasn't giving myself a chance to even get over anything that had happened between us. I was just choosing to cover it up with something else, something compulsive.

I didn't even let my anger subside, or my pain. I didn't even give a real friendship or intimacy a chance for us; I just wanted to control the situational subject and I used sex as my tool. The reality is if you play with fire you will get burned. Sammy hurt my feelings again just as I'm sure I've hurt his because I, like him, was not acknowledging my hurt to be able to move past it. The only difference this time was that I didn't take it personal.

⇥ EMOTIONAL UNAVAILABILITY ⇤

I think my relationship with Sammy was such a big one to me because I feel like I was trying to save myself in saving him. More than anyone else I'd dated, he expressed the part of me that I was protecting with all my defense mechanisms: my heart.

I remember a moment with Sammy when he was getting verbally abusive with me and I realized that the relationship wasn't right. I thought: *This is going to make me sick again.* Verbal abuse wears down my walls and I tend to fire it right back.

That is the pattern that occurs in unhealthy relationships without boundaries. We start acting in ways we don't want to and being people we don't want to be. That is one of the ways you can tell a healthy relationship from an unhealthy relationship.

I have realized that I can create my own happiness and security. I don't need other people to provide it. That was once a scary idea to me, but after looking into my habits and becoming more aware of my behavior, I decided it was actually not scary at all, but empowering.

Joey, Camry, and Sammy all had something in common and it wasn't their ages or their drinking or their inconsistencies. It was their emotional unavailability, something I'd experienced long before I knew what it was called. It is also something that took me a long time to name, and it was the catalyst for my relationship with my parents being so difficult as an adolescent. When I was younger, I felt they weren't always there for me emotionally. Even as a little girl I felt the despair of poverty in our home. There were many nights I cried as they locked themselves away in their bedrooms. Loreal would be asleep and I would be up and I felt very sad because I knew they were struggling. As a child I so wanted my mother to open up to me because I felt that I could love all her sadness away—kids, right. 🧓

As I grew, my mother became a great help with my new career, but she still didn't know how to be present with me. She and my father could be very distant. I felt they didn't understand me, and their emotional unavailability led to conflicts that felt like a violation of my personal identity. I felt like a prisoner in our home.

Now I know my parents did their best. I understand that they were stressed out and the truth is this is my account of my own life, theirs is probably different because everything has a reason, even if you don't understand it. Just like me, they were trying to learn and process some crazy life changes after we moved from our little town in Illinois to a new life in "Hollywood."

The entertainment industry and the whole Hollywood environment are so different from a Midwest life. It is not easy for people outside of it to adjust. And the industry wreaks havoc on even the strongest families—you can't imagine the number of horror stories we heard about how the industry broke families apart during the course of us living here.

But I realized that just like Sammy, I was in defensive mode too. I was just unable to see mine because I'm me. I had to step back before I could assess my feelings accurately. I couldn't name my emotional availability, therefore I couldn't see it in anyone else. And then once I saw it in other people, I was more interested in

pointing it out in them than in myself. I could have continued to ignore it, but my relationship with Sammy showed me that I needed to look inside to find the answers that explained why I was the way I was. Why didn't I choose loving people in my life? Why was it such a challenge to be vulnerable?

⇒ FEELING WORTHY OF LOVE IS ⇐
THE FIRST STEP TO FINDING IT

I have learned that you have to feel worthy of love before you can attract people who are good for you. That means being secure with who you are. You don't have to be perfect, of course. It's just that when you try to be your best, you attract people who want the best for you.

Another lesson I'm learning is that the depth of the excitement in your relationship early on has no impact over whether or not your current lover is the right person for you to commit to long-term. Another biggie—remembering that I can't change anyone but myself.

Learning to practice the art of acceptance in my love life has been really worth it, and I don't mean accepting unacceptable behavior from a partner. No one should accept abuse in any form. But I do mean accepting the fact that people choose to be who they want to be and no matter what you think, no one changes unless THEY want to.

Self-love isn't about being narcissistic or conceited. It's about caring enough to do your best for YOU. Self-love gives you peace and a feeling of wholeness that nothing else in the world can bring because it's YOU showing up for YOU. #YAYYOU!

Sometimes when I feel my self-love isn't where it should be, I will just close my eyes and take deep breaths while I pay attention

I Don't Belong to You

to my heartbeat and what I feel in my body. When I do this, I can feel the knowingness of me in comparison to the world. I quickly realize it's not that deep and that I can do this.

➤ SELF-KNOWLEDGE LEADS TO SELF-LOVE ⬅

Self-love comes with self-knowledge, and keeping a journal can really help you understand the influences and experiences that make you who you are. For years I wrote in journals. I started at twelve and stopped at seventeen and started typing them up on my computer and phone notes. I asked Joey to read one of my journals when I was trying to express to him my hidden anger. He never wanted to read them.

I would think to read them over myself, but I just wouldn't. Then for some reason, I finally decided to look through the pages of my journal, and I found my own clear-cut account of when and how the patterns that had caused me so much trouble were created. In those pages I realized through many childhood experiences WHY vulnerability was such a no-no. To be vulnerable in my home as a kid meant running the risk of getting those sensitive moments thrown back in my face, or worse, it meant being wholeheartedly open in a home with emotionally unavailable parents. So of course being vulnerable was the last thing I wanted to make it easy for me to be.

These behavior patterns may have been useful to help me survive my situations in the past, but things had changed and they were only causing me to repeat the same heartache just because I had gotten used to it, and it's really that simple, kids. We keep doing shit simply because we are used to it, that's why present-based practices are so important because they stop you from staying in the past and becoming a reactionary human.

Lauren Palmer

The truth was, I wasn't at home anymore. I had created better and healthier habits for myself and I was in the process of learning how to create healthy boundaries with the people in my life.

These things made it possible for me to see the behavior patterns that were hurting me, but I know now and I knew then that it would take consistent effort to completely remove these patterns. I needed to be patient with myself because it took more than a second for the habits to form and it would take more than a second for them to disappear.

I'm now more aware and I am able to see and understand that NO, that is not me. That's not ME, those were behavior patterns. We are not in control of the things that influence us when we are children. We can't judge ourselves on our ignorance. Once we know, we can only try our best to make the best decisions that propel us forward.

Practices like yoga and meditation, as well as therapy and prayer, have helped me realize I have to be a full glass before I can make it overflow with love for someone else. My self-discovery journey has become the ultimate love story and it's between me and myself (and God is the divine dance that connects us to everything else). I am learning to forgive those who have hurt me and understand why I have hurt others and myself.

In turn, it has made me a more patient and creative person. Even though some things were difficult, I don't regret the knowledge and the self-confidence I've gained from moving forward through all of that. Things hurt and people can be mean, but at the end of the day the experience you gain from any situation is invaluable to your life as a whole.

Life is an experience and it is YOUR experience. You come in alone and you go out alone. Though we do have one another and

I Don't Belong to You

are meant to explore all that we can within that, our journey is still OUR journey. We have to always remember that and not get so afraid to face it. We can't get to the point where we let our fear compel us to abuse the people or things around us.

I believe our relationships to one another are meant to teach us about *us*. To live life and all its woes and still understand that the point is to learn how to love and BE loved. Happiness comes when we know who we are and trust in our own abilities to create the lives we want. To have healthy relationships, I've learned that I have to know myself and accept and love myself before I can know how to accept and love others. I'm never knowing, only learning, and I accept that with joy.

Lauren Palmer

Hold the Phone!

ON USING TECHNOLOGY WISELY

> The human spirit must prevail over technology.
> —Albert Einstein

I remember the first time I was introduced to the Internet. My family and I were living in Robbins, Illinois. My mother has always been into communication devices. She was always on the phone when I was growing up, and when she heard about AOL dial-up, she found a way to get a computer so she could go online.

I believe she definitely was the first in her own family to even ever have a computer! My mom set up her email and started to experience the world of people through the Internet. She would use it to connect with other musicians and writers all over the world.

When my mother let my sister and I use it, we would always be on Disney.com, hahaha! I had so much fun playing the games on the site, it was a cool pastime. We'd had the computer about a year or so when my sister discovered the truly amazing and real point of the Internet. One day after watching an episode of Queen Latifah's talk show (the first one 😊) she saw a commercial about a website similar to ancestry.com, where you could find family members you had lost touch with or even those you'd never met.

Anyhow, my grandmother had three husbands, including my grandfather, whom she was with until he passed. Most of her children (seven altogether) shared a father, but my auntie Mattie shared a father with no one. This sometimes left her feeling somewhat separate from the rest of her immediate family.

Still, Auntie Mattie was one of the most successful of her siblings. She was a registered nurse (retired now) and made very good money. Auntie Mattie had her own place and was often known to have all the nieces and nephews over for pizza and movies!! She was very cool and still is.

When my sister found that website, she thought to search around for Auntie Mattie's father. We had only heard about her father referred to as some sort of mythical character. My grandmother left him in Memphis, Tenn., before coming to Chicago, and he was never heard from again. Loreal didn't think much when searching, just a pastime, but before we had known it, she'd found him!!

We were on the Detroit news with Auntie Mattie when she and her father had their first reunion. My mother couldn't believe it. We immediately drove down and the news got word somehow and came to cover the story and everything! My auntie Mattie was so happy, and that was a moment we have never forgotten.

When I moved to California, the last thing ony mind was the Internet. By the time my parents got me a laptop I was around the age of twelve. All I wanted to do was play Sims. Remember that? #THROWBACKTHURSDAY‼ 😂

I didn't have many friends because California is so spread out and it was difficult to drive to see everyone, especially since my

Lauren Palmer

family was new to the area and not in tune with the freeways. (That's really important in California, as crazy as it sounds.) So we often just stayed in the house.

⇥ CONNECTING ONLINE ⇤

I loved my family, but I really wanted to find ways to connect to other people! One of the only families we ever hung around with were the Pages. We met when I entered the *American Juniors* talent competition. 🎤 During the competition I met a little girl named Taylor Parks and her mother, Theresa Page, who was on the show too. Her family consisted of her mother, Theresa (hilarious, like Mother Teresa the nun, hahaha #GETIT); her stepdad, Damon; and little sister, Nia. I loved that family, and Taylor is one of my best friends 'til this day. 👯

I was always homeschooled once I moved to California because I worked out of town so much, but Taylor actually attended school for a short while when we were around twelve or so, and she kind of was my source to the real world.

This brings us to the Myspace era. 👥 I will never forget when she showed it to me. OH MY LORD MY MIND WAS BLOWN. #MINDBLOWN! Myspace was the shit maaaan! Hahaha, it was the one place that serviced your needs to connect with other people outside of your current reality.

I so badly wanted a profile, but as you may remember, there was that age limit. Taylor lied on hers 😄, but I was such a Goody Two-shoes back then. I was too scared to lie to my parents, but I was also lonely.

When I first told them about Myspace accounts, they said I couldn't have one, so I eventually lied about my age like Taylor and used other people's photos so that I could enjoy speaking to

I Don't Belong to You

someone other than the people in my home. Yes, y'all, that's right, I was what we today call a catfish! I chose the picture of a girl named Candace Cotton, aka Candi Cotton. . . . Hahahahahahaha.

That lasted for about a year. Then, at the age of thirteen, I asked my mom if I could make a private Myspace account that wouldn't interfere with my career or our privacy. She said yes, and Myspace became my refuge and my go-to place for companionship and sharing all my thoughts. That is when my relationship with social media began. As I grew up, the world of social media exploded with so many online sites, and I wanted in on them all! I wrote in my journals to give my feelings room to roam, yet nothing is quite like getting an immediate response from someone on the other end.

From ages thirteen through seventeen, all my profiles were private. It was so funny when I was filming *True Jackson, VP,* my cast members would make fun of my pseudonyms on Facebook, haha! It wasn't until Twitter was born that I decided to share a little more with my fans. I actually caught my mom clapping back on a fan from my "brand" page hard-core and I realized it was time to have just one page that I ran. 😂 I deleted my private account and began to just use my public account.

At first, using a public account was boring and weird because it was kind of the same as having a private one, lol. The only thing different was the followers, and the fact that I was accepting the idea of being a "celebrity." Twitter made me face my popularity, which for years was a part of me I pretended didn't exist. I did that for many reasons, I think. Partly because fame was never the drive, and partly because I didn't want to be put on a pedestal. I wanted people to see me as a regular person who'd worked hard to achieve her dreams.

Lauren Palmer

But like anyone who puts themselves out on front street, you must be willing to accept the people who love you and embrace them, while at the same time doing your best to ignore those who try to tear you down. I quickly discovered the "downside" of posting videos and selfies on Snapchat, Facebook, and other sites.

Being a public figure opens the door to all kinds of comments and criticisms that I expect on some level. As I've said, I like showing my fans the real me, but I've learned to keep some of the most personal things in my life private.

When I started dating an older guy back while on my television show *True Jackson, VP*, I wanted to share the news with the world—not with my family, but with the world. I was so happy in the beginning of my great love affair that I wanted my Facebook page to say "in a relationship." I wanted to show every photo of us together and post daily about the adventure that was our life together.

That's exactly what every other girl my age was doing or wanted to do too. But I knew a super public relationship was not for me. I wanted to keep people from thinking that my relationships were things they could also have an opinion about.

My work is out there in the media and it's understandable for some to critique or analyze that, but my personal life and relationships are not things I want open for public debate. Now, the fact that I was under eighteen and he was over eighteen helped shape my decision, but that wasn't what mattered most to me at that time.

In the end, my relationship fell apart despite my doing my best to shield it from judgment and naysayers. Still, I don't regret the protection I gave it because it's so easy to get distracted by the voices of friends and strangers when you're still trying to find your way in life or in love. I didn't want the opinions of others, whether friends or strangers, affecting how I felt about him or myself. That's the cool thing: Sometimes you don't have to share everything that's going on in your life. Sometimes you can keep your personal journey personal until you have it more figured out.

The thing about social media is that sometimes sharing can get addictive. It is almost like a drug that can take over your life. That addiction leads you to post, and post more at every turn, not realizing you have stopped living and instead have missed every moment stolen by the click of the camera. Pictures, personal details, and other private matters start to leak out, and over the course of more posts, you start telling more and more and more, until suddenly you're sharing every detail of your life.

Now, sharing can be a good thing, but it becomes a bit trickier when you are talking to the masses of people on the Internet— some of whom you know and some, not so much. After I hit sixteen and seventeen, my depression became unbearable. I had felt really lonely for a long time and it was hitting me hard, and I could not talk to my parents.

I started having a lot of negative thoughts. Even though in pictures you probably saw me smiling and appearing to be happy, there were times when I very much wanted to fall out of existence. 😩

At first, I wrote out my negative thoughts in my journal constantly, but eventually I wanted the world to hear me. I knew I couldn't scream out publicly without people responding. God is so amazing. When you need help, He reveals it in unique ways and through unique characters, but you have to be paying attention. At this time, I had a really good relationship with my makeup artist and hairstylist, Autumn and Jamika. I was grateful because I needed someone to talk to around this period of my life. My parents and I weren't relating very well back then.

⇒ USING THE INTERNET ⇐
TO SEEK KNOWLEDGE

Autumn would often share things with me, words, phrases, and quotations from important people. I would go home and look them up online. During this same time, I was often exposed to different lifestyles and ideas while working on the set. I started to explore those new things online too!

Now, I didn't believe everything I read, lol, but certain things I found on the Internet piqued my interest and I studied them in depth. I researched and double-checked things I'd seen before, forming my own opinions on the subjects. One of my favorite sites for quotations and gaining a different perspective was thinkexist.com. I looked up words and read the thematic quotes almost every day. The quotations were about all the different things I felt but didn't know how to express.

Then one day I thought to express my need to cry out subliminally—and kind of cowardly, lol—by posting quotes that reflected my pain on Twitter! By using the quotes from other people, I thought it wouldn't seem like I was trying to be a victim. Instead, I hoped people would think I was just sharing interesting quotations and thoughts.

When I tweeted the quotes that were meaningful to me, I got many responses and comments saying others felt the same way. Many of them would retweet and respond. Then we would debate and talk about those feelings.

It was sometimes uncomfortable, but mostly nice. It fed my

I Don't Belong to You

We're too busy documenting our lives to enjoy it.

need to connect and also gave me a sense of family. I know that sounds weird, but it gave me hope to know that other people—besides the mostly deceased men and women I was quoting—felt the same way I did. It gave me a sense that God didn't put me here in this world alone.

This experience inspired the concept for my talk show, *Just Keke.* ☺ The show covered topics of interest for my generation and served as a safe place where people could share their thoughts and feelings without fear of criticism or rejection. Before I knew it, I had a digital following.

⇒ THE GOOD AND BAD OF SOCIAL MEDIA ⇐

Sharing myself with these people became a very big part of my life. I had always had fun making videos online and being creative with my Myspace page and posting cool photos. But when Facebook, Twitter, and Instagram came along, it was different. With Instagram I could really show people my life and how it looked. On Twitter I could show them my thoughts, how my brain worked, and how I processed things. Social media was starting to grow at such a fast pace. I'm still not sure if anybody was ready for it.

Back then I became totally obsessed with social media and everything to do with it. I was always posting and expressing ideas or speaking out on topics on Twitter. It was my life, and up until this one time, I had never been severely ridiculed about much on social media.

But then I took a hit in the Twitterverse. They killed me on Twitter. No, seriously, they started tweeting that I was dead, even using the CNN logo to make it look official. I decided it wasn't personal, they were killing everyone that year. It was some weird

I Don't Belong to You

fad for a second because people were realizing they had the power to make anything they wanted trend if they hashtagged it enough times. 😂 😂 😂 😂 🙄

Anywaysssss, I decided to speak out about what was happening in Ferguson, Missouri, after Michael Brown was shot in August of 2014. The people were rioting and burning up all of the community's resources. I wanted to be there with them, but also let them know that the way some people were dealing with what happened wasn't in their best interest.

I wanted them to know that I understood, but the burning up of their own town and expecting the very same people who were oppressing them to hurry back and rebuild everything was just not realistic. But in their defense, a lot of the residents in Ferguson felt as if it was outsiders doing most of the rioting and causing trouble. My grandma Mildred told me that when Martin Luther King was assassinated there was rioting in almost all of the major cities, which left devastation in the black communities. To this day some of those neighborhoods have not been rebuilt.

As someone who grew up in a black suburb of Chicago, I understand that lower-income communities in America are supported just enough to keep them in poverty. I knew they were hurting because I was too, I just didn't want them to go through any more trouble, they had already gone through enough. I didn't want them to lose their town in the process! 💔

Not everyone agreed when I posted those thoughts about Ferguson on social media. Some felt I was too young to have an opinion on the situation at hand anyway. I was so heartbroken that the community I had turned to and been supported by was all of a sudden against me. 😭 🤢 It was very difficult for me to draw the line between my truth and the ignorance and judgment.

Lauren Palmer

Everything became so personal and I couldn't understand why. I was twenty, I had just broken up with Joey the year before. Camry and I just had whatever we had, and I wasn't facing a lot of the things that were bothering me. I was either trying to get into a relationship or into my work—anything but being home and feeling alone and dealing with the pain.

I knew there was work I had to do on myself. I realized that social media had become a major distraction. I was starting to abuse it and I didn't know it until I realized I cared way too much. It took a year and Broadway to get me to really take a step back before returning to the Internet and using it in a healthy way.

I've had it all, from people bashing my hairstyle, my acne scars, my singing voice, my acting skills, I could go on and on and on. I either laugh at myself or make it a game and see how well I can flip a negative into a positive. There was one instance recently where a mean-spirited comment caught my attention.

I posted a selfie where I was barefaced talking about my new tan lines. I had been at the beach, and I thought nothing of showing the real me to all of my fans and friends because I had done it several times before, and I like for people to see the real me. I stopped caring a long time ago if people were offended by my acne. It's something that I had to live with. I had to stop expecting other people to accept me, and I had to accept me. My fearlessness in sharing my imperfections is motivated by me wanting others who have gone through what I go through to have a moment of reprieve. It happens. We aren't perfect. So yes, I want them sometimes to see my acne scars and bad hair days because I want them to know that we all have them!

A blog called MTO took a screenshot and tried to create their own story, and the haters/cousins came out to play, let me tell you, hahahaha!!!!! The trolls called me "unattractive" and referred to me

I Don't Belong to You

as a "drug addict" and any number of other insulting and degrading names they could throw in there. To make matters worse, it was mostly young black men posting ugly comments. 💔

⇉ TROLLS IN THE TWITTERVERSE ⇇

I was perfectly happy to ignore the post until I saw the concerned responses from my female fans who were worried I'd taken the lowbrow attacks to heart. That is where I drew the line. I thought to myself how can I make this an empowering moment for all of us women?

After a few days, I began to think harder about the post's responses and even more about the young women (and some men) who seemed hurt by the poisonous arrows meant for me. Then it hit me! Those women (and some men) were facing the same mean-spirited trolls who had come after me every day of their own lives.

I really felt for them then, because some people are so hurt that the only way they can feel good about themselves is by insulting and putting other people down in the same fashion. #HURT PEOPLEHURTPEOPLE. I ended up making a post not about me but about embracing what's natural instead of hating what isn't perfect. It became #NOMAKEUPCHALLENGE and many girls tweeted me their photos just as I tweeted mine. It was a special moment. 🌷

Also, to the young men of color out there on social media who find it all too easy to attack women of color, I have a question: Do you understand what self-hate is? Take a moment to look it up so you can fully appreciate what it says about you when you put down someone of your own race or ethnic background, or, honestly, just another human.

Lauren Palmer

I can walk away from the painful things people carelessly post about me, because I live in a larger-than-life world of entertainment where you come to understand it isn't personal. But I didn't always, so I know there are many young people around the world who don't realize they can walk away from hurtful words, and that hurts my heart. They have to go to school, go to work, or even be in their own neighborhoods with trolls who think it is okay to shell out harsh judgments toward others. I wish I had some magic words to help those young people feel better—or better yet, a magic word to make those trolls fall off the face of the earth.

I don't have those magic words, but what I can tell you is to always keep your head up, respond with love to those who attack you online (or in person), and speak to your family, counselor, or a church group if it becomes too much to handle. Find ways to make yourself feel loved by YOU, do things for yourself, and appreciate those who appreciate you. You are loved and valued in this world.

Please understand that God created you in His own image, which means you are uniquely beautiful and divine. Don't let the ignorance of others make you think otherwise. What they are saying is about them, not about you.

I DO have a word for anyone who thinks it's okay to attack those around you simply because you have fallen asleep at the wheel. Think hard about why you're saying what you're saying before posting anything. The next time you want to go after someone because of the way they look or because their opinions or religious background doesn't agree with yours, take a step back and look in the mirror and ask yourself what you would feel like if someone said those same things to you or your family. Or have they already? And lastly, what's your point?

I Don't Belong to You

With one swipe of our phones, tablets, or computers, we can instantly be transported into the lives of those we know, and with one swipe we can also temporarily or permanently ruin someone else's life with our cutting words.

⇀ HIT PAUSE BEFORE YOU HIT SEND ↽

The same is true of reactive responses to your friends and those you love. This is a hard one for me, y'all! Sometimes you just want to send a big response right away, but once you send it, you can't take the words back. So I try to really understand what I truly feel first before communicating it to the other person. Sometimes I text myself. I know that sounds insane but it honestly works, lol! I will have a text conversation with myself like this:

Keke, what are you feeling right now?

> I'm feeling mad!

Why are you feeling mad? And are you really "feeling" mad or is that just your judgment of the situation?

> I actually FEEL anxious. I have anxiety about the situation.

Why do you feel anxiety?

> Because I am not in control.

Lauren Palmer

What is causing you to feel that
way?

> Well I really don't like
> when my friend texts and
> drives with me in the car.

Well what are you going to do
about that?

> I'm going to talk to my
> friend about how it makes
> me feel when someone
> texts and drives when I am
> in the car.

Texting myself helps me take a beat to figure out what I am really trying to say before I jump into accusations and/or reaction mode.

I think people should have privacy on their phones. We should be able to send whoever we want whatever we want privately. But the truth is that some things you can't take back. So whether it's a sexy photo I want to send to that boy I can't get outta my mind or a reactive text to my best friend, I try to play the movie forward and make sure that I won't look back and wish I didn't send it. There are people out there who won't respect your privacy.

The Internet and social media are still sooooooo new. They are like babies who haven't come close to reaching their potential. They are wonderful resources, but anything that is really great can be twisted into something terrible. I try not to hit send until I've considered the consequences. And we can do the same thing

I Don't Belong to You

when we are commenting on the photos or posts of our friends. I try to ask myself, Am I being cruel or kind? Funny or bitchy? Is it worth hurting someone or losing a friend over? Do I need to cut them some slack or say my piece?

We all have a very real need to welcome others into the good times in our lives, no matter where we are in our journey. If you are tempted to criticize, just remember we are all just trying to stay connected in this crazy, busy world.

⇒ KEEPING IT REAL ⇐

I reached a point where I got imbalanced with social media. I was allowing the Internet to become a substitute for real-life connection. The insecurities in my life and lacking esteem in other areas created an unhealthy sensitivity to the things people said to me and about me online. For a while, I felt pressure because critics online compared me unfavorably to my peers. They made it seem like we were in competition with each other, or that I had to be doing certain things to be perceived as successful or happy.

I got a bunch of piercings as a way of expressing myself, my creativity, and just evolving in general. People told me I was going crazy and not being myself. They said I was trying too hard. In reality I was just discovering who I actually was outside of the characters I portrayed as an actress. Outside of my "counterparts," I am an individual, incomparable, and I was slowly becoming ready to live that truth!

I began expanding spiritually, posting that I was reading up on meditation. Some claimed I didn't believe in God. I experienced so much hate that it became all I could focus on. I was really tired of people commenting on my life.

Lauren Palmer

I deleted all of my earliest pictures, thinking I was silencing the haters and shutting them "out." But in reality I was only hurting the people I was trying to connect with (tha kidz) and those who really loved me. Now I understand that it was my choice to let the negative comments speak louder than my inner peace—it was my past heartache and hurt that allowed those words to pierce through.

It was my subconscious calling out and trying to tell me there were some things I needed to focus on. That inner voice was telling me that I would not be able to see clearly and use my resources the right way until I worked on myself.

I knew the Internet could be a gift, but at that point it was more of a curse because of my perspective. I thought to myself that the only way I was going to be able to use social media to its true potential was if I stopped personalizing and removed my ego completely. #YOUSAIDWHATNOW!

YIKES. ●● I knew this was a major hurdle to jump over in my life, like fighting Bowser on Super Mario Bros., I had to beat this level! I came to hate that I cared so much about what was said about me on social media. Now, I think caring is important, but it's useless to care about what others think about your individuality. It's not the same as caring when you miss someone or hurt someone's feelings or want to make sure someone's okay, ya know? In my opinion at least. ♥

⇒ OFF THE GRID ⇐

Thankfully, my demanding role on Broadway provided the perfect opportunity to get off the grid without leaving me feeling like I was running away. My drive in my career gave me the push I needed because the truth was I had to focus on this role because it was so demanding physically and mentally. I also needed space to get my mind right. Worrying about being online was not helpful. I was giving too much of myself and needed to find balance again. It was really hard, but I felt that there was more to the picture and I was missing out by being all in my phone. #PUT THATPHONEDOWN. 🔼 📱 👉

For the first month on Broadway I wasn't using my phone because I was so busy. They had a vocal coach train me for my training period, but I wanted to continue with him once a week. I didn't want to fuck up and disappoint anyone. Whenever I get in that mind frame I put myself on a strict regimen that ensures perfection. 😌

My preparations and hard work on Broadway taught me many things that were useful when it came to using social media too. Self-control was a big part of it. I learned about controlling feelings of anxiety from my vocal coach, Bruce Kolb. I love him.

He is amazing, with his cute little belly, glasses, and a bald head! 🖤 Bruce was very stern but also sweet and fun. I would talk to Bruce about many things, often describing how I felt, and he mentioned something to me that a makeup artist named Sonia said to me before. She was very spiritual and intuitive. Sonia talked to me about learning to relax through breathing techniques.

Bruce explained that it worked both ways. If I didn't breathe correctly while performing, it would make me feel anxious and unable to connect the emotion to the vocal performance. He taught me that breath control can relieve me of anxiety and also make way for the spirit to shine through, which is what gives any song life. #SPIRIT. Bruce really helped connect the dots in a more technical way. He echoed Sonia's sentiments and connected them not only to life but also to music.

Bruce explained that we have to allow ourselves to experience

Lauren Palmer

life in the moment. It's about exploring the world around us rather than rushing around all the time. He said if I didn't do that I would miss out on life and wear myself out physically. He advised me to stay off my phone and social media so I could enjoy more of life.

I took his advice. I kept my phone down and tried to experience more of each moment and each day as it happened. I actually went out in New York with the little time off I was given. I walked around the city, enjoying the sights, and went to movies with my mom. She and I spent a lot of time together and it was good to get to know her as an adult.

Yep, it can be a little scary when you make the decision to take a break, but I looked at it like this: Taking a break gave me the time to make the people and opportunities in my life a priority, which is no small deal. Also remember, a tech break doesn't mean stopping cold turkey. It could mean simply not posting or reading other's posts until you've showered and had breakfast in the morning. Imagine enjoying a meal without the tech invasion, which then gives you the opportunity to be mindful, deliberate about what you eat, and to be present in the moment before you start the day.

We all need moments to simply rest our minds. You can take the time to doodle, think, create, exercise, and get clear. Every day, people put much more effort into taking time to check on social media than they do checking in with themselves, and that's when it's unhealthy. This allows past hurts, fears, or complacency to keep you on the same monotonous page in life, as you scroll through your never-ending newsfeed.

⇥ FINDING A BALANCE ⇤

My twenty-first birthday was August 26, 2014, and with that big step into young adulthood, I began to feel more mature and confident as an actress and as a person. By the time I finished performing in *Cinderella* in early January 2015, my feelings toward social media changed. Through prayer, meditation, and time off my phone, I was able to see a little clearer. There was still work to do, of course, but I felt the change and I shared it with my followers my last night onstage. 😲

Shortly after my Broadway run finished, I was cast on the new television series *Scream Queens*. I was so excited as I prepared for the pilot. I really wanted to be good for it, so I knew I had to remain focused and in tune. I went on a meditation retreat before we began filming for the first season. I also had my first experience with Reiki massage, and boy was it an experience. It was not gentle. Reiki begins like a light beating and gradually becomes more like a mugging.

There is a reason for the roughing up. The theory behind Reiki is that there is energy blockage in the body caused by a memory or a heartache or something in general you are holding on to that you don't need to. So the point is to work it out.

My Reiki massage was a very spiritual experience and it did call to mind certain hurtful things that I had forgotten. I was able to cry and let them go in that moment.

It was a beautiful experience and I was happy to have my feelings validated. While working on that first season of *Scream Queens* I also meditated, read into more spirituality and self-help books, and ate well. As a result, I had less anxiety than ever before. It also helped that my phone and social media were not playing such an important role in my life.

I wasn't checking my phone or texting all day every day. With much practice and concentration, lol, I spent more time talking to the people around me. I realized that I'd missed out on a lot of great experiences because I had been all into social media on my phone.

I Don't Belong to You

I'd finally begun to understand the point of life BALANCE. My creativity vault was expanding because of it. For the whole first year of *Scream Queens*, my relationship with social media went through a transition. I became more compassionate and forgiving of the hurtful or thoughtless things said about me.

I also became more of my own person. I took responsibility for my own happiness instead of expecting others to provide it. By the time I finished the show's first season, I had an ex-boyfriend and an ex–best friend, and I was back in counseling. I was doing even MORE self-work, as well as working on my spiritual side.

I decided to double up on self-discipline, forcing myself to face my issues head-on instead of creating situations that forced others to confront me with them. I didn't give a damn at that point what anyone had to say. I was just so happy to be getting help and realizing that it was accessible to me. 🦶 I was so happy to be doing everything to help myself while gaining a better understanding of what it meant to love myself.

⇒ LOOKING BEYOND THE HIGHLIGHTS ⇐

As my career has grown over the years, so has my need to use social media to reach the kids. But that reality doesn't mean I've strayed that far away from my basic decision to only post certain things about my life.

Think about it: Nothing is exactly what it seems, even on Instagram. It's pretty much all an illusion, even if you consider celebrities. The flawlessly beautiful, shamelessly rich, and famous people whom we follow aren't telling their followers the entire story of their lives day in and day out. They are showing us the highlight reel—the best of the best of their days, and a lot of us are buying directly into that while trying our best to follow in their

Lauren Palmer

footsteps. For the majority of us that's a winless battle that takes a toll on our self-esteem in the long run. And even if you can "keep up," how exhausting. #NOTHANKS.

Not only is it important to me to keep certain aspects of my life close to the vest, it's also really important to take time to think about what I'm saying and how it might impact someone else. I took action over my social media life by deciding where I'd draw the line when it came to talking about the people and places that meant the most to me. Just as I have boundaries with people in relationships, I have boundaries with social media that I won't cross and won't let anyone else cross when it comes to my online existence.

Still unsure? Maybe you need a bit more clarity to redefine your social media identity, and the only real way to get that is by taking a step back from tech devices while appreciating the many other ways you can stay connected in the world. I am as guilty as everyone else on some scale of creating a highly filtered presence on social media. I get it. I really do. But I try to remember not to compare.

When I see the posts and photographs of others, I remind myself not to compare my life to theirs because their journey is fit for them, as mine is for me. When you see your favorite celeb living a life full of star-studded parties, award shows, and around-the-world trips, also remember that isn't their entire life story. They are offering a highly edited version of their lives, one limited to just those aspects they want to share.

I remind myself that everyone experiences pain and hardships, no matter how rich or famous, and most would rather not broadcast that to the world. We can't get sucked into the vortex of "their lives are so much cooler than mine."

Cutting back on my own posts and social media helped me

realize this. I'd written a song, "I Don't Belong to You," shortly after I filmed the pilot episode for *Scream Queens*. Others had convinced me to hold off on releasing it, but after cutting back on social media, I gained courage and made positive changes. I became better at expressing myself. I was relentless in communicating to my label the importance of letting me release this song.

When I released "I Don't Belong to You" in October 2015, my relationship with social media had reached an even better balance. I was really starting to understand myself. I found so much freedom in that. I was happy to be myself in each moment.

FILTERING OUT NEGATIVITY, FOCUSING ON PURPOSE

I gained such compassion for and patience with myself. Through that, I became much more creative and productive. I wasn't bothered by negative comments. I took encouragement from both the negative and positive. I delighted in others enjoying the performance and when they hated it, I loved that it moved them period. How it moved them depended on the seat they saw the show from. #KNOWWHATIMSAYING?

I was filtering negativity from my thoughts, catering less to my ego and more to my purpose and the importance of why I do what I do. I'm not responsible for how people perceive things—that's their job. I'm only responsible for my intention—and my intention had become crystal clear.

My continued practices and my discipline put me in a position to be able to trust myself. I am not perfect. I still make mistakes always. But as Aristotle was summarized, "We are what we repeatedly do, excellence then, is not an act but a habit." That rings true to me.

Lauren Palmer

The quality of our lives is all about the habits we choose to keep and practice. Even when I fall off, there is muscle memory, and when I get imbalanced I know exactly what to do. As long as I am trying a little at a time I know I'm moving forward!

As the dark veil in my personal life started to lift, the personal work I did made the positive aspects of the Internet clearer. I focused only on productive ways to use the Internet. It all came from finding a better balance in my real life.

When we are balanced we are able to use things to our best advantage, and really that's the point I'm making. The Internet is such an amazing, magical tool in connecting us to all the things and people we had no access to before. That is powerful! In order to use it best, sometimes we need to take a step back and look at ourselves, making sure we are seeing clearly, through clean goggles.

Sometimes being able to use special gifts like social media means being responsible enough to put it to the side more often and appreciating other gifts that we may take for granted, like our bodies and nature—the grass, bees, food, water, and trees that allow us to breathe and thrive. We need them too to remain BALANCED. Without balance or making a conscious effort to be balanced we are not giving 100% of ourselves.

Being grateful for life and all we have in this world gives us a greater appreciation also for the online world that connects us to other humans. It reminds us why it is so important to treat each other with respect—online and off.

🙏 #NAMASTE. #LOVEISTHEGAG.

I Don't Belong to You

○ ○ ○ ○ ○ ○ ○ **9** ○ ○ ○ ○ ○ ⟨ ○

Heaven Is a Place Called Earth

ON SPIRITUALITY

Prayer is when you talk to God; meditation is when you listen to God.
—Diana Robinson

The first time I remember trying to conceptualize God was when I was about four or five years old. I was in the back room of my church, a church that I knew existed for as long as I knew *I* existed, lol!!

We had spoken about Jesus at home and I understood him somewhat, but I asked Sister Mary Kate, "How do I get to God? How could I get to God and get to Jesus? Could I look up in the sky?"

Before she could answer, I blew a kiss up in the air, hoping it would reach them in heaven.

I don't recall what Sister Mary Kate said or did next, but I do remember that for me it wasn't enough. For a long time, I felt that religion itself wasn't enough for me.

My father was raised Catholic and my mother was a Baptist. I grew up going to St. Peter Claver Mission Catholic church in my hometown. Our church was created because fifty years ago or so blacks were not allowed to worship at the bigger church, St. Benedict, in nearby Blue Island, Illinois. The black Catholics in the area signed a petition and the archdiocese gave them their own place of worship.

My father later became a church deacon, and my mom led the choir. My parents always had very strong religious beliefs, so not having a real relationship with God was pretty much out of the question. I'm happy they gave me the gift of faith and then allowed me to follow my own path on figuring out what it should or shouldn't mean.

Before my mom was the choir director of our church, Mrs. Mary Sabluski led the choir. She was in charge when I first joined. She was a tiny lady with glasses and a curly 'fro. She was Polish and she was a huge part of what made that church so special.

Mrs. Sabluski cared a lot about her faith and really used the music to translate that. The Catholic Church in general tends to be very rigid. Mrs. Sabluski wasn't that way. She realized that the standard Catholic choir songs were boring us out of our minds. 😩 So she recommended we all go home and watch the movie *Sister Act 2: Back in the Habit*, lol.

Literally one night during choir rehearsal that was exactly what she did. She had us all go to our nearest Blockbuster, rent the movie, and watch the way they flipped the songs to see if we enjoyed it that way better! Most traditional Catholic music is kind of slow. In the *Sister Act* movies, Whoopi Goldberg plays a nun who takes traditional church songs and has the choir sing them a little jazzier. 😎 Something you could move to. Needless to say, after we watched the movie, we enjoyed singing that way! Haha! 😊

Lauren Palmer

Mrs. Sabluski took us to church in a way that we could relate to, enjoy, and experience on a deeper level. When we sang like Whoopi's choir, we could feel the music in our bones and our hearts. We knew that we were tapped into a power that was bigger than ourselves because we lost ourselves in it.

Later in life, I realized that our choir director was teaching us a lesson that went beyond music and singing in church. She was showing us that there is joy and peace to be found in everything and every place in this world if you are open to looking for it.

I'm much more of a spiritual person than I'm a religious one, even if I did grow up in church singing every Sunday in the choir. As I have gotten older though, I've come to understand that religion is the telling of other people's stories on their journey of finding God.

I believe in personal growth and continual expansion. I know and believe that love is a fighting force in the universe and that God is pure love, and we are expressions of that love. For a long time, I felt that religion as practiced in the churches of my parents and grandmother weren't enough for me. I felt pressured to follow rules I didn't understand or relate to. The pressure to conform and accept their religion grew worse after my father became a deacon when I was about seven years old.

I also attended my grandma Davis's church. It was a much different experience, as I mentioned before, because it was so huge. In my home church almost everyone in the congregation knew one another. My grandma's Baptist church was huge and impersonal.

I spent most of my many hours in that church trying not to be bored out of my mind. When I was a little girl, I'd look for this one teenage girl (she could've been a tween, you know you can't tell when you're little; they're all "big" to you, lmfao) and make faces at her, trying to get her to laugh. LOL! I had fun just being a kid. I still do! I wish I knew that girl's name to see what she is up to. 🤭

Though I didn't always enjoy my grandmother's church because it seemed so serious, I loved what she taught me about spirituality, rituals, and practice. My grandma would sit me beside her bedside (even though she usually slept in her chair in the kitchen) and pray with me.

She taught me this prayer and we said it together every night.

"Lord now lay me down to sleep, I pray the Lord my soul to keep. If I should die before I wake, I pray the Lord my soul to take." 😇

Maybe the sentiment of trusting God to take care of me provided a sense of peace and security. It was being in church on Sundays with my family, going to Vacation Bible School, and praying with my grandma every night that deeply grounded me in my faith so much as a child that taking breaks from praying almost immediately made me feel empty and lost.

Prayer gave me something to hold on to as I began to find my way in the world. It gave me a comfort and a peace that extended beyond people, places, and material things, which is so important to have as we grow.

⤜ UNANSWERED QUESTIONS ⤛

I went to private school and they taught me about their faith in religious class, but even so I felt that God was so far away from that. I felt that He was there and had to be real, but the inflexible ways of the religious people at times made me feel disconnected

Lauren Palmer

and stifled. I felt as if I was just going through the motions. I felt there must be a way to know he was real for the believers. I thought there must be proof, right? That was a question I would ask myself for years.

I can accept not knowing everything about God and the way God works. I'm okay with doubting one day and then believing again the next. I doubt and then believe and then doubt again. I think if we are honest with ourselves, we know we all go through this in every facet of faith.

That's why I love the stories of Jesus, Buddha, and many of the other enlightened spiritual leaders who offer messages of love and hope. I honestly believe spirituality is something you feel in your heart and in your soul through your experience with humanity.

I think people often try to put God in some sort of box because it makes them feel safer and because that's where they put themselves. Growing and stretching as a person can be a scary thing because it means moving beyond what you know and exploring what you don't know on a consistent basis. It means accepting that you may know much less than you thought. 💀

Living fully means you can't always play it safe. I don't think we should put limits on what God can do, or on what we can do by his grace. I believe in my heart that we are all here to be loved and to spread love. Oh yeah, I also believe we can change spiritually over the course of our lives and that's okay too!

When I finished the seventh grade, my dad, now a deacon, started pressing me to take the required classes so I could receive the sacrament of confirmation, which is one of seven sacraments in the Catholic Church and supposedly gives us the gift of the Holy Spirit and strengthens our faith. My father truly wanted me to have that experience and while I did give it a lot of thought, I never committed to doing it.

I Don't Belong to You

I think somewhere inside of me getting confirmed meant committing to just one path for loving God. Even as a very young girl, I thought God doesn't belong to just one church or faith. He belongs to us all. He is everywhere and in everyone.

⇒ DIFFICULT TIMES AND PAINFUL MEMORIES ⇐

After our move to California, we weren't able to attend church the same as we had back home. I wasn't able to go to church regularly because of all my travel and my busy schedule, which also led to my falling out of the practice of praying every day. Our family experienced many changes in dynamics with our move and it often left me feeling like we had lost our sense of unity. I literally felt as if I couldn't connect to my siblings either. There was a dynamic that made us all unable to see clearly. I felt a lot of shame and guilt for the amount of money I made and attention I received.

At the same time I was growing and discovering new things about myself. One day when I was around twelve reading in my schoolbook, I came across a chapter about sexual abuse and the psychological effects it can have on a person. It triggered a moment for me from my childhood, one shortly after the incident with my cousin. It said that when people have been molested, especially at a young age, it is common they have shameful thoughts around sex thereafter.

The time after I was molested was very hard for me because my thoughts became immersed with sexual images and sexual concepts. What happened is that it created bad feelings and bad attachments around my sexual identity. For a long time, I suppressed thoughts around sex and felt shameful about the thoughts that would pop up. Around the age of fourteen, I finally stopped judging myself so much and accepted that, though my first experience was not a usual one, sexuality itself was a natural thing and it was okay to have sexual thoughts and that it was normal. I remembered that day I read that in my book. It was the day I reassessed my faith and I prayed my way out of the shame. Twelve-year-old Keke was having a revelation about seven-year-old Keke. It's like remembering something from the past one way and then receiving *knowledge* that allows you to process it in a healthier and more productive way. God and the Universe will present those opportunities in front of you and you will see them when you are paying attention! I know that sounds like a joke, but it's true. Whenever I look at my cousin to this day, I wonder if she has also carried shame around the event, and I hope she doesn't anymore. Or maybe she just wrote it off as two kids playing. That's what I feel makes life so paradoxical. Not everyone takes things the way you do, even if it happened to them too.

When I was around the age of seven, I would pray to God to remove my excessive desires to be sexual because I felt it became compulsive. I had become unfairly sexualized and it became all I thought about, which is a very human response I realized while reading my schoolbook. I guess during the time I felt the abrasive thoughts had subsided and when I moved to California my practice lacked, yet the baggage was still there.

That moment reminded me of the power of prayer. I realized as a twelve-year-old that when I was seven my practice of prayer and constant conversation with God helped me reclaim myself without all the sexual stuff clouding my head. This would be a reoccurring theme in my life: falling out of the practice of prayer and then regaining discipline and my sense of self once I had more consistency in that structure.

I relied on writing in my journals and praying to get me through. The journey has been excruciating at times, so I cut a lot

I Don't Belong to You

of it out of the story that is my life the moment I put it on the page, just because it was too hard to fully acknowledge! I prayed for God to send me a lifeline, and he did that periodically throughout my adolescence. Just when I would feel I was losing it, someone would enter my life and serve as a friend who I could talk to.

⇒ LOOKING FOR A LIFELINE ⇐

I'd met one of these lifeline people, a woman named Asha Kamali May, in 2004 or 2005 at a party after the NAACP Image Awards. She came up to me and told me congratulations on my nomination and that she was a dancer and choreographer. She gave me her contact info and told me to reach out if I ever needed anything. I thought she was beautiful and smart and I loved that she was willing to spend time with me.

There was a hole growing in my life because my relationship with my beautiful and very smart older sister, Loreal, started deteriorating after our move to California. I didn't think she stood up enough for me at home when I had conflicts with our parents, but of course, I wasn't thinking then that she was going through a difficult time herself. We literally uprooted our lives to move to California to pursue *my* dreams. When I went to film my first movie, Loreal and the twins stayed back a year while my mom and I went away and my dad stayed in LA to find work. That separation time itself was a lot. Loreal was only fourteen and trying to process all of that. She tended to withdraw when she was hurting. I was much more of an extrovert.

I felt this huge wedge building between us. Before I knew it, my sister and I barely knew each other. So I had this desire in my life for that kind of nurturing and it seemed like God was bringing

Asha to fill it. I could talk to her and share all the girly things that I so desperately needed to discuss.

Asha was a queen to me and still is. She graduated from Howard, was crowned Miss Howard University, and was a young adult in LA going for it! She choreographed my first music video, "All My Girlz," and she would dance with me often, one of the first professionals to nurture that gift in me. I was inspired by the fact that she took time out of her day to spend time with me. She taught me the value of putting time into mentoring other young people.

I could talk to her, even though it was difficult for me to open up about my home life because of shame. The little bits I did reveal to Asha were never judged. Instead, she related her story to me, showing me her scars. She was brave and that gave me strength unbeknownst to her (oh SHHHTT I'm getting teary writing this. Smh.). Her humanity gave me another reality option, life after pain and grief and family difficulties. She was and still is an inspiration to me, like a sister.

When I started *True Jackson, VP*, I felt that I had found two real-life angels who were like mothers to me. They were two more lifelines sent from above. I felt that my prayers of wanting a better relationship with my mom had finally been answered. I say that respectfully at a time when that part of my mom was not accessible in our relationship. She was focused on doing so much with my career out of love for me, but I needed affection and that was something she did not understand for a while because it was not what she received herself.

There were other times I had trusted people and shared with them the internal things I was working through, but they often judged me and my family. I ended up hearing later that they'd told someone something, which made me even more guarded than before.

I Don't Belong to You

I wanted to get into a better situation, not throw away and irrationally judge the last. I knew my situation wasn't the best at home, but these two women helped me to see the positives. They helped me to understand that happiness was my *choice*. They helped me teach myself to shift my perspective. The years I had with them during *True Jackson* were honestly God sent because those were my most depressed years.

Of course, after *True Jackson* went off the air and I was approaching eighteen, it was all about getting out of the house! Once I got out, all I could think about was the fact that I was out, not why I wanted to go. Slowly but surely I watched as I slipped into an uninspired pattern.

I felt that I wasn't being conscious in my actions and I kept feeling like I was trying to get out but didn't know how. This is when my relationship with Joey was seconds from ending. It literally started to feel like shackles on my feet, while my relationship with my family was deeply fractured.

I had nowhere to turn and my prayers to God, not often but sometimes, were usually vacant. I was completely disappointed and felt I had accepted that as just my life even though something deep was telling me that wasn't true.

⇒ GETTING OUT OF A RUT ⇐

How? How, I wondered, could I get out of this rut? I somehow stumbled on the word *codependency* one day. I said, "Hmm, does this apply to me? Am I in a codependent relationship?" I started NAMING the things in my life that had power over me and the things that gave me power over them.

That's how I see life: Once we name the things in the dark that we hide from and we are afraid to speak about, they no longer have power over us. Instead, we have power over them and we see beyond the illusions they play on us with fear and the idea that we in some way are not worthy of a happy life.

In disguise, my codependency had the power over me. Once I took off those stupid 👓 with the fake 👃 I was able to see that my relationship dynamic was a big part of why I felt so drained emotionally. I then was able to make a clear choice on how I chose to proceed once I realized my relationship was one of the problems.

⇒ GOD CAN'T BE INTELLECTUALIZED ⇐

My search for that *more* wasn't romantic, even though at times I got sidetracked by romance, haha (refer to chapter seven 😄). It has always been about me, just as it is always about you! Our life experience is our life experience and that was what I was finding out.

I remember while filming the pilot episode of *Scream Queens* that soon afterward, I had to do promo for *Brotherly Love*. I had been searching and searching, spiritually and metaphysically, for my inner strength and my connection to God and I just had hit the point of realizing that God can't be intellectualized. He can only be felt.

I so badly wanted to feel his truth because I didn't want to talk about what I didn't understand. I remember crying in my mother's arms, breaking down to her that I felt like a fraud—a fraud for believing in God because I was really starting to question Him and I was doing everything right.

Right!? Why was I still so lost?

My mother was calm and told me that God is something you feel, but it was okay if I could not feel him just yet and it was okay if I questioned Him because we all have and do at times. That was

I Don't Belong to You

the point of the journey and the point of faith. I realized that was the truth, and I would have to let go and accept it.

⇀ A NEW MASTER ↽

Another lifeline, Sonia, the Korean makeup artist I worked with, invited me to her home one day. She said we are all students and teachers to one another. She always said, "I will teach you all I know and can do and then introduce you to a new 'master.'" That is what she called it. I just associated that with a person being a master at their practice 'cause, uhh, I ain't looking for a master. 😳 •• 😔 #TOOSOON.

When I was at Sonia's house she taught me a few Korean flows of practice. The practice was all about getting into the movement. Pretty much I would spread my arms up to the top of my head and then to my heart. After, I would kneel and then do a version of child's pose, which would be me sitting on my feet with my hands reaching out in front of me. I would do this many, many times. Sonia told me you should do it really as many times as you can! However, it ain't as easy as it looks. Hahaha, it's a #PRACTICE.

After she showed me the flow, Sonia told me she was going to do some energy clearing in my body. It reminded me of *The Karate Kid*, Bruce Lee, and Jesus, hahaha, mainly because she was speaking about universal energy that we all have access to use to help us heal ourselves and others. It reminded me that Jesus prayed on the mountain with the disciples.

I always felt that Jesus' story wasn't meant for us to just buy into, but to acknowledge that we too are God's children just as he is. Jesus wanted us all to know that we all had a universal power, but so many of us felt unworthy and still feel unworthy because of our life story lines.

Lauren Palmer

We so quickly believe we are incapable, but we are not. It's similar to when the martial artist Bruce Lee accessed his universal power. Many suggest that is the power that allows you to heal yourself. It gave him such crazy strength. Being in tune with your spirit allows you to control your breath and use it as an engine as opposed to letting it control you in your humanity. It's using the intellect behind your thoughts, which you can only do by removing the need to please "self." That means ego, not the self that is your human body that needs your love.

Sonia had me lay down in her bed and she just told me to close my eyes. All I could feel was her waving her hands over my body. As she'd get to a spot she felt had what she was looking for, she would work through it. It felt kind of like a massage but different. Because she would touch a spot, rub her hands together, and hover over the section she was treating. I remember feeling slightly lighter on my feet afterward.

We walked downstairs to get something to drink because I was thirsty. I saw her pull some watermelon juice she made out of her fridge. I asked her what her diet was and she was similar to vegan but even more severe. Her food was very limited. Yet, she was so strong and vibrant. Was that why?

She told me the food that we eat plays a major part in how our brains work and when we eat the things that are no good for us it's easy for us to feel uneasy or not confident. It's simply because our senses are being dumbed down by our food, what we are seeing, and our lack of practices, if we even know any TO practice.

Sonia's whole teaching was that we are like earth—rocks/bones and water make us up, and more of us is water than bones a.k.a. rocks, just as it is with earth. She told me the importance of water intake and how it truly regulates our entire system as it serves as a cleaning agent/magic superglue.

Sonia put me in contact with many spiritual people, including a Native American man in Nevada named Ed. I've only spoken to him on the phone, but we talked a lot while I was performing on Broadway. Sonia believes he is just a spiritually advanced man, like a tribal "elder" from one of those cool movies. 🙂

During my Broadway show, I was getting over Camry, learning to not obsess over my phone, and beginning to start wobbling on my own two feet. I read inspirational things online and in some books, but I also would call Ed. He would encourage me, telling me I'd be all right and I was doing fine. He always told me to be gentle with myself and more supportive.

Ed encouraged me to have fun and not cage myself in but trust myself to know what's right. He reminded me that it was the simple things, like brushing my hair or giving myself a hug, that can build my sense of self. I found his words very useful.

I've had several spiritual advisors. They are like mountain guides who take you up to higher levels of spiritual experience and perception. #ASCENSION. The best and most authentic spiritual guides help you figure things out for yourself by sharing information and knowledge, showing you many paths rather than demanding that you follow just one.

After working on the pilot for *Scream Queens*, I returned home and met up with another spiritual teacher I met through Sonia. She had a small studio in Koreatown. I went in, and it was a little hard to understand the woman because her English was a little broken. I followed as much as I could and I honestly loved that the language barrier made us use other senses to understand each other. At first she put my hands on these electric things. She

Lauren Palmer

told me that she was taking a picture of my aura, getting a telling of my chakra balance.

Hmmm, I thought, *chakras?*

She showed my colors and explained to me a bit about how they get unbalanced and how I keep them balanced. I remember her telling me how much more creative you are able to be when you learn how to keep yourself balanced. That was huge for me to hear because that's what started this whole thing!

⤜ FINDING THE PATH TO HAPPINESS ⤛

I was feeling passionless and that just wasn't okay, but I was taking the right actions to access that freedom again—the freedom of being myself and being enlightened in my purpose while understanding how it connects to my gifts.

Shortly after my aura reading, Sonia's friend laid me down and I was prepared to go through something similar to what I had done at Sonia's house. It was just as I had suspected, and I enjoyed it just the same. I felt lighter and as I started to relax more I would go into a deep sleep, hahaha, which was apparently a good sign. 😊

She had suggested after many energy-clearing sessions that I try out this Sedona retreat and I immediately wanted to. I was feeling as if I was finally on the path to happiness and I really was willing to try anything that didn't make me hallucinate or that sounded like a cult, hahaha. 😄

I wanted to experience other ways of releasing emotions, since for so long I had hidden them. My parents, of course, were really worried and kinda persuaded me to take Jamie with me, lol. I gave in, but it was in that time I experienced Reiki, as I mentioned in the previous chapter. It was an experience! This damn lady had the strength of Muhammad Ali!! 😄😄😄😄 She beat on me lightly and then fiercely. 😫

She explained there can be energy blockage in the body because of bad memories or a heartache that you haven't let go of. Some even believe these energy blocks cause a buildup of excessive cells, which create the possibility of having a mutating cancer cell.

The idea is to work it out of the body and release it. It was a very spiritual experience and I did let go of a lot. It was a beautiful practice and I was happy to validate my own feelings. "Me" was feeling very loved and respected by me and pleased at all the new ways I was allowing my human body to find refuge.

During my trip to Sedona, they had me watch an amazing 2010 documentary movie called *I Am* by Tom Shadyac, the comedian and director of movies including *Ace Ventura: Pet Detective.* The documentary has its funny moments, but it is not a comedy. It shares his study of the nature of humanity and human connections. He was inspired to do this after recovering from injuries received in a serious bicycle accident. Without spoiling it for you, this inspirational film was all about our responsibility to each other. I thought it was amazing and really put the world in perspective for me.

After that, I really thought I had it figured out. I was preparing for my first season of *Scream Queens,* and I had decided after the Broadway show to move back in with my family to better our relationship. I even tried a transcendental meditation course with a man by the name of Light Watkins.

He taught me some ancient Indian practices on how to enter the transcended state of our minds, similar to that Johnny Depp movie, haha. This takes us deep into our unconscious and,

Lauren Palmer

through consistent practice, clears out all the years of gunk that have turned you into a less "pure" version of yourself.

⇒ THROUGH THE PAIN THERE ⇐
IS STRENGTH CREATED

All things were looking good at this point. At home I was even able to share with the twins, Lawrence and Lawrencia, a little bit of what I learned, and they were receptive to it. Then I met Sammy, and if you forgot just scroll back to chapter seven and remember. 😐

I was at the end of the season when most things fell apart but I pulled myself back up and in turn I found myself a new therapist, adding yet another practice that would help keep me balanced mind, body, and soul. All the while I was losing all the fucks there were to possibly give, because all that mattered to me was being well. 🙍

The only thing that was important to me was getting right with who I was so that I could see more clearly and start to recognize who I should and shouldn't have as a major part of my life. That's when the true benefits of self-work showed themselves in my music career. Approaching the end of my first season of *Scream Queens*, even with all the drama, all the work I'd done on myself gave me the courage to be able to present my song "I Don't Belong to You" to my fans.

Before then I was not ready to speak my truth and express that part of myself without asking for permission. I was still too closed off from who I was to be able to express the totality of who I was in that moment without being insecure and questioning my choice based off others. And that is the opposite of what being an artist is about! Every artist you have seen, I promise they faced

I Don't Belong to You

some shit in their lives, that's the only way you get to shine without guilt or worry for others. Through the pain there is a strength created and almost a love for others that makes you even more conscious of how important it is to be who YOU are in the world.

I was starting to realize how it not being about "me" played into the whole story of life. When you are given a platform it's important to share the truth. What truth? *Your* truth, how you got here, and what you're saying now that you're here. No, not everyone with a platform uses it that way, but those who do receive something more valuable than gold. They receive peace.

➤ LETTING GO OF EGO ➤

When you are being true to your heart, you are doing God's work. Even though I had my financial ups and downs, my career was still active, but why was I not at peace. Why? Because I wasn't being fearless and true to my heart, which in turn wasn't letting me do God's work, which in turn left me feeling purposeless.

That's the cycle we exist in when we choose to feed our egos. Our egos are the most ignorant parts of our humanity. Our egos are the human dysfunction. Our egos make us believe that we are more important than anything else on this planet. Our egos are our identification with our form, meaning we are attached to our humanity. Not realizing that humans die and that there is no way around it.

Trying to satisfy an ego that's always afraid because it never knows when it's gonna "go" is a living H-E-double-hockey-sticks. But many times in our society, especially the American society, we are encouraged to service the flesh. In turn that makes us afraid and when you are afraid you act compulsively, which is never the best response to life.

Lauren Palmer

We become very divisive people, which leads to the even bigger illusion that we are separate in this world, alone. Nothing else really does exist in this material world other than our unity. United we are one, but separate we are not using our full power. Yes, we have individual spirit, that's the unexplained, but UNITED we are the one big spirit. It's like "You are not a drop in the ocean, but the ocean in one drop." 😌

We aren't really here to make a name for ourselves; we are only here to be here for each other. That's why God put us here TOGETHER! To love and be loved. Not to have a bunch of money, not to have some cool cars 🤑, love. Sorry to break it to ya, but I promise that living by that is the only thing that has given me my moments of peace. 😎

⇥ EYES OPENED ⇤

After breaking up with Sammy my eyes became super open to my problems. It was becoming clear to me that my problems would find me no matter where I went because they were MY problems. Even if the person around me was good, I wouldn't see it because I was blinded!

Once I finished *Scream Queens'* first season my main focus became my music. I did some dating here and there but ultimately it was all about me focusing on keeping myself creatively open and learning to better myself. When I came back to California I decided I was ready to move back out of my parents' house and I ended up having my best friend move in my new place with me. I set up my yoga for two days a week, working out at least three times a week, eating a high-protein, low-carb diet (as I prepared for my movie role in *Pimp*), and speaking with my therapist once a week. I was feeling good, but there was more.

I Don't Belong to You

I'd been working on this book since my days on Broadway and it has probably been one of the most therapeutic things I've done in this period of my life. For so long when I was dating Joey I wanted him to read my journals. I would always ask him to read them because, like I said before, I guess I felt they could explain my disposition. He would *never* want to read them.

I forgot the details of what was in my journals, but I always remembered that they were special to me and explained where I'd been. I think subconsciously I knew what was there but had practiced pretending I didn't for so long that I'd forgotten what I was pretending about. 🫤

It's like I remembered being depressed but I hadn't validated all the reasons why. I guess it's how people clinically explain PTSD, it's like a disassociation. So even though the things in those journals happened to me, I had to separate from them mentally in a way in order to deal with life as "me," lol. If that make sense??

Well, during the month of April 2016, I decided to hang out with Sammy for the first time after we split. I told you how that ended in chapter seven, and I again thought I meant more to him than his drinking. Sammy wasn't really an asshole but his drinking made him one, and I couldn't understand why I still wanted to subject myself to that. Or how I didn't realize that that's what I was doing.

⤳ REVISITING THE PAST ⤶

Finally it had come to me. Something told me to go look at my journals. They had always been just a reach away but right then was the only time I felt the need to read them. I opened up my journal and immediately started laughing at so many funny childish things I had forgotten! I soon realized I was very overworked

and completely isolated out of my parents' fear of my celebrity, mainly my mom's.

My mom, as I've said before, has dealt with a lot of anxiety in her life. I even remember she had nightmares about me being attacked when we moved to California. She was afraid of what happened to other child stars before me. She did not want me to *end up like them*, so much so that I felt she isolated me like Rapunzel.

Then I got to a page that had tearstains on it, and as I started to read I felt as if I was hearing about a girl I used to know. I started to read my accounts of abuse I experienced in my home as an adolescent. That was not at all conscious in the giving or receiving end. "Forgive those, for they not know what they do."

Moving to California was traumatic for my entire family. My dad always drank. He had nine brothers who drank to celebrate birthdays, baptisms, funerals, and other family events. They came together and drank as a tradition. But when we moved to California there became levels to his drinking. My dad wasn't raging from moment to moment, he was a period drinker. He could binge and then not binge but sometimes the mood swings caused by *not* bingeing created eggshells to walk on. I don't think it's possible to explain how traumatic these dynamic shifts in our family were after moving to California, but I believe they were for all of us.

My dad had worked all his life. He fought so hard to financially sustain a roof over his family's head and here I was, working like an adult, making more money by age twelve. I can't imagine the effect that had on him, and it isn't my place to suggest, because I honestly don't know what triggers other people.

What I do know is my father loves me, but, whenever you are

I Don't Belong to You

stressed, adding any kind of chemical influence can have an adverse effect. My mother never drank, but she dealt with anxiety ALL HER LIFE. My mother did not always have help from anyone when handling my career, she did so much of it on her own and she experienced much ridicule and sexism. When I think back, I wonder how she did it, I wonder how she managed.

My moment of truth had finally arrived after reading my truth through my journal pages. I realized I had to express my suffering. I had to go through with bringing it to light so I could lament. I had to start the process and the actual ACTION of forgiveness. My inability to accept my feelings and actually take the steps to forgive had made me emotionally and mentally sick all those years.

I started screenshotting and texting my mother my journal entries. I later regretted that because I realized she probably couldn't sense my energy through the text. That's one of the biggest problems with texting important things, the lack of context. As I was texting she told me she started having a panic attack.

I was so scared because this was not what I wanted! I didn't want to upset her with my truth, I just wanted us to acknowledge it. I just wanted her to know I was starting to see again. I wanted her to know that I wasn't distracting my pain with Joey's pain or Camry's pain or Sammy's pain, but that I was looking at my own!

⇒ A MENTAL BREAKTHROUGH ⇐

This was a mental breakthrough. #POSITIVE! I left my house immediately and headed to her house. I called my mother because she had stopped replying to my texts. The moment I texted I was on my way she called and her energy was not at all how she described. It went from talking to her panicking to her being com-

Lauren Palmer

pletely emotionless and dismissive. I was so confused and it was starting to feel all too familiar. My mom already knew I'd prepared a letter to my dad concerning his drinking. She was a part of my whole self-discovery process, encouraging me to speak about my feelings as I discovered them. I'd already shown her the letter to my father earlier in the week, but was waiting to read it to him that weekend.

Once I got to my parents' house I saw that my mother was not open. I saw that she was hiding, and as much as I wanted her to not be afraid and just be real, I was also hurt that she was reverting back to old habits. These were her old defense mechanisms, the ones that made it hard for us to relate when I was child.

She started to tell me I was using my dad as a scapegoat for Sammy's problems. 💔 That gutted me to the core because I couldn't understand how she couldn't see the mirror image of my family relationships with those I'd called friends. I felt again the dismissiveness I'd felt as a child, the manipulation of my words. I remembered my helplessness.

She started to patronize me, asking what was wrong with me, was I having a mental *breakdown*? She was flipping things on their head as well as she had when I was a teen, trying to silence me with her efforts to embarrass me. She was worried that I was going to wake my siblings and dad. Just then they did start to wake to the commotion. I tried to speak but she jumped on my words, trying to paint this picture that I was wanting trouble for my family.

Again, I was gutted. I was trying not to personalize and to see the situation for what it was, but as she said, "Go 'head and say your attack on the family!" it was as if I TOO was not a member of THE FAMILY. AGAIN, I was GUTTED. I started to say forget it, "Fuck it then, since I'm attacking the family I'll leave!"

I Don't Belong to You

I was so hurt in my heart and we were all screaming and all I saw was my little brother silent and my little sister crying. This is why I was here, to break the cycle of hurt and suffering, unaddressed feelings. My little sister pleaded, "Please, Keke, don't leave like this, you can't let the anger take over you. Please. I love you."

I knew the reality was that my mother didn't want my dad to feel jumped on, but her choice of words painted me as an enemy and she prejudged the situation before any of us got a chance to experience it. I was willing to read my dad my letter. I read it but ultimately felt the moment had been ruined.

My dad and I shared words, and one thing he said struck me: "Keke, you never told me you felt this way. If you had, I would've worked on a way to fix it." This was true, I hadn't ever told him how I felt. It wasn't even about him changing at the drop of a hat, it was about me expressing how I felt—he was right, I never had until this moment. I didn't sit on that thought for long because I couldn't get my mother's words out of my head.

I let my father speak to me, but moments after, as my mom started to speak, I remained silent. My expression showed the truth. Every kind word she said was negated by every dismissive word she'd said since I'd entered the door. Every memory and every heartache she gave started to ring in my thoughts.

I started screaming them back at her!!! "Nah, I'm FAKE! I made up my abuse, I made up my heartache, and I blamed it on Dad! That's what I did, because really I'm hurt about Sammy! I'm having a mental breakDOWN that's what's happening."

My mother was regretting it all—the moment she said it, the moment I repeated it, and the moment my family heard it. She didn't mean that; she's human.

The doors were locked and my mother wouldn't let me leave, they wanted me to stay with them and talk, but I had become the me who never got a chance to speak. I remember during some *True Jackson, VP* years when I would have violent thoughts. I couldn't understand where they were coming from, but in this moment I'd realized it was the unreleased emotion trying to express itself in my thoughts. This rage I was expressing was necessary, just as sadness was a necessary emotion for the character in the Pixar movie *Inside Out*.

⇁ THE HEALING BEGINS ⇀

I was hurt and angry that I had been misunderstood *again*, even as I was trying to get them to understand. I felt like a little girl again, like I was trapped in a home and held prisoner, except this time I was free and could be heard. My mother was in tears as she said, "Keke, I know I'm not perfect and I don't mean the things I've said and done. But I am sorry and if you love me you will teach me."

Her words struck me, and even in my rage I made a conscious choice to accept them while still deciding to express my rage. I heard her, but I wanted her to still hear me.

I finally found my way out of the house through the garage as I watched my little sister give me her last plea. I know this sounds dramatic, but this is the reality and art DOES imitate life, lol.

I blocked my mom's texts after that, but I did read the texts my sister sent. I felt her words, but I was personalizing. My story, my experience, my pain, that was all I could feel for that time and for a few days after.

Only a few days passed before I got outside of myself and remembered what my mother had said. "If you love me, you will teach me." I also recalled the words my father said: "I would've done something to fix it."

I Don't Belong to You

Those were the words I had been waiting for all my life. Though they didn't come when I wanted them to, they came when they were supposed to and I was not going to allow my anger or fear to let me down this time and not communicate what I wanted. Even if it didn't end the *way* I wanted, I owed it to myself to follow through with this process of forgiveness. I was going to come through for me because now I had the tools to know how. 😌

I met back up with my family and introduced family therapy as an idea for us as well as our old tradition of family night as a good add-on. We made a promise to take actions of forgiveness by actually doing the work it takes to rebuild a relationship and a family, by BEING A FAMILY.

Reading those pages in my journal showed me firsthand why my relationships with men were in the state they were in. I had disabled many alarms back then so that I could survive the present situation without being in a constant panic. I continued to repeat the same patterns accepted by me during that time of invalidation, even when having other options as a now-grown woman. The pain and emptiness I felt through the page was excruciating to read, I felt as if a weight had been lifted but almost as if it was lifted after already crushing me. 💔

I was able to read through the pages where all my defense mechanisms were built. It became like a cheat sheet for all the things Keke does to trick herself because she forgot her brain could do that without her knowing, haha. 🙄

Truly, once you teach your brain something by making it a habit, unless you stay conscious of it, your brain can reuse and make decisions without you. #WHATEVERYOUPUTINCOMESOUT. That is what happened to me! That was all. I went to sleep at the wheel when dealing with the stress of my job and my family. It was too much to bear so I let go of the wheel. Very human thing to do. 🎩

Lauren Palmer

We were a family who had hurt and didn't know how to fully communicate our feelings in the healthiest way. It's so strange how I so often, even to this day, thought I was great at communicating my feelings when I grew up in a home with poor communicators in that regard, lol. #HINDSIGHT. My mother grew up in a distrusting home, having her guard up. From her understanding, and her relationship with her mother, that's how you toughened your child up and prepared them for the world. Remember the story I told about my grandmother? From an early age she encouraged distrust of others, even family. However, as a not-so-normal teen not going to school every day, all I heard were my parents' and my immediate family's point of view of me and the world, and then that of other people at work. At work it was always hard to trust people because I was the star of the show and felt that's why people were nice to me. It wasn't like I went to school and developed a social dynamic not influenced by my career. My parents didn't know, and neither did I, about how much the entertainment industry could affect and change our lives and the way we looked at things. Instead of my family talking, instead of us getting counseling during this time, we all just held it in. At some point I decided not to trust anyone and to always keep my guard up. I agreed to see it as me against the world and my prize was loneliness. If you want to own being misunderstood, then that's what you will be because that's the only way you will allow yourself to see it. The love and the companionship, the relationships I wanted to have even with my family were paralyzed with that one promise to myself that I didn't realize I had made. If there's anything I've realized in my twenty-third year, it's that forgiveness is the key that unlocks all the doors of happiness. I couldn't forgive my parents; I wasn't giving them a full second chance for the mistakes they made

I Don't Belong to You

while raising four children. #NORMAL. Yet they forgave me. Constantly. I said horrible things to my parents like most children do, and they never held me to it. They didn't stop taking me to work every day, they didn't move back to Chicago when I got out of line. They had compassion because they knew what I was dealing with even though I was too young to understand what they were dealing with. That is love!!! That is real love that is unconditional and that is the greatest message I got from my parents. My parents never gave up on me, even when I gave up on myself because I equated their love for me with my career, because that's the perception I decided to agree with. I held on to all the hurt in my life and allowed it to isolate me. When the reality is, no, you don't have to let people walk all over you #BOUNDARIES, but love is a choice. A choice that involves growth and forgiveness and trial and error. An action that leaves judgment in the past and effort toward a brighter future in the forefront. Someone really important to me once told me "no one gets it right on the first try" and this is what we must remember if we want to be happy. Happiness means letting go, and when people choose to look past your faults maybe you can do the same.

I realized there is no meeting God without going through pain and FACING IT. When you do that, you understand the point. Without going deep within yourself, you can't understand the depth of God. We never want to face it, but once we do that's when the whole forgiveness thing comes in. That's when your personalizing stops and your compassion for humanity and the appreciation of the experience of life comes in.

Forgiveness is WORK and that's what I was doing with prayer, with my PRACTICE, with my learning of different practices. I didn't know it, but that was what I was doing, working through my pain and forgiving those who had hurt me, including myself, so I could be as free as I was when I came into this world. The reward of doing that work is knowing God.

⇒ THE BENEFITS OF BEING SPIRITUAL ⇐

Spirituality is a choice. It's a choice to either see it this way or that way. The truth is what you make it, but no matter how badly you see it, the next person can choose to see it as great. That isn't anyone's fault, that's someone's choice, just as easily as they see it as good, you can too.

This is what free will is. We get the chance at life, and really it's simple: Love and be loved. We are the ones who choose to make it complicated, and it's usually because we know no different.

For those of you who aren't quite sure where or how deep your faith lies, that's okay. We all have our journey of faith. Being aware of your spiritual needs can bring a positive change in your life. You can get spiritual answers to some of the most intriguing questions, including who you are and what your purpose in life is.

I have much respect for every religion and spiritual practice that exists today, and I know we are all on the same journey, some of us are just taking different roads to get there. There is no right or wrong way, just different paths in growing consciousness, the source of joy and peace.

Whenever I had questions or felt lost, I researched religions and spiritual practices I was curious about. I loved learning about different faiths and other ways to find peace in my soul, including traditional Christian service.

As an adult, I actually went back to my home church, St. Peter Claver, and got a powerful message as a now adult person from

I Don't Belong to You

the father, lol. In short, he had stated his interpretation that the original sin was not so much about Adam and Eve eating from the tree, but that they hid it from God. It was their own shame that isolated them and in turn made them feel lost in the world. It was their belief that they were separate from God that symbolizes humanity's current relationship with God and the "sin" that we are all born with—the curse of disbelief and unworthiness.

Father said the "original sin" that apparently casts the illusion on humanity is that we are somehow not connected to God and each other *always*. When in reality no matter what religion or practice or color or age or sex, our consciousness is birthed from only one consciousness (God). HOW COULD WE BE SEPARATE? NO, it's our HUMANITY that can overshadow our consciousness with personality (EGO) that stops us from staying in constant contact with that heavenly consciousness in which our creator resides. 😭

⇉ MEDITATION AND PRAYER ⇇

In my ongoing spiritual journey, I like to practice both meditation and prayer. Through meditation, I'm continuing to learn how to block out all the noises and distractions of the world and just focus on God. The ability to talk to God with comfort and ease is such a transforming experience that during those times, I can actually feel Him ordering my steps for the day.

When I take time for prayer, whether it's an hour to open the day or a heartfelt check-in at the end of the night, I know I am tending to the most important relationship in my life. Just knowing that gives me peace and I feel more grounded in the source of my life. I feel more tuned in to the people and the world around me.

Lauren Palmer

Prayer isn't an item to add to your agenda and then to be checked off each day. Prayer is the soul of life, the rhythm of one's day, the disposition that you bring to everyone and everything else. There is no right or wrong way to pray, just let your heart speak. The fullness of God is everywhere. God is not a man in the sky, a man away and apart from you. God is an energy, the consciousness that gives breath to all life.

What that means, simply put, is when we commune with anything we are communing with God. When you commune with your best friend, you are talking to God in some way. When you're crying a big cry about your recent breakup or lost job, you are crying out to God.

God is always listening, always responding to us in ways we can understand and immediately access. The question is—are you listening too? He could be talking to you through the waves of the ocean or through a shooting star bursting in the sky. Does something as simple as a butterfly on your car window serve as a reminder of a different kind of beauty in God's eyes? #MAGIC ISPERCEPTION. #WHATISAMIRACLE.

CONSCIOUSLY commune with God and then listen for His response!

FINDING THE PATH TO ENLIGHTENMENT

Growing up religious can make you feel as if there is one way to know God, but there isn't. Religion is just the journey of someone else's path of enlightenment! What is yours? Are you like Moses right now when he was questioning God? Or are you Horus, losing your eye to circumstance?

All these stories, told in parables, are stories of *the human experience* when reaching enlightenment. We each live our versions

I Don't Belong to You

of these stories of life and they are all meant to teach us to appreciate the earth on which we stand.

You can look at the actual sun as the sun of God TOO! It gives us water and light and allows for the trees and bees to grow. These are the parts of those stories that we forget because we put ourselves at the top, or we just praise the faces of the religion instead of the teaching of their stories.

I believe that through God we can do all things. There is no need to intellectualize faith beyond that. We can let go of what can't be explained and make that leap of faith. It's our choice, yours and mine, and we should choose wisely.

As my spirituality has deepened, I have found numerous ways to achieve the inner peace my mother so often speaks of. I have so many memories of her saying "Peace be still," and it took me a long while to figure out what she meant. What she was saying was not too different from what my vocal teacher Bruce said. It is in the stillness that we can best communicate with God/Universe.

All through the day I talk with God, asking questions either in my head or out loud depending on my day ahead or the challenges I'm facing. Every day I try to do a little bit of yoga and pray to God before I go to bed. Guidance comes to me as I'm hearing things or seeing images, or with anything I feel myself strongly drawn to. Whenever I feel overwhelmed or find myself dwelling on the past, I bring myself back to awareness by taking a deep breath and whispering, "I'm here now."

Our spirituality changes, shifts, and grows as we age. Though I feel pretty strong in my connection with God, that doesn't mean I don't have my doubts from time to time on what and who God is in my life. Feeling doubtful isn't a great place to be but I realize there are a few seeds of disbelief in all of us because we all live in a material world that forces us to want to question what we cannot see. We are humans, haha, and it's only in those moments where we can choose to be motivated to dig deeper.

The spiritual advisor Deepak Chopra wrote, "God exists as a field of all possibilities. God is pure consciousness, the source of all thoughts, feelings, and sensations . . . God is One but diversifies into the many—he makes possible the observer, the observed, and the process of observation."

In the end, I believe that being spiritual isn't about understanding God, it's about seeking Him and welcoming His presence into every aspect of your life.

10

#Growingnotgrown

ON GIVING BACK TO THE COMMUNITY AND ACTION STEPS TO BE A RESPONSIBLE SOLDIER OF LOVE

What you want is in what you don't want to go through.
—R. Kelly

When I was growing up in Illinois, every Saturday and Sunday my dad would get up early and go to the old folks' home and help out, donate blood at the blood bank, volunteer at a homeless shelter. He eventually served as a deacon in our church. He didn't make a big deal about it. I'd ask him where he was off to and he'd say, "Going to see a man about a dog." I hated when my parents said that, lol.

Very early on I understood there was something important he was doing; however, it took many years before I would really understand personally how substantial service is to life. When he started to truly study to become a deacon, I realized what a major part of his practice that was, and we were proud of him for giving up his free time to do it. I could see that it brought joy to my father to do for others.

I often heard my dad speaking with members of our church about what needed to be done in the community and how it could be accomplished. He was always about "the people" and not just black people (because we are black, lol), but *everyone*. As a boy, his family called him "Michael," like the Michael character in the television show *Good Times*, because he was all about the community, or tha *kidz* as I would say. 😏 #DESTINY.

My dad raised me to believe that we have a responsibility to the other humans around us. This would be a major theme in my life, though it took me a while to really step outside myself and realize what it meant to practice it. I have always been a people lover and I used to get my feelings hurt often—caring so much about how other people felt about things that didn't concern me, haha.

My mother always made me feel like that was a special thing. Yet deep down, I knew that HAVING strong feelings was better than not having any at all. It took a really long time for me to understand emotions.

For whatever reason, I always had an affinity for people and a strong empathy for others— I hated for anyone to be in pain. I believe that quality plays a huge part in my personality. I know what it is like to struggle, I know what it's like to have to deal with dark feelings, and I have nothing but love for others who sacrificed and fought, even when they are over my head.

Growing up I had many friends whose families were barely getting by. My parents didn't have it easy and they did all kinds of things to try to get us a better life. As a child I remember feeling— not actually intellectualizing, but feeling—sometimes the sadness from my family. I so badly wished for our household to never suffer. No one spoke about it and that made the feelings I had so much harder to express.

My family and I were poor in our Illinois hometown days, but back then we had our most intimate family moments. We often

Lauren Palmer

had movie night and I remember watching the movie *Claudine* about a poor single mother in Harlem played by Diahann Carroll. She had to hide her job as a maid so she could still get welfare because she couldn't have kept her family together otherwise. That was a personal reality for us, and one for many people in our community. Both of my parents always worked, but it was years before I realized that the lady we cleaned up for who came to visit us every so often worked for Section 8 (the federal program that provides subsidized housing for low-income tenants), and she was checking to make sure my family was qualified to live there and met all the requirements.

I realized later that it's such a systematic game for people in poverty to qualify for federal subsidies. It was personal for me and other African Americans who grow up in poverty. Either it was not helping the people who needed it well enough or it was pigeonholing the community from being independent. Too often, people really believe the lie that they can go no farther than where they are. After I moved to California, though my options in life got bigger I also realized the sense of community is often stronger in towns like the one I grew up in. Or at least I know it was strong in Robbins.

We had problems, but the people who lived in our little town were very close. We knew the cops, the post office workers, and the county government members. My relationship with my family and our overall sense of community got worse when we moved to Cali. Back in Robbins, we were poor, but we had one another. Family was most important in Robbins because we weren't easily distracted by *things*. We had very little, but at times, a little was enough.

Once we moved, I was always performing to bring happiness to those around me. There was so much sadness from racism, being poor, and the suffering passed down from generations of unreleased feelings about slavery/segregation/integration. Our suffering was from many things. My grandma experienced much emotional trauma and she put that on her children, and they placed it on my generation, because she never dealt with it completely and that's just how the cycle continues.

Entertaining her and my family and other relatives became my purpose, to ease our collective suffering. That's actually what my music mentor R. Kelly told me years later. He said: "Keke, your suffering is where you find your purpose." My purpose and my mission growing up was to bring happiness where I went! I would do anything to bring joy to my family and those around me. I hated so much to feel their sadness, but I delighted in the service of bringing them joy!

I always believed in magic, and as I grew, people often told me never to lose that belief. It was like they were saying don't lose the magic of believing in your life. So I always wanted to hold on to the belief of living a positive and progressive life and the excitement of bringing joy to those around you.

I would dance, sing, and act a FOOL as my grandma Davis would say, hahahahaha. I remember I had this one show called *The No No Way Show*, hahahahahaha, and my uncles on my dad's side would entertain my ideas and die laughing at all the different characters I played and the topics I wished to discuss on *The No No Way Show*.

It made me so happy, sooooo happy to perform for them, and for everyone around me. At every sleepover, I was the one

Lauren Palmer

wanting to choreograph a dance routine or competition just to pass the time. I found a way to perform and entertain no matter the situation. It was the best, because singing and dancing were my favorite things and they brought joy to others too. I loved that feeling.

Once I became an actress I did the same thing, though I wasn't really conscious of it. Connecting to people was the reason I started performing and the reason I enjoyed it so much. I was doing it for the connection, but I wasn't completely AWARE that was my real purpose.

⇒ PASSION COMES WITH PURSUING ⇐ SOMETHING BIGGER THAN YOURSELF

FAME, as you call it, can make you a victim, a hero, or a saint. It's up to you and the world to determine what you are "seen" as, but the best reason for achieving or reaching for success is to touch the lives of more people in positive ways. You become more aware of "you"—who you are and what you are meant for—the more you can touch others and lift them up. When you are not conscious of your connection to your purpose, it's easy to become uninspired or to start misdirecting your gifts. I strongly believe passion only exists when the pursuit is for something that you feel is bigger than you.

When my mother read the script for *Akeelah and the Bee* she was so excited because she saw its greater purpose. She had been excited about other projects before, but I realized she felt something special about this film. She was thrilled at the thought of me winning a role in it, of course, but she also kept saying that the movie would last a lifetime and that it would really inspire hope and touch the community. There was that word again.

Hmmm, I thought, *community means something.*

I Don't Belong to You

12 DAILY REMINDERS

1. The past cannot be changed

2. Opinions don't define your reality

3. Everyone's journey is different

4. Things always get better with time

5. Judgments are a confession of character

6. Overthinking will lead to sadness

7. Happiness is found within

8. Positive thoughts create positive things

9. Smiles are contagious

10. Kindness is free

11. You only fail if you quit

12. What goes around comes around

VEX KING, BONVITASTYLE.COM

I prepared hard for that *Akeelah* role and my mother made it a family thing, lol. As I mentioned earlier, we all read the script together—my dad, lil' bro and sis, and older sister. Then my mom would put on spelling bees for my sister and me to compete in for junk-food money, hahahaha. It was her way of helping me learn those big words for the auditions.

I actually had to go through seven auditions, which was exciting and entertaining and nerve-racking. We knew it would be a powerful movie and an important role for me, so I was stressed too. But I learned to work with that energy as an actress, instead of against it. Working on the film was mostly fun.

There was this one huge memory from a day on set when we were shooting the scene where Dr. Larabee tells Akeelah about his daughter and opens up about why he left Akeelah hanging for her national spelling bee competitor. Well, Laurence Fishburne scolded me because I was laughing during his close-up. It really hurt my feelings and turned into a huge thing on set. 😠

Years later, I realized that, even if he had been assertive, he was truly trying to show me that it's necessary to give respect to our fellow actors. Which is something that I take very seriously to this very day. 😊 #THANKS. I also remember they weren't too worried about my schooling on the set and my mom threatened to take me away if they didn't let me get my mandatory hours. But it was mostly fun on the *Akeelah* set because I was finally around kids again.

When I'd first moved to Cali it was about a year and some change without a school type of setting where I was surrounded by other children. The other kids really thought I was some special being to be cast in the starring role. I thought if only they knew where I was really from and what my life had really been like. I hated being put on a pedestal.

I Don't Belong to You

Once I filmed *Akeelah,* word quickly spread around and something happened that I hadn't expected. I became a spokesperson of sorts for the community. Literally, everywhere I went even strangers were telling me things like "You are a beacon" and "Thank you for helping my child." I would hear these things and I would appreciate them, but I think they also kind of scared me. I didn't want to take them too seriously or let them hit me too deep. Something made me afraid, even though I loved touching people and had been connecting with people way before anyone knew who I was.

I realized later that what scared me at first is that people were thinking of me as some sort of a role model, and I didn't yet feel ready for that; I didn't feel that I was qualified. I thought being a role model meant being perfect and as far as I knew I was a regular kid with regular problems and insecurities. I had always loved making other people happy and helping them forget their pain, but this was a whole new level and it made me anxious at times.

Looking back, I was uncomfortable because of the responsibility I felt went along with that. I thought about regular people who had become celebrities and inspirational leaders, and how some of them, like Michael Jackson and Tupac and the Reverend Martin Luther King Jr., were attacked because of it. It used to scare me! I started to take on their story line in so many ways. Our minds have nothing to draw from but what we've already seen. The heart can see manifestations of a different future, but sometimes we scare ourselves with what we have seen before. I was afraid someone would make up lies about me or shoot me. I was afraid of losing my identity, and losing the magic that came with it.

I was still figuring out who I was and that made it strange to have other people telling me I was an inspiration to them. I

Lauren Palmer

wanted to be able to relate to others like a normal person. I realized much later that maybe some would ridicule me, but there would be others who'd love me. It was part of being in the light. That's where you live when you are living in your truth, following your purpose, and to live in fear is to live in the dark.

People also are often struggling with things you couldn't fathom and that's why we show mercy and empathy and never forget that it ISN'T PERSONAL. All the people who are living their truth went through s%^t. I was afraid to face that, but nothing good happens when you hide your truth and live in the dark. We all have to face dark times and challenges, but that is part of life. When you fight through and make it to the light, it makes life all the better because you feel better inside. Looking back, I realize that back then I just needed to keep living and have enough experiences to draw from and better understand the importance and value in living out front and not being afraid to shine my light fully. Things take time, I think so often we rush things instead of just letting life happen. #ALLWILLBEREVEALED.

⇒ STAYING GROUNDED ⇐

My mother helped me get a handle on that. In fact, after *Akeelah and the Bee*, she focused on getting me a publicist to make sure the community knew my name. Mom would get really upset with this one publicist because she didn't understand the value of me being a positive force in communities like the one I'd grown up in.

My mother was often approached by others who wanted me to come into the community and give talks or speak about my experiences. Sometimes she asked organizations and groups if they would allow me to speak to the kids. I just told my story of growing up and working to become an actress. She saw the importance

I Don't Belong to You

of me reaching out to those who were still living in poverty. My mom knew that if other young people back home and in similar poor communities knew that I was one of them and saw that I had been successful in following my dreams, they could do it too. That one publicist didn't get it, because she'd never been in our situation. She was clueless.

After my speeches, those in the audience would come up and, again, they were using words like *hope* and *inspiration* when speaking about me. As I said, I knew what they meant but I didn't quite understand exactly how I was "all of that" by just living my life. I understood only as much as I knew, not as much as there was, if that makes sense?

I truly did enjoy going and hanging with the kids in those neighborhoods. When I was younger it was the best because they felt I was famous but not that famous, so they could relate to me and we could talk like normal. As I got older and busier as a performer, my favorite part about giving talks at schools started to change because kids weren't always able to see me as being just like them and someone they could relate to.

I slowly became more of this "celebrity" person and I took it personally that they didn't accept me as their own anymore. That skewed my judgment for a while because I allowed their feelings of separatism to separate us. I honestly felt that there was nothing I could do to change that so if that was what it was, then that's what it would be about: my "fame."

For a long time, I was a slave to that.

Those were the *True Jackson* years, when I was dealing with problems at home and some depression, and it became a lot easier to give in to what people thought than to practice giving them another perspective. I just wanted to be left alone because I let my inside voice get silent, so I closed myself off for a while.

It wasn't until I got on social media that I realized I could kind of humanize myself so others related to me a little more. I tried it with Twitter first, then Instagram, and it really helped for a while. Then, as I noted earlier in the book, I got unbalanced in the area of social media and had to take a step back and work on myself.

During all that time spent working on myself, I was getting rid of things that were weighing me down and blocking me from being my best. All of my work to be a better person was creating a light, a way for my purpose to shine through. When we work on ourselves to be clearer "thinkers" and more AWARE of following our hearts and our intuitions, we start to realize that all of the things we've been looking for were always there. We accept who we are, which makes us more willing to put ourselves out there and serve others within healthy boundaries because we are no longer taking things personally.

⇒ A HUMBLE MENTALITY ⇐

This is called a "humble mentality"—a way of finding fulfillment and happiness by thinking less about your material needs and more about the emotional intelligence of those around you. It's about using your gifts and talents to better influence others forward in positive ways. When I live with that attitude, it seems to benefit everyone, me included. I feel better about myself when I reach out to people, just like my father did. He worked to instill that concept in me.

A little before my *True Jackson* years, and then during them, my parents encouraged me to do community outreach with Bernice King, the daughter of the Reverend Martin Luther King, who dedicated his entire life to elevating the lives of others. When we worked together, Bernice and I would tour museums to learn

I Don't Belong to You

about the history of slavery, the Civil War, and the Civil Rights Movement. There were photographs and stories of old slave ships before the Civil War as well as videos of the riots and demonstrations in the 1960s.

It was both eye-opening and heartbreaking for me. It all felt SO close even though I was only a child (that speaks to collective consciousness and energy that lives on past death, whether it be positive or negative). I felt the suffering of the people even though I'd never met any of them. During these trips I would usually be on the road with my dad and he would always say things about how the people from his time—like the acting couple Ruby Dee and Ossie Davis—did more for the community than just entertain them. They were activists, bravely fighting for equal opportunity and against discrimination.

I think he believed they could be role models for me because they were devoted to a cause bigger than themselves, and they were respected and admired for standing up for those who were oppressed. Dad also spoke fondly of the late Muhammad Ali. I loved how my father talked so warmly about how that great man made him feel. I could feel his love and admiration. Even though my father never met Muhammad Ali, he never forgets how Ali made him feel. I recognized the importance of that and never forgot it. I mean, here my father was teaching me positive and useful tools from inspirational people he'd NEVER met. That's POWERFUL and it works the same way with negative and nonuseful tools. #YOURBRAINISA COMPUTER. #BECAREFULWHATYOUFEEDIT.

⇒ REACHING OUT AND FINDING PURPOSE ⇐

These were powerful lessons to learn. They helped me grow as a person. I began working in television at a young age, surrounded

We mature with the damage,

not with the years.

—HPLYRIKZ.COM

by so many adults and given so many responsibilities. It made me grow up fast in some ways. I was often overwhelmed emotionally. The entertainment and music businesses have their fun sides, but they are truly businesses. When you are dealing with agents and contracts and sizable amounts of money, you can easily get caught up in the numbers game and lose sight of your purpose and passion.

I was reminded of this when I tried to release my second album. I felt so boxed up because my label at the time fought me on it. It was as if they blamed me because my first album wasn't a success. It was all about the numbers to them, so I started to associate musical success with numbers too.

I was afraid that my second album might fail. I lost the fearlessness, the joy of singing and entertaining and the point of it all. It had become personal, which it never is, and the struggle is remembering that. The interesting thing was that during this time, I learned that the best way to overcome my fears and sadness was to reach out to other people and do something for them.

My parents' lessons on using my gifts to benefit others came through once again, and it was reinforced by similar inspirational encounters I had around this time involving a couple of personal role models who I looked up to, Will Smith and Rihanna. They showed me an example of people who think of others and have somehow stayed true to themselves by encouraging others.

I know this personally because when I was going through some hard times with my career and family and I was super stressed out, I talked with a mutual advisor about how to resolve them. He represents a lot of actors and performers. He told me that it wasn't unusual for someone who'd had career success in the entertainment business to go through these things. He encouraged me to give myself time to deal with the changes in my life and not to act without thinking things through with a long-term perspective.

His advice was helpful and I listened to it. I was still processing it a few days later when I got a cell phone call from a weird number. I didn't recognize it so I didn't take the call. I let it go to voice mail. Then a few hours later, I checked the message and I couldn't believe what I heard. It was Will Smith!

He said something like, "Hi, Keke, this is Will Smith. I heard you were having a hard time and I just wanted to tell you that I know what you are going through. Don't let it get you down. Just take your time and you'll be fine. This will pass. I'm in Hong Kong making a movie now but if you want to talk just give me a call or text. Hang in there, Will."

I'm paraphrasing, but that was the sentiment. After hearing that, I remembered that we shared the same advisor, and I figured he must've mentioned what I was going through to Will. I was so touched that Will Smith took the time out of his schedule to reach out to me. He also made me a happy birthday video for my sweet sixteen, something I'll never forget. 😄

Sometimes when I am overwhelmed with things, I tend to think that no one else has ever had the same problem, lolol dramaqueeeeen. Will Smith reminded me that I wasn't alone and that others had made it through similar challenges. His few words had a real impact.

Another lesson I learned was to reach out to others when they touched me. So one day a few years later, I hit up Rihanna on Twitter. I became a real fan after "We Found Love." The visuals for the song truly brought tears to my eyes, and though I didn't share her experience exactly, I felt the sentiment. Life could be hopeless and painful, but that is where the love often is met. I told her she in-

I Don't Belong to You

spired me and that I hoped she continued to have a lot of success and a happy life. Again, I was surprised when she DM'd back!! She wrote, "Keke you are a light, just keep embracing God's anointing and you will be blessed." 😮 😄 😄 😄 😄 😄 😄

I was just thrilled, and even more thrilled when she started following me on Twitter and Instagram. She was showing me love and letting me know I was acknowledged in the world. The singer Brandy did something similar for me. When we met, she gave me my first journal to write in, and in the front she wrote, "I am who I am because you are who you are." It took me a while to understand that quote, but the fact that she gave it to me really got me into writing in a journal every day, which is really a great release and honestly has brought me much peace throughout my life. The written word is powerful.

Brandy lifted me up. The same goes for Queen Latifah, Chaka Zulu, Ludacris, and many others that continued to show me the possibilities in life and the support given to you when you are being a force for the good.

⇥ CREATING A BALANCE ⇤
AND FINDING HAPPINESS

Service to others really is a healing force and a way to get your magic back. On my lowest days, bringing a smile to others brings me happiness. When I was younger, I overdid this and tried too hard to always be a people pleaser, but around the time I was twenty-one, my personal work helped me to be stronger and gave me more understanding, more insights, and self-knowledge. I learned how to create a better balance by first getting myself right and then creating healthy boundaries that allow me to be of the best service to others.

Lauren Palmer

We often judge ourselves and our experiences, but my EXPE-RIENCE is what gave me the INSIGHT to even understand the purpose for my gifts and my passion. It also helped me to see the truth I always knew as a kid, the magic of using my gifts. I realized that we are meant to experience life fully and completely. We also have the free will to make choices that help us sustain our personal best and to be the best we can possibly be.

There is no real happiness when everything is motivated by SELF. Loving ourselves is good, but there is nothing rewarding or inspiring about chasing material success, status, or fame. 👎 I've seen that in my own life and in the lives of others chasing fame and fortune. Will Smith helped remind me that even the biggest celebrities take the time to get outside themselves and touch the hearts of others because that's what makes it worthwhile.

I think we all know the benefit of serving others. We just get lost sometimes, usually when we buy into the hype that happiness comes with wearing designer clothing or owning a mansion. #THEPOINTOFADVERTISEMENT.

We forget that it's not about things at all but connecting to the people whom you share this world with. 🕴️

⇥ BEING A HERO IS EASIER ⇤
THAN YOU THINK

Or how about being someone's hero? We all enjoy movies and television shows about superheroes like Iron Man, the Avengers, Blade, the Fantastic Four, Catwoman, Wonder Woman, Storm, Superman, and Supergirl. Kids of my generation grew up wanting to be Teenage Mutant Ninja Turtles or Power Rangers. (If any Hollywood producers are reading this, I'm available to be the Pink Ranger! 😃 #DEADASSTHO.)

I Don't Belong to You

I'm stronger because I had to be, I'm smarter because of my mistakes, happier because of the sadness I've known, and now wiser because I learned.

We all have magic. You and I have the power to change the lives of those around us for the better, what's more heroic than that?

Do you want to save the world? Start next door and work your way up. We can teach a child to read. We can drive an elderly person to the doctor or to church. You can go up to that shy little girl next door and tell her she's beautiful. I can visit hospitals and nursing homes and perform for people who haven't had anything to smile about in a while.

I mentioned earlier that I am empathetic to a fault. It's almost like telepathy, my superpower! I can't walk by a sad-looking child or adult without trying to lift them up or noticing that there is something they are hiding. I have fairy-godmother syndrome. I want to wave my wand and make everything better for everyone I meet.

For the rest of my life I will remember that Will Smith, Rihanna, Asha, Brandy, Ludacris and his manager, Chaka, and Queen Latifah were among those who reached out and touched me with their kindness. I want to be remembered by others for doing the same thing. Don't you?

What is more heroic than reminding someone they have value? Well, helping them add to that value might be even more heroic. Teaching someone to swim, dance, sing, ride a bike, drive a car, or use the Internet are all powerful gifts and heroic deeds.

So the next time you think to yourself, *I could use a little help right now*, I suggest that instead of waiting for it to come, you reach out and help someone else and see what happens. Maybe, just maybe, you'll get the help you want by helping another human in need. And even if it's nothing to you, you never know who will think of you as that hero!

Whenever I've lost my bearings and am focused on other people's ideas of success, it gave me anxiety and made me depressed. Yet when my focus was sharing my gifts with those who were willing to receive them, I always felt happiness and peace.

It wasn't until this past year that I realized what I had been searching for was finally here. I was afraid before, but that fear only kept me further away from myself. Now that I'd become exalted in my own personal truth I was able to see clearly how it wasn't and is not scary to spread your jewels across the world. Not only that, but how NECESSARY it is, because when you release yourself from suffering, you can not only help those around you but you can also remove your ancestors' pain that you carry. All of humanity's ancestors, not just our ancestors that we base off of color or origin. I finally saw my purpose. I accepted my struggles as part of the journey. There is no need to take on the suffering of our ancestors.

I've learned to be grateful for the gifts I've been given. I've learned that when I get anxious and scared, I can breathe in and breathe out and keep moving forward. I remind myself that anything that happens, good or bad, will make you better eventually. Peace comes from within, so know that everything will be all right. And know that happiness and fulfillment come in using your gifts and your passions for God's will (spreading LOVE!!).

⪜ KINDNESS AND ACCEPTANCE ⪛ ARE GIFTS WE CAN ALL SHARE

When we suffer, we can find release and joy on this earth by accepting ourselves and accepting others. Most of all, we should be kind to each other. Kindness is such a simple concept. Do unto others as you would have them do unto you. It's the Golden Rule! Jesus said it himself during the Sermon on the Mount. He also said, "Love thy neighbor as thyself." If you are not consciously

Lauren Palmer

working to live in that positive space, how can you expect to see positivity in the world around you?

No matter what shade of black, brown, or white our flesh may be, we are all part of HUMANITY. African Americans, Hispanics, Caucasians, Asians, Native Americans . . . our ancestors all struggled and suffered. We are here because some of them persevered and survived. We owe them our respect. We should honor their suffering by ending it wherever and whenever we can in ourselves and in others. By acknowledging it and lamenting it instead of holding on to it and unconsciously handing it down to generations to come.

We are all in this together, part of a collective culture. We are all connected and we all need to look out for one another.

When one of us is hurt, we all hurt.

When one of us is kind, all of our lives are given the opportunity to be elevated.

⇉ KNOW BETTER AND DO BETTER ⇇

My experience as a black person definitely helps me relate personally to people of all races and colors who've faced prejudice, discrimination, and injustice (which is ultimately everyone, in their own way). I hurt for those who have suffered, but I also respect and honor those who survived and thrived. Through the struggle, we emerge stronger and more resilient.

We were put on this earth to experience life together, and if we give each other support and love, we will all benefit. That serves the common good. Sometimes we forget that we are all family. That's the dark side of human nature rising up, but hatred, jealousy, and cruelty serve no good at all. Personalizing your experience cuts you off from other people and the shared

I Don't Belong to You

human experience of pain, happiness, joy, and perseverance that we can all relate to though we come from different backgrounds.

I believe in my generation and know that we can pick up where our ancestors left off. Look around and you see young people of all races, sexual ties, and colors hanging out together, dating, marrying, and raising families together.

That gives me hope that we are on the right path. We still have many things to overcome, of course, and it isn't about immediate results. We need to fight for greater access to higher education, for decent wages, more workplace opportunities, and other societal problems we have inherited from previous generations. We can change them for our future children even if we do not see the changes for young adult lives.

What kind of world could we create if we all decided to show our parents that we could do better and be better? I credit my parents' generation for doing some great things. What if we picked it up and advanced it? What if we eliminated war, poverty, and racial hatred entirely?

When they were my age, people of my parents' generation talked a lot about bringing more peace, love, and understanding to the world. Many of them worked hard to promote those important goals. Now it's our turn.

Part of growing up is learning that the world is bigger than you. Life is not just making yourself happy. It's about facing individual and collective pain and thinking universally. We are universal. My pain is your pain and my story is your story.

Maybe you aren't a black girl named Keke, but I know you have your own story. The purpose of a human life is to improve yourself so that those small seeds planted play a part in changing the world at large. The journey is getting over ourselves enough to

Lauren Palmer

honor the gifts that our spirit brings so we can use them to heal the world.

We are not out here alone, to be separate from each other, or to make money and be rich. We were put here together to experience life in the fullest, including its ups and downs. We must learn to look to each other for the love and support we need. At some point, we forgot that we are a family. We can get so caught up in pleasing our flesh and our desires.

We don't leave this earth with our money or our cars or even our bodies. The only thing that lives on after we are gone is the way we made people feel, the things we've given them that are eternal and can never be diminished.

So, I ask you, what's your magic? What is your tool? What pain have you discovered from your own personal story that you can use to heal humanity?

ACKNOWLEDGMENTS

$\mathcal{W}$ow . . . first of all THANK YOU. Thank you to everyone that has had anything to do with making this book possible. The Universe, God for giving me LIFE, and the earth on which I stand for making it possible for me to even survive in this galaxy! Sorry I'm so dramatic, but this is me, lol, and these words written on this page note that I, too, was here. That I had a story, I had a human life, and there were many people who were a part of it and hopefully I was a real part of theirs too.

There are many people I would like to thank. I'd like to thank my mother, Sharon Palmer, for always believing in me and seeing in me what sometimes I'd forgotten, for loving me for me (but also keeping the bigger picture in the forefront of my eyesight), for never letting me forget the purpose of living and of telling your story. For reminding me of the responsibility we have to ourselves and others and the magnitude that our actions hold. I am thankful to my father, Lawrence Palmer, for showing me what it means to love and to be selfless and to be courageous. For showing me that bravery sometimes is silent and sometimes underappreciated, but that the act of doing good is doing good when no one is watching. I am thankful to my sister, Loreal Palmer, and her husband, Frank, for showing me what love can do. Seeing how they have allowed their love and love for their children transform them is quite magical. I am thankful to the TWINS Lawrence and Lawrencia! Thank you for giving me hope, strength, laughter, and a team. No matter how dark my road got, I could look to you two and know why I had to keep going, why I had to switch it up and keep going for something BETTER!

I am thankful to the Davis (my mom side) family for giving me attitude, sass, and the ability to stand up for myself! I'm thankful to the Palmer family for showing me what it means to stick together, to value family, and to always laugh no matter how hard times are. I want to give thanks to chi-townnnnnn aka ROBBINS, ILLINOIS, for making me a hustler, for showing me what the bottom was so I could create the blueprint to get to the top, and for showing me what wrongs were happening so I could have the drive to make shine a light on what was right. #MISSION.

Special thanks to North Star Way and Simon & Schuster for publishing and believing in this book. I honestly don't know how to thank you—my publisher Michele Martin and the entire team, the North Star kids, for understanding my purpose for this book! You are the real deal.

I'm thankful to my agency—Jan Miller, CEO, probably the coolest lady you'll ever meet! HAHAHAHA! And to my agent, Lacy Lynch. Damnnnnn Lacy, we did it!! You are the true definition of a ride or die. Through this entire process I have loved and appreciated you. I have been more than grateful to have you on my team. You have been more than a team player; you have been the MOTHERF*CKING MVP and THAT'S THE GAG. I really couldn't have done this without you and I don't tell lies. #LINCOLN.

Acknowledgments

Truly, I am grateful to the depths of my soul and so is Mildred Davis. For it is her to whom I dedicate this book. God bless.

Below I want to give specific thanks to all the kids, all the peeps, all the players who had a part in making this whole thing possible:

The editorial squad: Javen Benton, Destiny Modeste, Shatika Rembert, Josh Caldwell, Suzy Butin, and Chelsea Irvin—for all the hard work and emoji checking.

To Wes Smith, for stepping in and stepping up; Lauren Auslander and the team at PMK; and Doreen Wilcox for her early support.

And to the rest of the Simon & Schuster: Cindy Ratzlaff—Director of Brand Development; Diana Ventimiglia—Editor and supporter of my words, dreams, and visions; Hilary Mau—Sales Coordinator; Irene Kheradi—VP Executive Managing Editor, Production & Copy Editing; Amanda Mulholland—Assistant Managing Editor; Emma Powers—Managing Editorial Assistant; Hilda Koparanian—Senior Production Manager; Alexandre Su—Senior Production Editor; John Vairo—Associate Director, Art & Design, for using his amazing creativity to make me a FLY cover; Lisa Litwack—Senior Director, Art; Liz Psaltis—Director, Marketing Adult; Jean Anne Rose—Director, Publicity; Hazel-Ann Mayers—EVP & General Counsel, Simon & Schuster Legal; Jaime Putorti—Director, Interior Design; none of this happens without each and every one of you.

Acknowledgments